Toward an Anthropology of Ambient Sound

D1744148

This volume approaches the issue of ambient sound through the ethnographic exploration of different cultural contexts including Italy, India, Egypt, France, Ethiopia, Scotland, Spain, Portugal, and Japan. It examines social, religious, and aesthetic conceptions of sound environments, what types of action or agency are attributed to them, and what bodies of knowledge exist concerning them. Contributors shed new light on these sensory environments by focusing not only on their form and internal dynamics, but also on their wider social and cultural environment. The multimedia documents of this volume may be consulted at the address: milson.fr/routledge_media

Christine Guillebaud is a senior researcher at the French National Centre for Scientific Research (CNRS), and member of the Centre for Ethnology and Comparative Sociology (CREM-LESC), based at the University of Paris Nanterre, France.

Routledge Studies in Anthropology

Toward an Anthropology of Ambient Sound

Edited by
Christine Guillebaud

Routledge
Taylor & Francis Group

LONDON AND NEW YORK

First published 2017
by Routledge

2 Park Square, Milton Park, Abingdon, Oxfordshire OX14 4RN
52 Vanderbilt Avenue, New York, NY 10017

*Routledge is an imprint of the Taylor & Francis Group, an informa
business*

First issued in paperback 2019

Copyright © 2017 Taylor & Francis

The right of Christine Guillebaud to be identified as the author of the
editorial material, and of the authors for their individual chapters, has
been asserted in accordance with sections 77 and 78 of the Copyright,
Designs and Patents Act 1988.

All rights reserved. No part of this book may be reprinted or reproduced
or utilised in any form or by any electronic, mechanical, or other
means, now known or hereafter invented, including photocopying and
recording, or in any information storage or retrieval system, without
permission in writing from the publishers.

Notice:
Product or corporate names may be trademarks or registered trademarks,
and are used only for identification and explanation without intent to infringe.

Library of Congress Cataloging-in-Publication Data
Names: Guillebaud, Christine, editor.
Title: Towards an anthropology of ambient sound / edited by
    Christine Guillebaud.
Description: Abingdon, Oxon ; New York, NY : Routledge, 2017. |
    Series: Routledge studies in anthropology ; 38 | Includes
    bibliographical references and index.
Identifiers: LCCN 2016052999 (print) | LCCN 2017013011 (ebook) |
    ISBN 9781315755045 (E-book) | ISBN 9781138801271 (hardback :
    alk. paper)
Subjects: LCSH: Sound (Philosophy) | Sounds—Social aspects—Case
    studies. | Noise—Social aspects—Case studies.
Classification: LCC B105.S59 (ebook) | LCC B105.S59 T68 2017 (print) |
    DDC 304.2—dc23
LC record available at https://lccn.loc.gov/2016052999

ISBN: 978-1-138-80127-1 (hbk)
ISBN: 978-0-367-86905-2 (pbk)

Typeset in Sabon
by Apex CoVantage, LLC

The multimedia documents of this volume may be consulted at the address: http://milson.fr/routledge_media

Contents

Figures

Tables

Audiovisual Documents

- Chapter 1

  1. In the street [2'26"]. Olivier Féraud, 2008. A boy expressly goes into the streets after the New Year's family midnight festivities to use fireworks. For many people, fireworks have to be used down in the street. It is a way of investing and appropriating the street as the space of noise at this moment.
  2. A few minutes of the Quartieri Spagnoli resounding at midnight. Olivier Féraud, 2008. Some vocal reactions to firecracker's detonations can be heard [2'26]. Midnight is marked by a great detonation that can be heard at mark 38 second of the recording.

- Chapter 4

  1. A morning at Saktan Tampuran Bus Stand (Trichur, Kerala). Video [04'53"]. Image: Christine Guillebaud, 2008.
  2. The Lottery car. Saktan Tampuran Bus Stand (Trichur, Kerala, India). Video [03'16"]. Image: Christine Guillebaud, 2008.
  3. Successive stages of deceleration and reacceleration based on the lottery sound recording [01'21"].
  4. Extract from a "Work Song" from *Cinderella*, Walt Disney. Video [01'21"].
  5. Accelerated voice with "comic" effect followed by the "fast-forward" technique, experiment based on the lottery sound recording [00'47"].
  6. Excerpt from a radio broadcast (France Info).
  7. Parisian Tram announcement (Line 3b). "Ella Fitzgerald—Grands Moulins de Pantin" Station.

- Chapter 5

  1. "An approach Bell at Kouchi Station" (1955–1975). Source: Ima Yomigaeru Kokutetsu, 2010, Columbia Music Entertainment. CD 3, Track 19. ASIN: B003800360. EAN: 4988001300908.
  2. "An Arrival Bell at Fukui Station" (1955–1975). Source: Ima Yomigaeru Kokutetsu, 2011, Columbia Music Entertainment. CD 6, Track 3. ASIN: B004WLXTZQ. EAN: 4988001475200.

3. "An Active Window Bell at Yonezawa Station" (1955–1975). Source: Kokutetsu, Furusato no Eki, 1999, Pony Canyon. CD 1, Track 26. ASIN: B00005FR22. EAN: 4988013000506.
4. "A Departure Bell at Ryougoku Station" (1955–1975). Source: Ima Yomigaeru Kokutetsu, 2010, Columbia Music Entertainment. CD 2, Track 1. ASIN: B003800360. EAN: 4988001300908.
5. "Ue Wo Muite Arukou: an Arrival Melody at Kawasaki Station" (2008). The song, translated "Sukiyaki" in the US, was major hit in Japan as well as American pop chart. Its author, artist Sakamoto Kyu, was born in Kawasaki. Source: Keikyu Eki Merodi Original (Japanese), 2009, USM Japan. CD 1, Track 6. ASIN: B001PBQLHY. EAN: 498805551146. An excerpt of a live recording can be found on YouTube.

- Chapter 6

1. Soundwalks with Strathdevon School Pupils on 28th April 2011. Recorded by Heikki Uimonen & Viika Sankila.
2. Three Homework Recordings by Strathdevon Primary School Pupils Finlay, Megan & Leah on Wednesday 27 April 2011.

- Chapter 7

1. Recorded ambiance in front of the Azbakiyya Park, by al-26 yūlyū, Downtown Cairo, April 14, 2011 at 3:25 p.m. (Recorded by Vincent Battesti).
2. Walk between Talaat Harb square and Sherif Basha street, Downtown Cairo, November 4, 2009, 7:45 p.m. (Recorded by Vincent Battesti).
3. Same day, about one hour later, walk between al-Bibani square and ḥara al-Meɛamār, Darb al-Aḥmar, Old Islamic Cairo, November 4, 2009, 9:05 p.m. (Recorded by Vincent Battesti).
4. "*Roba vekkiyya!*" cry of the ragman/junk gatherer in the street, recorded from the seventh floor of a Haussmannian-like building, in a pedestrian area, Downtown Cairo, November 6, 2009, 8:57 a.m. (Recorded by Vincent Battesti).
5. In the outstanding traffic ambiance of the Ramsīs square, the cries of the microbus touts can still be heard by the potential fares, in Cairo, November 2, 2003, 11:24 p.m. (Recorded by Vincent Battesti).
6. A street greengrocer's cry in the residential Doqqi neighborhood, Cairo, December 5, 2009, 1:21 p.m. Her cry is very modulated and difficult to perform but highly recognizable by the potential customers. (Recorded by Vincent Battesti).
7. Street demonstration against an American invasion of Iraq, a few left-wing intellectuals met and enjoyed coming back to the street (unthinkable for a long time), on the sidewalk in front of Sayeda Zeynab mosque, Cairo, February 15, 2003, 1:21 p.m. (Recorded by Vincent Battesti).

8. Street demonstration for the January 25 Revolution, and against the military, by protesters of different social classes on Talaat Harb street and Tahrīr square, Downtown, Cairo, October 31, 2011, 10:38 p.m. (Recorded by Vincent Battesti).

9. At dusk, birds that populate a huge villa's garden, in the chic residential part of Mansuriyya, country suburb of Cairo, February 25, 2007, 7:00 p.m. No doubt those who can afford to enjoy such a sound ambiance in Cairo are a very happy few (this bourgeois villa belongs to a former minister and businessman). (Recorded by Vincent Battesti).

10. Same day, two and a half hours later, ambiance in a local café of Suleymān Gawhar (Doqqi), with patrons playing *tawla* (backgammon) and dominoes, smoking *šīša* (narghilé), February 25, 2007, 9:30 p.m. (Recorded by Vincent Battesti).

11. Saturated sound space in the popular neighborhood of Sayeda Zeynab during her *mawlīd*, the annual saint's festival (for a week), Cairo, October 1, 2002, 11:26 p.m. (Recorded by Vincent Battesti).

12. Religious sounds (prayer from a small mosque nearby) heard in a composed ambiance with other incidental and accidental sounds during a walk inside an informal overcrowded market in Azbakiyya, Downtown border, Cairo, February 19, 2007. (Recorded by Vincent Battesti).

13. Religious sounds (Friday's sermon from the local mosque) heard in a composed ambiance with other incidental and accidental sounds, from an apartment in the neighborhood of Suleymān Gawhar, Doqqi, Cairo, February 16, 2007. (Recorded by Vincent Battesti).

14. Cries close to screams of young peddlers selling T-shirts at night on Talaat Harb street, Downtown Cairo, April 14, 2011, 8:20 p.m. With the revolution, people took up the street again, especially vendors. In strong competition, they cry or scream to draw customers, but nonetheless they sometimes cooperate to create a specific street ambiance. (Recorded by Vincent Battesti).

15. Saturated sound space during the popular annual saint Festival of Sayeda Zeynab, during the *leyla kebīra* (the last and greatest night of the *mawlīd*), Cairo, September 24, 2003, 0:37 a.m. (Recorded by Vincent Battesti).

• Chapter 8

1. Two neighbors talking from their apartment windows. Travessa do Terreirinho, 27/6/2012. (Recorded by Iñigo Sánchez Fuarros).

2. *Visitas cantadas* participants arrive at Largo da Severa and the *fado* performance starts. Largo da Severa, 22/9/2012. (Recorded by Iñigo Sánchez Fuarros).

3. Interaction between the *fado* singers and participants in the Visitas cantadas. Largo da Severa, 22/09/2012. (Recorded by Iñigo Sánchez Fuarros).
4. The muddled sound environment in the vicinity of the Praça do Martim Moniz, 1/9/2012. (Recorded by Iñigo Sánchez Fuarros).

- Chapter 9
    1. Rambla Santa Monica. 2007. (Recorded by Ciudad Sonora).
    2. Loudspeaker in the beach, 21/06/2007. (Recorded by Ciudad Sonora).
    3. Poblenou Park, Barcelona, 22/07/2007. (Recorded by Ciudad Sonora).

- Chapter 10
    1. Gysin, *I Am That I Am,* YouTube, January 2011.
    2. Jandl, *Devil Trap,* YouTube, April 2011.
    3. Chopin, *Chercher,* YouTube, February 2011.
    4. Chaton, *Décade,* http://aj.chaton.free.fr/, 2009.
    5. Heidsieck, *La semaine (Passepartout 5),* in Bobillot Jean-Pierre, *Heidsieck, poésie action,* Paris, Jean-Michel Place, 1996.
    6. Cage, *Roaratorio,* disk 1, part 4, New York, NY, Mode records (mode 28 / 29), 1992.
    7. Gould, *Solitude Trilogy, Three Sound Documentaries—3 The Quiet in the Land,* CBC Records, PSCD 2003–3, 2000.

- Chapter 11
    1. Person 1
    2. Person 2
    3. Person 3
    4. Person 4
    5. Person 5
    6. Person 6
    7. Person 7
    8. Person 8
    9. Person 9
    10. Person 10
    11. Person 11
    12. Supercollider/livecoding very simple demonstration (by Vincent Rioux)

Contributors

Vincent Battesti (CNRS, Laboratoire Écoanthropologie Ethnobiologie, Muséum national d'Histoire naturelle, Paris, France)

Tripta Chandola (Digital Ethnography Research Centre, RMIT University, Australia)

Anne Damon-Guillot (Jean Monnet Saint-Etienne University, CIEREC, France)

Jean-Charles Depaule (CNRS, Laboratoire d'Anthropologie Urbaine, Ivry-sur-Seine, France)

Olivier Féraud (Méditerrannée Aix-Marseille 2 University, LAU-IIAC, France)

Christine Guillebaud (CNRS, Laboratoire d'Ethnologie et de Sociologie Comparative, Paris-Ouest Nanterre University, France)

Claire Guiu (Department of Geography, University of Nantes, Espaces et Sociétés ESO, France)

Pierre Manea (Department of Sociology, Keio University, Japan)

Vincent Rioux (Department of Digital arts, École Nationale Supérieure des Beaux-Arts, Paris, France)

Iñigo Sánchez (Instituto de Etnomusicologia, Universidade Nova de Lisboa, Portugal)

Jean-Paul Thibaud (CNRS, Centre de Recherche sur l'Espace Sonore et l'Environnement Urbain, Grenoble, France)

Heikki Uimonen (Sibelius Academy, University of the Arts Helsinki, Finland)

Acknowledgments

This book is a result of the MILSON program (Anthropology of Sound Milieus), based at the Centre de recherche en ethnomusicologie (Research Center for Ethnomusicology) at the Laboratoire d'Ethnologie et de Sociologie Comparative (Center for Research in Ethnology and Comparative Sociology) of the Université Paris Ouest-Nanterre (2011–2015). We warmly thank the Fyssen Fondation for funding this project, along with the French partner institutions that provided us with precious logistical and intellectual support: Ecole Nationale Supérieure des Beaux-Arts de Paris, Université Paris Lumières, and the Maison de l'Archéologie et de l'Ethnologie.

Many thanks to scholars who presented papers during our workshops and/or took part in discussions with the team, such as Pierre-Albert Castanet, Tripta Chandola, Alain Corbin, Anne Damon-Guillot, Danièle Dubois, Claire Guiu, David Howes, Bernard Lortat-Jacob, Pierre Manea, Rosalia Martinez, Bruno Messina, Stéphane Rennesson, Iñigo Sánchez, Jean-Paul Thibaud, Heikki Uimonen, and Corsin Vogel.

Jean-Paul Thibaud, sociologist and international specialist in urban ambiances, graciously accepted to write an afterword, "The sonic attunement of social life." We express our hearty gratitude to him for the thought and writing of this text, which illuminates the cross-cutting nature of our endeavor and opens new research perspectives.

This volume also benefitted from the expertise of several translator colleagues. We sincerely thank Juliette Rogers, Jessica L. Hackett, and John Rogove for rereading and/or translating the chapters of this book and Laurence Fayet for help formatting it for publication. Last, we would like to thank Routledge for the interest shown in our manuscript.

Introduction: Multiple Listenings

Anthropology of Sound Worlds

Christine Guillebaud

Sound environments—composite worlds that are produced, perceived, and listened to either intentionally or coincidentally—have attracted a boom in interest over recent decades. The disciplines applied to their study have diversified tremendously since the foundational work of Murray Schafer (1977) and Pierre Schaeffer (1966), expanding to include acoustics, psycholinguistics, architecture, urban studies, and the sound arts. This upturn in interest was long thought to be proof of a deep cultural fact, that analysis of hearing lagged behind that of sight, rooted in the centuries-old ranking of the senses in Western thought. This recent research has largely made up for the imbalance. Today study of the sensory environment is predominantly interdisciplinary, to the point that previous academic limits are being redefined in favor of more overarching fields of study, as attest the range of terms used to describe them: history and anthropology of the senses (Howes 1991, 2003, Classen 1993, Corbin 1994, Colon 2013); sensory practices (Ingold 2000); auditory culture (Bull and Back 2003); acoustemology and sound anthropology (Feld 1994, 2000, Ricci 1996, Feld and Brenneis 2004, Féraud 2010, 2013); sounded anthropology (Samuels *et al.* 2010); the history of sound technologies and sound studies (Bijsterveld and Pinch 2012, Sterne 2012). This volume contributes to this rapidly expanding field in which anthropology is fully assuming its place. It aims to ethnographically decipher everyday ways of living and doing, with a particular interest in how ambient sound produces social relations, how sound productions are invested with meaning locally, and how ways of listening are forged and oriented differently depending on the ethnographic context being considered.

The question of sound is more relevant than ever in the Western world, and this is likely even truer in countries of the global south. Worldwide rankings of the most noise-polluted cities include the megalopolises of Mumbai, Cairo, and Tokyo. There as elsewhere, decibel counts are measured scrupulously according to standards set by national and international organizations.[1] Sound pollution has now become one of central governments' major concerns in the management of public space and infrastructure. If this conception of "pollution" is legitimate from the perspectives of public health and the improvement of citizens' quality of daily life, it does raise a few issues in an anthropological undertaking such as ours. Ambient sound is produced and altered by a wide range of materials and surfaces, weather conditions, and media upon which its propagation depends (such as air and temperature). However, by nature it is also immaterial and part of daily sensory experience. We should account for this inherent complexity by treating it as a composite material, the perception of which necessarily draws from a vast spectrum of ways of paying attention spanning simple inattention to ordinary sounds all the way to specific forms of listening, such as listening to acoustically salient sounds that organize or prompt human activities. Indeed at the local level, a simple physical decibel level count taken near an intersection, hospital, or school says nearly nothing of how residents and passers-by use and listen to the space. It says nothing of how they perceive ambient sounds or how they appraise and appreciate the sensory environment. The notion of "pollution" just as arbitrarily puts thousands of everyday commercial and ritual activities with all but incomparable sound characteristics on the same level. Examples are not hard to find: festive uses of fireworks, various calls to prayer, loudspeaker systems and all manner of sound distortion, local sales methods (itinerant street vendors, bazars, markets, etc.), very dense transportation network signaling, commonplace ways of initiating interaction with others, or even multiple ways of conferring cultural identity on a place and its correlate, for residents to form a community. Sound's place in numerous areas of everyday, ritual, and political life has yet to be discovered, and this book is intended to contribute significantly to study of this unassuming level of public life. There is much left to explore, this time on an empirical base expanded by necessity: the everyday sounds of houses, streets, and neighborhoods, of rituals and celebrations, and of commercial activities and stations all deserve our full attention. The undertaking is all the while guided by the social and cultural contexts that give meaning locally, thus distinguishing it from the collection of acoustic environments for the quantitative analysis of "nuisance" or "pollution." Likewise, it sets itself apart from work intending to preserve or conserve ambient sounds for memorial or heritage purposes.[2] This book is primarily devoted to understanding the *sensory* modalities of the production of sound environments, decrypting the range of local knowledge and the imaginaries they inspire in a given group or society.

Provincializing[3] Our Sonic Perception

Several methods were already at our disposal to meet these objectives. Some disciplines have already formulated and experimented with situated approaches to urban sensory manifestations. Architecture and urban studies (Augoyard and Torgue 1995, Grosjean and Thibaud 2001) and psycholinguistics (Dubois 2009) have established recording protocols and methods for analysis of perception and its associated discourse. Although these are established methods today, they were clearly forged mainly for the analysis of urban spaces, and moreover in field sites found for the most part in Western Europe and North America.[4] At the same time, the anthropology of sound has usually focused on the sound perceptions of natural spaces like the forest (Feld 1994, 1996, 2000, Gell 1995) or everyday and ritual life in rural settings (Ricci 1996, Panopoulos 2003). It is only quite recently that anthropological studies have turned to the ordinary sounds of the city, including those conducted by contributors to this volume such as Olivier Féraud (2010) on sounded forms of sociability in Naples and Tripta Chandola (2010, 2012) on sound perception in Delhi's Govindpuri slum. Others set out to explore the everyday sounds of institutional sites like hospitals in the United Kingdom (Rice 2013), sound mechanisms in places of worship such as South Indian Hindu temples (Guillebaud 2009, 2015), or the spatiality of calls to prayer from Kenyan mosques (Eisenberg 2013). In work of this kind, immersion in other sound milieus, encountering different ways of interacting in public, and the obvious need to work in the language of local interlocutors result in different strategies and temporalities than those of typical urban ambiance studies.

This division between disciplines and the location of field sites is well known, a result of the "Great Divide" between "us" and "them" that has already been exposed and historically contextualized by several authors (Fabian 1983, Lenclud 1992). The study of sound perception currently tends to foster the circulation of methods among disciplines. Soundwalks (Westerkamp 1974, McCartney and Paquette 2012) and commented walks (Thibaud 2001), which were especially well tested in the fields of art and architecture, have recently been applied in the anthropology of sound. Several authors of this present work also adapt experimental protocols to their research sites and thus further develop analysis of the cultural dimensions of listening (see especially the contributions of Battesti, Guiu, and Uimonen). At the same time, anthropology is used more than it used to be in the theoretical exploration of our perception of the sensory environment. One example that comes to mind is "Ambiances in Action," one of the themes of the Second International Conference of the Ambiances network (Montreal 2012)[5] or the "Translating Ambiances" theme chosen for the first meeting of the eponymous International Research Group (Nantes 2014).[6] At this meeting, the cultural dimension of perception asserted itself forcefully as the group worked on investing lexical fields associated with the notion of "ambiance" in various languages, such as *atmosphère* (French), *ambiente* (Spanish), and *omgivelser* (Danish).[7] In the process, participants discovered that certain terms—*hygge* (Danish), *barzakh* (Arabic), *stimmung* (German)—did not always have a strict equivalent in translation. This linguistic perspective was also at the heart of the symposium "Le son pris aux mots" (Sound in words) (Paris, 2014),[8] which set out to address the variety of verbal and grammatical resources in play in sound perception using various ethnographic examples. The keynote address by Danièle Dubois and Matt Coler was the occasion to highlight the diversity of linguistic constructions: in English, for example, "What I perceive" asserts a distinction between the "object" of perception and the perceiving "subject," a relationship that proves irrelevant in certain native American languages (see also Coler 2014).

In continuity with these recent anthropological and linguistic reflections, one especially relevant point to our argument must be emphasized: a significant part of the world, in all its cultural and sociolinguistic diversity, remains to be explored. How do residents perceive the sound environments of Delhi or Tokyo? What are the social, religious, and political perceptions of the residents who listen to sound environments? How are they thought to be effective, and what specific knowledge exists about them? To reply to these fundamental questions, this book employs empirical work from a variety of cultural contexts in India, Italy, Egypt, France, Ethiopia, Spain, Scotland, Portugal, and Japan. While not aiming to be exhaustive, this volume offers a situated approach to sensory environments by tracing their forms, acoustic dynamics, and sociocultural contexts of production and perception. It moreover presents a series of recent studies on cities undergoing great structural change, be they national capitals (Lisbon, New Delhi, Cairo, Tokyo), urban and cultural centers (Naples, Barcelona, Trichur), or even smaller cities (Choisy-le-Roi). They are intended to enrich the study of the sensory environment by using higher-contrast empirical foundations than work to date, in what we hope is a less geographically divisive way.

Sound Versus Sonic

Conceptually, we started with the chart of oppositions suggested by the psycholinguist Danièle Dubois and the ethnolinguist Matt Coler. Dubois discusses variations in the conceptualization of the notion of "soundscape," as well as its methodological consequences for investigating the perceptual aspects and meanings of sound environments related to the concept of "ambiance" (Dubois 2012). In collaboration with Matt Coler, she has recently expanded this comparison to the concepts of "*milieu*" and "*umwelt*," producing the following table:

Table 0.1 Variations in the conceptualization of the notion of "soundscape." Compiled from Dubois (2012: 686) and Dubois and Coler (2014).

Soundscape (///landscape)	*Ambiance /milieu/ umwelt*
Visual analogy	Multimodal
Map (2-D)	3-D
Frontal perception	Immersion
Sound (acoustic)	*Sonic* (sensorial property)
Objectivist (physical-sciences centered)	"Subjective" (psychology and social sciences)
Analytical	Holistic

This volume is definitely situated on the right half of this table, among studies focused on the perceptional qualities of sound milieus. The underlying distinction between object and subject is a theoretical precondition for many of the contributions to this book, which indeed deal more with "ambiances" and "milieus" than with "soundscapes." More specifically, the work presented in the book is strongly ethnographic,[9] but not in the sense of being limited to a discipline, since it brings anthropologists and ethnomusicologists together with a geographer and an artist. It is more a matter of proposing a research policy that entails observing everyday practices from as closely as possible. It concentrates on ordinary scenes of life and interactions observed at the scale of particular places (a street, neighborhood, station . . .). It also proposes paying closer attention to phenomena and concerns a wide range of sound events, including voices, footsteps, firecrackers, bell chimes, and birdsong, sometimes compounding each other and sometimes layered onto other sounds. Several contributions capture such events in real situations of immersion (see Féraud, Guillebaud, Manea, Battesti, Uimonen, Guiu, Sánchez, Rioux) and offer new analytical categories as a result. For example, Olivier Féraud proposes the neologism "soundcial" (socio-sonic) for approaching everyday postures that simultaneously invest acoustic and social space, like everyday life in the streets of Neapolitan working-class neighborhoods or celebratory sonic activities, such as the popular practices of fireworks and firecrackers (Chapter 1). Vincent Rioux sheds light on the characteristics of individual sound perception with the notions of "sonosphere" or "aural sphere" and its fundamentally shifting nature, opening and re-shaping itself, "encompassing whatever sources attract its attention (. . .) including both active listening and passive hearing" (Chapter 11). Last, we must acknowledge that although we initially became aware of the classic opposition between objectivity and subjectivity in terms of disciplines, this, too, will be challenged repeatedly throughout these chapters. Surpassing the confrontation between the production and reception of sound milieus, ecological and pragmatic approaches additionally invite us to consider the world of sound as existing "in between" object and subject, something that might challenge their opposition. One example that comes to mind is the self-generated character of the sound milieu and the collective dimension of perception that emerges from the multiplicity of ticket-sellers' calls in a bus station in India (Chapter 4).

This volume also proposes testing existing methods in new field sites, especially methods for analyzing discursive appreciations of sound milieus. Indeed, it is easy to get inhabitants and users of a space to speak while perceiving by using soundwalks in-situ, and/or after the fact by using reactivation protocols or questionnaire-interviews that include listening to selected sound recordings, among other techniques. These methods are used extensively by the authors in the volume. Vincent Battesti recounts two complementary experiments he conducted with residents of Cairo in order to be able to analyze verbalizations as close as possible to those of their personal and daily experience. The first consists of an "aural postcard," using reactivated listening of recordings of ambiances in order to pick up Cairo residents' common terminology for describing and qualifying the general ambiance (for example, "atmosphere," *gaw*) in various sites and/or of typical sound events. The second experiment, called "mics in the ears," modifies the soundwalk method by equipping informants with binaural microphones and earphones prompting more contextualized verbalizations; at the same time, he noted how informants behave in the street, move their heads, and more generally interact with their socio-ecological environment (Chapter 7). In another chapter, Heikki Uimonen uses Sound Preference Tests and Recorded Listening Walks to learn about the modalities of verbal appreciation of the inhabitants of Dollar, a Scottish village. They build on earlier studies, one by the World Soundscape Project (Simon Fraser University) dating back to 1975, and two important Finnish studies in which the author had participated a quarter century later (*Acoustic Environments in Change*, 2000 and *Soundscapes and Cultural Sustainability*, 2009). Uimonen's approach here addresses the micro-community of Dollar's local Strathdevon Primary School and puts the results of previous studies into perspective with his recent observations in the field. He implemented the same protocols, combining statistical and qualitative methods, along with participative ethnography by the students. The author thus compares liked and disliked sound categories across three generations. Analysis of materials at the scale of the Strathdevon Primary School reveals processes of enculturation "in making sounds and evaluating sounds" by members of the same acoustic community and changes in associated cultural values (Chapter 6).

Through the studied cases, this volume suggests working in a broader palette of languages, which also gives access to other local conceptions. This volume does not, however, overlook other modalities of perception and hearing that are rarely approached through discourse "on" sound. The significant non-language component of perception (Pink 2010) calls for equal interest in local ways of bearing oneself and moving around, and more broadly in how individuals act and act together in situation. The ecosystem of phenomena and the physicality of sound experience are also addressed in the ethnographies. Sound events are sources of corporal, spatial, and territorial inscription, relying heavily on the places where they emerge. Claire Guiu studies this territorial dimension in her chapter on "the sonorities of urban transformation" in Barcelona (on the Ciudad Sonora Project). Her team set out to characterize sounds in coastal zones that have recently experienced urban development and district renewal, from the Moll de la Fusta to the Forum of Cultures. She analyzes their sonic organization and dynamics, which is largely subject to laws and regulation. She identifies the simultaneous presence of discontinuous events and notable soundmarks that have come to the area since the 1990s, like the sound of helicopters, airplanes, conversations, footsteps, shouts, and whispers. She demonstrates that the ambient sonority and associated discourse contribute to a "process of the appropriation, qualification, spatial organization and transformation of place" (Chapter 9). Another member of the Ciudad Sonora Project, Iñigo Sánchez, pursued this same hypothesis in a new field site, the working-class Mouraria neighborhood of Lisbon, and presents his analysis in a separate chapter. Although the neighborhood is located near the city center and its touristic attractions, the neighborhood has historically been considered a "territory on the margins of the city." The author closely followed a massive urban renewal program, the QREN-Mouraria Action Plan (2011–2012), and set out to give an account of its impact on the everyday sensory environment. Based on three examples from the urban environment (the *Largo da Severa*, the *Praça do Martim Moniz* and the *Largo do Intendente*), he demonstrates how musical styles (especially Portugal's nationally recognized Fado music) and new sounds are given new life in public spaces as numerous other soundmarks have changed or disappeared. The author also notes that "reshaping the milieu of sound can be a powerful tool in transforming the urban dynamics of a given place" while demonstrating precisely how this requalification of space can also lead to intense conflict. The controversies pitting bars and local authorities (the city) against each other in the neighborhood especially contest the qualification and lived experience of these "noisy" sounds, issues that manifest divergent cultural interests today (Chapter 8).

What Is Listening?

As we have said, this volume pays considerable attention to the perception-related aspects of sound milieus. But what is listening, and how can one understand the listening attitudes of the other? The auditory experience is a complex phenomenon because it involves a variety of ways that the subject may pay attention, depending on sound sources' acoustic characteristics, their spatial organization, and the cultural dispositions of the perceiving subject that is giving them meaning. In common parlance, the difference between the terms "hear" and "listen" already mark two distinct ways of comprehending hearing, one passive and the other active, that situate the work of the ear in a process of selectivity and intentionality. These ways of "hearing" and "listening" are not mutually exclusive and are usually combined in a given situation—for example, in relation to the criteria for the acoustic salience of certain aspects of sound (intensity, frequency, duration, timbre), our daily habits, or even new experiences that develop our ear for new sonorities. They also heavily rely on the perceiving subject's subjective dispositions (age, gender, skills) and the actions mobilizing him or her in a given situation.

From a theoretical perspective, several authors have described and modeled how we listen in great detail. This starts with Pierre Schaeffer, who identified "four ways of listening," the pioneering model employed here. Schaeffer indeed proposed breaking listening down into four terms, first presented on pages 113–114 of his *Traités des Objets Musicaux* (1966) based on four verbs in common use in French: *écouter* (to listen), *ouïr* (to be aware of), *entendre* (to hear), *comprendre* (to understand).[10]

Table 0.2 Four ways of listening (Schaeffer 1966: 113).

4	1
Comprendre	*Ecouter*
(to understand)	(to listen)
3	2
Entendre	*Ouïr*
(to hear)	(to be aware of)

Starting with common sense, Schaeffer divides these four terms into two general ways of listening. The first, *écouter* and *comprendre* (across the top of the table), conform to a degree of "objectivity" in audition.[11] The term *écouter* refers to comprehending sound as a result, as being caused by something or the presence of someone. Sound is an "event" in this case, and the person who hears it perceives it as an "indication," meaning that it gives information about its source. The other term, *comprendre*, involves wondering about a sound's "meaning" by introducing the subject into a certain domain of "non-sounded" values. This semantic kind of listening is characterized by speech, everyday language. According to Schaeffer, it also concerns all kinds of "meaningful" listening, such as music, which he also took as an example. The second way of listening, comprised of *ouïr* and *entendre* and found across the bottom of the table, imply a "subjective" character. *Ouïr* presupposes that the hearer perceives a sound of an as-yet-undefined character and that this perception is "raw," whereas *entendre* takes this as a step toward determining the nature of the sound itself; the listener has thus "chosen" some of its components. Schaeffer also introduced a vertical division between types of hearing according to their "concrete" or "abstract" relationships to sound. Schaeffer presented the complete and more complex table on page 116 of *Traités des Objets Musicaux*.

Schaeffer makes several subsequent refinements to enhance and improve reading of this diagram. Of particular relevance here is his distinction between the two "listening pairs." The first sets "natural" listening apart from "cultural" listening. In sector 1, natural listening is presented as universal. Concerning humans as well as animals, it makes sound a way to inform oneself about an event. It becomes cultural (sector 4) when it is the object of explicit conventions. The second pair opposes "mundane" listening and "specialized" or "practitioner" listening and highlights the differences between the perceiving subjects' skills and the quality of their attention.

Table 0.3 Four ways of listening (Schaeffer 1966: 116).

4 COMPRENDRE / Understand	1 ECOUTER / Listen	
- for me: signs	- for me: indications	1 and 4:
- before me: values	- before me: exterior events	Objective
(language-meaning)	(agent-instrument)	
Emergence of content from sound, and *reference* to and *confrontation with* non-sound notions.	*Emission* of sound	
3 ENTENDRE / Hear	2 OUÏR / Be aware of	
- for me: qualified perceptions	- for me: raw perceptions, rough sketch of the object	2 and 3:
- before me: qualified sound-object		Subjective
Selection of some particular aspects of sound	- before me: raw sound object	
	Reception of sound	
3 and 4: Abstract	1 and 2: Concrete	

The first, mundane, is more intuitive and "open" (p. 122) and leaves the subject available to what his ears perceive. The second, more specialized and "closed," involves training and skills permitting the ear to choose and intentionally hear what it "wants to hear and elucidate" (p. 121).

One of the strengths of this model is that, instead of considering listening in relation to the kinds of sounds around us, it puts listening in a range of concrete and objective relationships to sound materials, although in practice these forms of listening usually combine and fluctuate. It makes it possible to escape the logic of genre categorization that begins with qualifying what we hear rather than wondering about how we hear it.

We note in particular that sector 4 is often explained using the examples of languages, Morse code, bells, or warning horns (p. 121) as so many "signs" to be decrypted and understood. In a surprising way Schaeffer also includes music (admittedly making its relationship to meaning more complex) as a form that "deliberately diverts (without ceasing to hear it) from the event and circumstances that it reveals relative to its emission, to cling to the message, signification, *values* borne by the sound" (p. 121). However, although the confrontation of listening with non-sound notions may be broadly and overtly established in the diagram (sector 4), the illustrative examples are ultimately more reductively presented, often concerning a linguistic relationship of the signified/signifier type. This inclination to make our relationship to the non-sounded strictly semantic (more a tendency than an assertion in Schaeffer) is problematic. It might best be understood by situating him in his disciplinary background (an engineer by training rather than a social scientist) and in light of his body of work focusing on the notion of "sound objects," which he encourages us to appreciate for their intrinsic qualities, and specifically without regard for their signification or cultural context.

This type of "semantic" relationship is also found in Michel Chion's presentation of his three listening modes. Heir to Schaeffer, Chion took up some of the older categories and adapted them into three terms: causal listening, semantic listening, and reduced listening. Causal listening corresponds perfectly to sector 1 of Schaeffer's diagram, and "consists of listening to a sound in order to gather information about its cause (or source)" (Chion 2012: 48). Semantic listening more specifically concerns the interpretation of a message, as with spoken language but also other codes such as Morse code (Chion 2012: 50). Last, reduced listening, which was also borrowed from Schaeffer, is a "listening mode that focuses on the traits of the sound itself, independent of its cause and of its meaning" (Chion 2012: 50). In Chion's sharpened redefinition, semantic listening implicitly picks up the features of Schaeffer's sector 4, identified by the verb "*comprendre*/understand" or by the expression "cultural listening." As we mentioned earlier, Schaeffer made ready reference to languages and codified languages but also to music and more broadly any form of listening that confronts acoustic and non-sounded dimensions, including values. In an anthropological approach such as ours, this also seems problematic, reducing the cultural to languages (or even music) and correspondingly, limiting description of this kind of listening to the purely "semantic." For music, credit is due to ethnomusicology for having particularly well explored this listening relationship favoring pragmatic and performative descriptors. Ritual music, whether it is shamanic, related to possession, or for communion with the divine, especially presupposes forms of listening that are far more complex than a signifier/signified relationship. Music's relationship to the non-sounded has been approached as a "continuum" with the natural environment (Legrain 2014), as a manifestation in an underworld situation in Andean cosmologies (Martinez 1996), or as a process of bringing non-human agents into presence. It can concern divinities simultaneously called, manifest, and represented through sound (Guillebaud 2008, Prévot 2014), "sonic beings" independently animated by and in the sound (Brabec de Mori and Stoichita 2012, Brabec de Mori and Seeger 2013), or forms of "personification" (or "musical living") that find themselves at the heart of musical emotion (Bonini Baraldi 2015). This relationship to things other than sound, which we will deliberately leave as open as possible, is still wide open for exploration where ambient sound is concerned. The non-sounded is commonly hastily pigeonholed as merely indicational or causal listening. In this book we take up Schaeffer's invitation to enrich the "cultural" dimension of the model by approaching mundane listening through specific ethnographic case studies. The first step is considering examples of sound events that concern neither language nor music. Our approach *confronts* listening to ambient sound with non-sounded notions, without presuming they are of a strictly semantic order.

The first part of the book explores these concepts in detail. The study of pyrotechnical practices in Naples contributed by Olivier Féraud notably demonstrates how the intensity (loudness) of these actions locally denotes a strong social demonstrativeness and social expressivity. He shows that intensity is generally negatively perceived by the Neopolitan middle class, which associates non-festive firecracker noise with delinquency, incivility, and social instability, while those who like firecrackers associate them with the cultural values of courage, virility, and risk-taking (Chapter 1). Anne Damon-Guillot also highlights a division of a cultural order in her study of the texts of Jesuits and Franciscans who went to Ethiopia in the early modern era to convert people to Catholicism. She demonstrates how the Europeans' sonic sensitivity was embedded in a proselytizing project characterized by a fundamental dichotomy. The missionaries used powerful sounds (such as bells, the preaching voice, and fireworks) to convert people, whereas the daily and ordinary sounds of Ethiopia—like groans or weeping—were described with an eschatological vocabulary (Chapter 2). A similar *othering* process is analyzed by Tripta Chandola in her study of the "obscene voices" of the women of Govindpuri, a slum settlement in Delhi. She emphasizes the particular sonic (and emotional) manifestation of the slum's highly gendered, violent, and volatile materiality that is found in these performances (Chapter 3). These three case studies specify the capacity of ordinary sound milieus to constitute, reinforce, and/or contest social orders. Through them we can see how actors connect to and disconnect from each other, perform acts of belonging or exclusion, or communicate and cut themselves off from each other.

This volume's more focused approach to phenomena will also make particular underdeveloped (or ignored) dimensions emerge from Schaeffer's model. We are thinking in particular of the temporal dimension of sound and the context in which we perceive and listen, especially in relation to the actions we are engaged in at the time (walking, working, praying, taking the train, and so on). These dimensions were put into precise relation by the sociologist Henri Torgue (1999) in his template for reading our systems for listening. He first distinguished between three kinds of listening: mundane listening, musical listening, and musician listening. In this model, the first (mundane listening) possesses exactly the same characteristics as those previously described by Schaeffer (Sector 1) and Chion (in "causal listening"). Torgue defines it with a much more explicit temporal dimension and sets it radically apart from "musical listening":

> Everyday listening corresponds in a way to a state of waiting interrupted occasionally by the emergence of conscious perceptions. It is a state in which modulations of attention adapt to a number of diverse situations. In daily life this kind of listening may range from the limits of drowsiness to the sharpest attentiveness, as when one is quite watchful of everything that happens (or could happen): the sentinel, the waiting soldier, etc. (. . .) Listening does not belong to the musical order: sounds play the role of indicators, attesting to actions that go beyond them, are only the indicator of an experience. In this kind of listening, if sound provokes

a response from the person who hears it (psychometric or affective), it is not just because of its sounded nature, but by its signification in the chain of meaning, not as the very subject of reception.

(Torgue 1999: 27)

After this presentation, he defines "musical listening" in which "sound has a direct action on the person hearing it. Emotional, psychometric, or semantic action" (Torgue 1999: 27). This reference to agency, which had not appeared in earlier models, is important in that it emphasizes that any kind of sound can be the object of a "musical" listening since it is the sound's *capacity for action* that is in play more than its intrinsic nature. Last, "musician listening" is symmetrically defined by actor-hearers' capacity for action, themselves acting *on* sound instead of sound acting independently on them. This kind of listening is rather close to Schaeffer's "specialized listening" when he spoke of the specific skills of an acoustician, musician, or even Native American of the Plains to listen to the galloping sound of a horse (Schaeffer 1966: 122). It thus resembles what Schaeffer put under the verb *entendre*/hear in his diagram (sector 3), moreover designated by Chion as a modality of "reduced listening." What ultimately distinguishes these three authors from each other is therefore the dominant criteria they selected. As we have seen, time and action are fundamental for Torgue, who added only an outline for a new descriptor, "register." It corresponds to the "intentionality of sound," but it appears the author left it rather rough in this diagram, open to future development. To round out his diagram, Torgue last describes the "states" associated with the three types of listening (which appear in separate columns) according to the retained descriptors or criteria.

From this presentation, we see that the main theoretical models fully agree on mundane or causal listening, and on identifying specialized, reduced, or musician listening. However, the authors struggle to find terminological consensus on relationships to meaning, as their variety of labels demonstrate (semantic listening, non-sounding, cultural listening, musical listening). As we pointed out earlier, it does seem difficult to treat language and music at the same level, and recently some anthropologists have asserted

Table 0.4 Three kinds of listening (Torgue 1999: 28).

CRITERIA		STATES	
Attitude	Diffuse	Metabolic	Analytical (concentrated)
Time	Present/Indefinite	Anamnesis (Retrospection or "retro-audition")	Repetitive (Projection)
Action	Residual sound	Of sound	On sound
Register	Emotion	Identity	Information/ Transcendence

that they should be considered under different analytical paradigms. According to Michael Houseman, relationships to non-sound elements cannot be reduced to a signifier/signified relationship, precisely because music is by nature "plurivocal"; among other things, it depends on "a multiplicity of plans of intelligibility" that language does not have (Houseman 2013: 238). Although the first two models remain vague on the kinds of non-sound confrontations hearers experience, Torgue's model opens up the pragmatic aspects of listening, its temporal passage, and its established relationships of agency (the action *of* sound versus action *on* sound) as very fruitful avenues for study. The relationship to meaning remains somewhat vague in the latter model too, since, as we have seen, it appears in the definition of mundane listening when the emotional and psychometric effects of everyday sounds are concerned.

The distinction between mundane and musical listening is not entirely obvious either, especially if one considers the criteria of action. Some chapters of this volume demonstrate how everyday sound has the capacity to become operative itself (a modality that is not music's exclusive prerogative), and without the perceiving subjects modifying their "diffuse attitude" or relationship to the "present time" that define mundane listening. Pierre Manea's chapter is enlightening in this regard. He offers a historical and phenomenological study of sound signals in use in the overcrowded trains of Tokyo, from the electric bells used in the early twentieth century to contemporary departure melodies. The temporal organization of this progression of tones (approach bell, arrival bell, and departure bell) also corresponds to the differing levels of indexicality conferred on them by the status of "sound-effect signals" that can effectively manage traveler behavior and daily crowds (Chapter 5). Purely acoustic crowd management is also addressed by Christine Guillebaud in her study of an Indian bus station. She shows how ticket vendors' cries function according to a principle of "multiple attraction" that creates effects of presence and relationship as well as collective self-management, which is ultimately rooted in sound events' capacity to generate simultaneous actions (affordance) that assure the daily continuous flow of travelers (Chapter 4).

Last, specialized, reduced, and musician listening have not received much attention from anthropology to date. Two chapters of this volume help to fill this gap. They focus on artistic practices and performance by showing the work of specialists in sound poetry and sound arts. If this kind of specialized listening confirms that perception is connected to a concomitant action on sound (especially in sound synthesis and the use of recording equipment), it also engages other forms of listening at the moment of on-site performance. Once again, the relationship to *meaning* is a dimension cultivated by these artists who try to shake up or transform our relationship to everyday sounds. Jean-Charles Depaule's chapter devoted to scenes of sound poetry mostly of the latter half of the twentieth century shows how some inherited categories came to be upended by the acoustic work of creators such as Bernard

Heidsieck, Ernst Jandl, Henri Chopin, and Brion Gysin. Most of them permanently freed poetry from the yoke of the written text by experimenting with the voice's many performative dimensions and/or incorporating recording techniques of the time into their creations. To the multiplication of the possibilities of work on sound material itself (phasing, cut-and-paste, echo effects, reverberation, distortion) also correspond an increasingly asserted blurring of the boundaries between articulated language and non-linguistic modes of expression (shouted, hummed, aspirated, etc.) or even between sound and noise. The article also pays particular attention to the consideration that musicians and sound artists (Luigi Nono, Luciano Berio, John Cage, etc.) gave to everyday sound milieus, with an eye to creating original works in which mundane, musical, and reduced listening could constantly flow into each other. But in the end, what sound practices are we talking about? "Sound poetry, poetry of sounds, of noises?" wonders Jean-Charles Depaule himself (Chapter 10). In the final chapter, Vincent Rioux describes the artistic experiment he conducted in 2009 on the occasion of the destruction of a fifty-year-old footbridge for pedestrian traffic between downtown and a shopping center in the city of Choisy-le-Roi, France. An on-site artistic project was created to mark the end of "an organic part of the city," including post-contact improvised dance (by the Comipok' collective) and computer-based live sound compositions by the author. An outdoor and multichannel sound installation was developed, inspired by theoretical reflections on individual and collective listening in urban settings. Sound material was collected through informal interviews of inhabitants, who were asked to talk about their use of the footbridge, their memories of it, and its future disappearance. Unlike a purely discursive analysis, their speech was then reworked in real time (timbre, prosody), live-coded as the author reassembled elements, and broadcast in the performance space. The voices became sound materials upon which the artist acted by remixing them with other prerecorded materials while broadcasting the result through speakers discreetly spaced along the bridge. Through the infinite combination of possible effects and the artist's improvisational work, the system helped dancers, pedestrians, and the sound milieu interact with each other by providing "a flexible set of textures to play with in order to create an ever-changing ambiance." Through this sound space, both composed and shared, the author demonstrates the composition of "an ambiance just slightly out of kilter with everyday life that would relate to a mode of modified presence" (Chapter 11).

At the end of this brief presentation of some of the main theoretical models for listening, one fundamental question remains. It concerns the ratio between the previously chosen descriptors for distinguishing between these models. As we have seen, these descriptors present fundamental oppositions between indicator and sign, the natural and cultural, and sound objects and agents. Are the criteria governing these oppositions equally important to the identification of the kinds of listening described here? Is it possible to know the precise moment when one form of listening shifts to another? How to account for mixed or "liminal" forms?[12] Although this book does not hold the definitive answers, it does provide a wide range of ethnographic and artistic case studies that will make it possible to explore and compare our multiple ways of perceiving the sound environment.

Notes

1 In particular, the "WHO Guidelines on Community Noise" edited by B. Berglund and T. Lindvall (1995), an updated version of the document published by the World Health Organization in 1980. Accessed December 2, 2015, at www.who. int/docstore/peh/noise/guidelines2.html.
2 Of particular interest are the British Library's *Save our Sounds* archive program, or the report of the *European Acoustic Heritage* program (Kytö *et al.* 2012).
3 Term coined by Dipesh Chakrabarty in *Provincializing Europe: Postcolonial Thought and Historical Difference* (2007).
4 There has been more recent work to emerge on urban ambiances in Brasil (Thibaud and Duarte 2013) and Egypt (Said 2013).
5 See the conference proceedings, edited by Thibaud and Siret (2012): http://halshs. archives-ouvertes.fr/AMBIANCES2012
6 The "Translating Ambiances" Groupe de recherche international (International Research Group) is certified by the French National Center for Scientific Research (CNRS). See: www.ambiances.net/seminars/gdri-translating-ambiances.html
7 See also the comparable study on the term "soundscape" by Danièle Dubois and the European research group COST TD0804: http://soundscape-cost.org
8 Organized with the support of the University Paris Lumières (PLUM). See the MILSON collective website: http://milson.fr/je/upl-november-2014/ programme-2014–2
9 Readers are invited to consult the audio and/or video recordings that each author provides as ethnographic illustration or for analytical support. These examples are indicated in the body of the texts with references in the format of "Document 1" and can be consulted by author name at the following address: http://milson.fr/ routledge_media
10 The inherent complexity of this model is notably due to the fact that it uses commonly used verbs but goes on to attribute them with specific meanings that may sometimes lead to confusion when applied outside of Schaeffer's theory. It remains relevant nonetheless.
11 Later in the work, Schaeffer requalified the term "objective"—focused on the object of perception, not the activity of the perceiving subject—more ambiguously as "intersubjective" or "collective" (p. 119).
12 See the 23rd ICTM colloquium titled "Between Speech and Song: Liminal Utterances" hosted by the Research Centre for Ethnomusicology (Paris-Ouest Nanterre University, 2015): www.ictmusic.org/23rd-ictm-colloquium

References

Augoyard, Jean-François and Henry Torgue. 1995. *À l'écoute de l'environnement. Répertoire des effets sonores*. Marseille: Editions Parenthèses.
Berglund, Birgitta and Thomas Lindvall, eds. 1995. "WHO Guidelines on Community Noise." *Archives of the Center for Sensory Research* 2 (1): 1–195.
Bijsterveld, Karin and Trevor Pinch, eds. 2012. *The Oxford Handbook of Sound Studies*. New York: Oxford University Press.

Bonini Baraldi, Filippo. 2015. "La douceur, critère d'appréciation esthétique chez les Tsiganes de Transylvanie." *Cahiers d'ethnomusicologie* 29: 23–41.

Brabec de Mori, Bernd and Tony Seeger, eds. 2013. "Considering Music, Humans and Non-Humans." *Ethnomusicology Forum* 22 (3): 269–286.

Brabec de Mori, Bernd and Victor A. Stoichita. 2012. "Sonic Beings? The Ontology of Musical Agency." Panel convened at the 12th EASA Biennial Conference (10–13 July). Nanterre: Paris Ouest Nanterre University.

Bull, Michael and Les Back, eds. 2003. *The Auditory Culture Reader*. Sensory Formations Series. Oxford: Berg.

Chakrabarty, Dipesh. 2007. *Provincializing Europe: Postcolonial Thought and Historical Difference*. Princeton: Princeton University Press.

Chandola, Tripta. 2010. *Listening into Others: In-between Noise and Silence*. PhD Thesis, Queensland University of Technology, Brisbane.

———. 2012. "Listening into Others: Moralising the Soundscapes in Delhi." *International Development Planning Review* 34 (4): 391–408.

Chion, Michel. 2012. "The Three Listening Modes." In *The Sound Studies Reader*, edited by Jonathan Sterne, 48–53. New York: Routledge.

Classen, Constance. 1993. *Worlds of Sense: Exploring the Senses in History and across Cultures*. New York: Routledge.

Coler, Matt. 2014. *A Grammar of Muylaq' Aymara: Aymara as Spoken in Southern Peru*. Brill's studies in the Indigenous languages of the Americas. Leiden: Brill.

Colon, Paul-Louis, ed. 2013. *Ethnographier les sens*. Paris: Petra. Coll. Anthropologiques.

Corbin, Alain. 1994. *Les cloches de la terre: Paysage sonore et culture sensible dans les campagnes au XIXᵉ siècle*. Collection champs-Flammarion. Paris: Albin Michel.

Dubois, Danièle, ed. 2009. *Le sentir et le dire. Concepts et méthodes en psychologie et linguistique cognitives*. Paris: L'Harmattan.

———. 2012. "Dénommer, définir, identifier, décrire une ambiance: A Semantic Analysis of the Word 'Soundscape'." In *Ambiances in action / Ambiances en acte(s): International Congress on Ambiances, Montreal, Sept 2012*, edited by Jean-Paul Thibaud and Daniel Siret, 683–688. Montreal: International Ambiances Network.

Dubois, Danièle and Matt Coler. 2014. "Sounds, Languages and Meanings: Ontologies or Umwelten?" Communication at the *MILSON conference "Le son pris aux mots" (20–21 nov.)*. Org. by Christine Guillebaud, Rosalia Martinez and Vincent Rioux. Paris: National School of Fine Arts.

Eisenberg, Andrew J. 2013. "Islam, Sound and Space: Acoustemology and Muslim Citizenship on the Kenyan Coast." In *Music, Sound and Space: Transformations of Public and Private Experience*, edited by Georgina Born, 186–202. Cambridge: Cambridge University Press.

Fabian, Johannes. 1983. *Time and the Other: How Anthropology Makes Its Object*. New York: Columbia University Press.

Feld, Steven. 1994. "From Ethnomusicology to Echo-Muse-Ecology: Reading R. Murray Schafer in the Papua New Guinea Rainforest." *The Soundscape Newsletter* 8. www.acousticecology.org/writings/echomuseecology.html.

———. 1996. "Waterfalls of Song: An Acoustemology of Place Resounding in Bosavi, Papua New Guinea." In *Senses of Place*, edited by Steven Feld and Keith H. Basso, 91–135. Santa Fé: School of American Research Press.

———. 2000. "Sound Worlds." In *Sound*, edited by Patricia Kruth and Henry Stobart, 173–200. Cambridge: Cambridge University Press.

Feld, Steven and Don Brenneis. 2004. "Doing Anthropology in Sound." *American Ethnologist* 31 (4): 461–474.

Féraud, Olivier. 2010. *Voix publiques: Environnements sonores, représentations et usages d'habitation dans un quartier populaire de Naples*. PhD Thesis, Ecole des Hautes Etudes en Sciences Sociales, Paris.

———. 2013. "Ethnographier les environnements sonores." In *Ethnographier les sens*, edited by Paul-Louis Colon, 117–144. Paris: Petra.

Gell, Alfred. 1995. "The Language and the Forest: Landscape and Phonological Iconism in Umeda." In *The Anthropology of Landscape: Perspectives on Place and Space*, edited by Eric Hirsch and Michael O'Hanlon, 232–254. Oxford: Oxford University Press.

Grosjean, Michèle and Jean-Paul Thibaud, eds. 2001. *L'espace urbain en méthodes*. Marseille: Éditions Parenthèses.

Guillebaud, Christine. 2008. *Le chant des serpents. Musiciens itinérants du Kerala*. Paris: CNRS Editions.

———. 2009. "Musique mécanique et temple hindou: Histoire controversée d'un dispositif visuel et sonore." *Terrain: Revue d'Ethnologie de l'Europe* 53: 98–113.

———. 2015. "The Dēva/Asura sound categories and their spatial distribution in the Maṇṇarśāla Nāgas temple (Kerala, South India)". Paper delivered at the International Symposium *Sound perception of places of worship (of different religions) via a multidisciplinary anthropological and acoustic approach* (3–4 November, Paris: Musée du quai Branly).

Houseman, Michael. 2013. "Postface. Rira bien qui rira le dernier. À propos de l'humour musical." *Cahiers d'ethnomusicologie* 26: 231–239.

Howes, David, ed. 1991. *The Varieties of Sensory Experience: A Sourcebook in the Anthropology of the Senses*. Toronto: University of Toronto Press.

———. 2003. *Sensual Relations Engaging the Senses in Culture and Social Theory*. Ann Arbor: University of Michigan Press.

Ingold, Tim. 2000. *The Perception of the Environment: Essays in Livelihood, Dwelling and Skill*. New York: Routledge.

Järviluoma, Helmi, Meri Kytö, Barry Truax, Heikki Uimonen, Noora Vikman, and R. Murray Schafer. 2009. *Acoustic Environments in Change & Five Village Soundscapes*. Tampere: University of Applied Sciences and University of Joensuu.

Kytö, Meri, Nicolas Remy, and Heikki Uimonen, eds. 2012. *European Acoustic Heritage*. Tampere: Tampere University of Applied Sciences; Grenoble: Cresson.

Legrain, Laurent. 2014. *Chanter, s'attacher et transmettre chez les Darhad de Mongolie*. Paris: EPHE, Collection Nord-Asie 4.

Lenclud, Gérard. 1992. "Le grand partage ou la tentation ethnologique." In *Vers une ethnologie du present*, edited by Gérard Althabe, Daniel Fabre, and Gérard Lenclud, 9–37. Paris: Maison des sciences de l'Homme.

Martinez, Rosalia. 1996. *Musique du désordre, musique de l'ordre. Le calendrier musical chez les Jalq'a (Bolivie)*. PhD Thesis, Université Paris X, Nanterre.

McCartney, Andra and David Paquette. 2012. "Walking, Listening, Speaking: The Soundwalking Interactions Project." In *Ambiances in action / Ambiances en acte(s): International Congress on Ambiances, Montreal, Sept 2012*, edited by Jean-Paul Thibaud and Daniel Siret, 189–194. Montreal: International Ambiances Network.

Panopoulos, Panayotis. 2003. "Animal Bells as Symbols: Sound and Hearing in a Greek Island Village." *Journal of the Royal Anthropological Institute* 9: 639–656.

Pink, Sarah. 2010. *Doing Sensory Ethnography*. London: Routledge.

Prévot, Nicolas. 2014. "Music, Spirits & Spirit in Bastar, Central India." In *Dialogues with Gods, Possession in Middle Indian Rituals*, edited by Tina Otten and Uwe Skoda, 229–246, Berlin: Weißensee Verlag, Indo-European Studies in Politics and Society 6.

Ricci, Antonello. 1996. *Ascoltare il mondo, Antropologia dei suoni in un paese del sud d'Italia*. Roma: Il Trovatore.

Rice, Tom. 2013. *Hearing and the Hospital: Sound, Listening, Knowledge and Experience*. Canon Pyon: Sean Kingston Publishing.

Said, Nora Gamal. 2013. "Cairo behind the Gates: Studying the Sensory Configuration of Al-Rehab City." *Ambiances*. http://ambiances.revues.org/252.

Samuels, David W., Meintjes Louise, Ochoa Ana Maria, and Thomas Porcello. 2010. "Soundscapes: Toward a Sounded Anthropology." *Annual Review of Anthropology* 39: 329–345.

Schaeffer, Pierre. 1966. *Traité Des Objets Musicaux. Essai Interdisciplines. Nouvelle Édition*. Paris: Éditions du Seuil.

Schafer, Murray. 1977. *The Soundscape: Our Sonic Environment and the Tuning of the World*. Rochester: Destiny Books.

Sterne, Jonathan, ed. 2012. *The Sound Studies Reader*. London: Routledge.

Thibaud, Jean-Paul. 2001. "La méthode des parcours commentés." In *L'espace urbain en méthodes*, edited by Michèle Grosjean and Jean-Paul Thibaud, 79–99. Marseille: Éditions Parenthèses.

Thibaud, Jean-Paul and Cristiane R. Duarte, eds. 2013. *Ambiances urbaines en partage: pour une écologie sociale de la ville sensible*. Genève: MetisPresses.

Thibaud, Jean-Paul and Daniel Siret, eds. *Ambiances in action/ Ambiances en acte(s): International Congress on Ambiances, Montreal, Sept 2012*. Grenoble: International Ambiances Network.

Torgue, Henry. 1999. "Aspects de l'écoute." In *Espaces, musiques, environnement sonore. Quels liens entre les recherches sur l'environnement sonore et la musique?*, edited by Björn Hellström and Nicolas Rémy, 27–34. Grenoble: Cresson.

Westerkamp, Hildegard. 1974. "Soundwalking." *Sound Heritage* 3 (4): 18–27.

Part I
Listening into Others

1 Noising the City

Revealing Popular Neapolitan "Soundciabilities" in Pyrotechnical Practices

Olivier Féraud

Daily social postures, as can be observed in most popular areas of Naples, often show particular sonic intentionalities. Sonorous attitudes demonstrated in interactional situations in public spaces where inhabitants convene and converse from windows, balconies and streets illustrate the community's sociability strategies. A set of these invisible sociability strategies can be unveiled by listening to the place they occupy in the public space. This kind of "soundciability" is the subject of this chapter, as observable in the Neapolitan context.

Even if many current studies deal with human perceptive dimensions of the sonic environment, their methodologies rarely properly attest to an ethnographical approach. Deep and close observation performed over a relatively long period of time of the way people practice, listen to and produce their sonic environments lets us tackle some social and cultural aspects to which neither classical acoustical nor psycho-perceptive approaches give access. Using categorical questionnaires or quantitative evaluations, these approaches usually focus on individuals' perceptive processes, or are limited to quantitative measurements of acoustical phenomena, giving priority to experimental protocols that ignore or do not give enough importance to the sociocultural dimension of the sonic relation between people and their environment on one hand, and between people as sociocultural groups on the other hand.[1] The ethnographical approach lets us focus on the fact that the sonic dimension of many human contexts can often be an explicit mark of social organization and social relations. Despite the development of the anthropology of senses that, among other things, pointed to an occularcentric worldview (Howes 1991), and in spite of audition being considered as a less minor sense than olfaction, touch or taste in the Western system of thought, sound has only recently been taken into consideration in social and cultural studies. The introduction of sonic preoccupations into anthropological field research (Feld 1994, Ricci 1999) is closely linked to the popularity of the term "soundscape". Originating in an eco-art background (Schafer 1977, Truax 1978), soundscape was developed later within the artistic field (Dauby 2004) and the sound ecology field.[2] The term is now quite widespread in different fields, such as perception of environment (Amphoux 1994), psychoacoustics (Dubois *et al.* 2006), bioacoustics (Oba 2006), environmental acoustics, urban studies or history of senses (Corbin 1994, Fritz 2000, Gutton 2000). Following the epistemological positions of these studies, soundscape can be used as a theoretical or methodological tool, or as a concept, in order to reveal a variety of qualitative aspects, such as assessment, identification, spatial positioning, meaning or aesthetic reception.

Even if these ambient studies attest to a real attention to human reception of ambient sounds, the term "ambiance" is often used as a global sensitive perception of environment (Tixier 2011)[3] mixing different senses and representations without really taking into account the actor's sociocultural heritage. One could venture to say that the fact that these studies hardly surpass the individual level of perception hinders them from being considered as anthropological approaches. Furthermore, statistics never truly deeply reach social and cultural aspects. The problem may stem from the term "soundscape" itself. From a Shaferian "point of view", listening to the "sounds of the world" would be equivalent to the contemplation of a panoramic viewpoint. Considering the relatedness between "soundscape" and "landscape", the term inevitably induces a frontal positioning; it places the individual as a spectator in a position of contemplation. Although such a listening experience would be possible in a concert hall, listening to a recording represents only an isolated aural experience. It does not properly represent the everyday human sonic experience of surrounding sounds. In his criticism of the term "soundscape", Tim Ingold compares sound to light more than to vision, recalling that sound "is neither mental nor material, but a phenomenon of experience" (Ingold 2007). Following this position, we do not hear a soundscape when we listen to our surroundings. In the same way light immerses, "sound is not the object but the medium of our perception. It is what we hear in" (Ingold 2007). This question of the frontality of the sonic perception focuses on immersion by pointing out the fact that we "hear in" more than we "hear something", as a commingling within a context.

Following this position, it is possible to affirm that just as being an inhabitant of a popular Neapolitan area implies taking part in the social environment and the interrelations, it also implies being a part of the sonic environment. Living in such a place as a part of the social web necessarily induces actively taking part, whether through sounds or silence, exuberantly or discreetly, in the social strategies of interaction. Within the popular Neapolitan context, such "soundcial" (socio-sonic) postures can be revealed by focusing on two types of notable sonic postures that show a particular investment of the acoustic and social space. The first type, in a microsociological approach, is intrinsically linked to the daily outdoor life in popular areas: everyday interactional situations that imply the use of loud, or "public", voices both in the domestic context and during vocal interactions with street sellers.[4] The second is a sonic action linked to celebration: the popular practices of fireworks and firecrackers.[5] Popular pyrotechnical practices can be considered as loud sonic actions that confront the urban sonic dimension convening a large audience, denoting demonstrativeness and expressivity. I would like to focus precisely on these pyrotechnical practices that involve particularly loud sonic action.

This reflection shall be carried out by discussing the term "noising", considering it as a way of investing spaces through actions using loud sound as a medium. A definition of "noising" can be found in the Urban Dictionary as "the act of people causing a nuisance or making a noise".[6] "Noising" appears as an interesting term to express the way people intentionally use sounds as actions, to diffuse something other than exclusively sound, in a large space (in the sense of social—or public—space). Considering "noising" in this way provides an occasion to explore "noise" in terms that go beyond its simple negative connotations. Indeed, even if the term "noise" has been questioned by many authors,[7] in most studies as well as, more generally, in the Western-oriented cultural history (Schwartz 2011), "noise" usually carries negative connotations, by referring to acoustic pollution and nuisance. Noise can be all the unwanted sounds masking what should be correctly heard or listened to, or what we do not usually pay attention to but is nevertheless disturbing or embarrassing. In this reflection, I suggest that we should cease framing noise "through a restrictive geometry of appreciation" (Schwartz 2011), but rather consider it as a porous sonic phenomenon involving people, intentionality and sociability.

Considering the way other Neapolitan sociocultural groups hear and stigmatize sonic environments of the Neapolitan popular areas as a dual pollution, that is sonic pollution as well as social pollution, it is easily understandable that noise is generally a question of judgment, an opinion projected toward others.[8] Observations from the popular area inhabitants' "point of listening" (Chion 1985) reveal that the sonic environment not only results from social disorganization and incivility but also from an intention, and that this intentionality is aimed more at producing loud, rather than disturbing, sounds. In French, the translation of the word "noise", *bruit*, derives from the verb *bruire*, which means to produce sound. However, *bruit* or *bruire* is also linked to the idea of rumor, as in the first verse of this seventeenth-century French song: "*Vostre bruit et vostre grant fame me fait vous amer plus que fame.*"[9] As Michel Chion (2007) relates, in classical French literature, like in Molière or Racine, "the term *bruit* [. . .] does not refer to a sound, even less to an animal cry, but to news, fame, reputation, honor (or dishonor), quarrel or rumor . . ." We will retain this meaning, considering that noising, in such a popular Neapolitan context, does not entail making untimely noises but rather a way of making oneself public, as a commingling with the social network. The aim of this reflection is to reveal what can be expressed behind the loudness of such social postures. We will not only explore what Michel de Certeau (1994) calls "ways of doing", but also listen to some Neapolitan "ways of noising".

Firework Practices as Acts of Noising the City

Fireworks let us see how intentional sonic acts can be extended to the level of the city. Popular practices of fireworks exemplify social, ritual and emotional ways of being noisy in the streets, of making the streets noisy and of noising the city. A strong taste and a shared interest for fireworks are clearly present in the Neapolitan context. Fireworks are experienced as a properly traditional way of expressing celebration. More generally, fireworks are claimed as a Vesuvian tradition by all Neapolitans who feel a sense of cultural belonging to their region, in reference to the Neapolitan craft industry, the Neapolitan pyrotechnical reputation and the historical background.

- **Document 1:** In the street [2'26"]. Olivier Féraud 2008. A boy expressly goes into the streets after the New Year's family midnight festivities to use fireworks. For many people, fireworks have to be used down in the street. It is a way of investing and appropriating the street as the space of noise at this moment.

The practice of firecrackers (called *botti*) and fireworks (commonly called *fuocchi*) has increased in the last decades, even if some public security awareness campaigns have recently tried to curb it. Traditionally used during the New Year's celebrations and for religious processions, firecrackers have progressively come into competition with fireworks in various celebration frameworks, such as marriage or baptism. The firecracker lover's attraction to more powerful explosives, linked to the immoderate use of fireworks among the popular classes, has provoked a loathing sentiment within the middle class. Oral testimonies easily associate firecracker noise to noise pollution, delinquency, incivility and social, economic and cultural instability. Yet, firecracker lovers insist on different values, such as pleasure, emotion and courage. For young firecracker lovers who consider themselves as street boys, firing impressive and noisy explosives allows them to experience and confront the fragility of the body with the potential destructive danger of fire, power and loudness. During this experience of explosion, sound and smoke, the skin, ears and nose are challenged through something that represents a set of cultural values experienced as a way of living the image of a popular Neapolitanity tinged with economic instability, social violence and traditionalism. Through the *botti* and *fuocchi* dialectic, distinct realities coexist. Observing these different practices in their own settings reveals divergent relations with the sonic environment and the public spaces.

Fireworks and Firecrackers: Some Collective Representations

Before pursuing further, it is important to return to the crucial distinction between fireworks and firecrackers. This distinction is technical as well as socioeconomic and cultural. Classical fireworks, called *fuocchi* (diminutive

Figure 1.1 Boys discussing after having fired a big *candela romana* in the street around 01:00 a.m. on New Year's night in the Quartieri Spagnoli.

Photo: Olivier Féraud (2005).

of *fuocchi d'artificio*), are first of all used and appreciated for the art of light. That is the reason why they are also called *luce colorate* (colored light). Loud sound is, of course, also an important dimension. But unlike fire-crackers, the aural appreciation is not the noisy aspect of the sonic production. As domesticated noise, fireworks produce a structured configuration of whistles and well laid-out detonations, which are coordinated with the light choreography.

A third designation is *Bengali*. The visual fireworks are often considered as less local than firecrackers. On one hand, this denomination reminds us that, in popular thinking, fireworks were first a Chinese invention. *Bengali* is also a hazy "orientalist" reference to the actual Neapolitan Chinese market without taking into account any precise geographical origin.[10] The Chinese community actually occupies a large part of the economic scene in Naples, which is one of the biggest commercial ports in Italy. Inasmuch, the majority of the family-used low-cost fireworks are Chinese products. Traditionalist discourses criticize this market, insisting on the popular and accessible nature of this product that encouraged some abusive uses, like F1, a 55-year-old man employed in the social administration: "[. . .] a few years ago, families called the pyrotechnist out for important fireworks . . . now everything is Chinese products!"

Critics also point out security arguments, denouncing the cheap quality of these Chinese products, compared to the historical Neapolitan firework industry, which is seen as an art form. Such discourses are a mark of the competition between the Neapolitans and the Chinese. Even if each year firework use is the cause of a great number of accidents, these critics of Chinese fireworks often overstep the subject of the fireworks themselves and aim rather at the presence of the Chinese in general.

The fireworks called *botti* are small or large pyrotechnic devices that are simply intended to offer detonation and smoke. The term *botta* refers to the sound as well as the act. In Italian it means "blow" as well as "noise", in the sense of a noisy action with a violent connotation. In other terms, the physical object *botta* (firecracker) is denoted by the sound that it produces. This sound is not only a loud sound; it is also a powerfully oriented noise. Firecrackers are predominantly used by young men and children in the popular areas at different times throughout the year and/or just for fun. Passionate members of the middle class also use them on limited occasions, such as celebrations. In terms of socially oriented practice and in terms of a sentiment of sociocultural belonging, globally, fireworks appear as appealing more to a middle class, while firecrackers are always associated to the street as popular space of expressing celebration, and in a pejorative sense to instability, insecurity, with frequent reference to the Camorrista underworld (as shall be developed later).

Fireworks Within the Family Circle

Pyrotechny is a family affair. Generally, all members (children, parents and grandparents) share a common taste for detonation, lights and noise. Rich families often have a trusted family pyrotechnist, in the same way some have a family doctor, who knows the family circle, knows the family's preferences and provides safe fireworks. For most families the New Year's celebration fireworks represent a quite important expense. Fireworks, more specifically, are always the affair of men, both young and old. Adult men also frequently show a passion for fireworks, associating them to masculinity and virility, but also to the games of their youth.

Young boys are initiated to fireworks by their father or grandfather. Fa., a student living in the city center, relates:

> Firing and using firecrackers has always been a family affair . . . When I was younger, my father used to sell firecrackers and to set them off, it has always been like that . . . My father doesn't fire anymore, certainly because he is older now . . . But adults also fire, like 40 or 50 years old . . . Whoever enjoys firecrackers sets them off.

Girls are more naturally oriented toward "colored lights." In the family circle, girls are allowed to participate in the lighting of small-sized and harmless fireworks, such as *candele romane* (called "roman candles" in English), which can be described as hand-held torches diffusing a colorful and incandescent panache. Commonly, the fireworks used by families are small or mid-size colored whittling rockets, and lightning torches and fountains.

Figure 1.2 Girl holding a fired *candela romana* on a balcony during the 2005 New Year's night in the Quartieri Spagnoli.
Photo: Olivier Féraud (2005).

Before developing the aesthetic, emotional and sociocultural values associated to fireworks, it is important to detail other distinctions within the *botti* category.

A Typology of Firecrackers

Different types of firecrackers can be categorized according to legality, size and power. The biggest and most powerful among them is called *bomba*, which can be presented as the most "illegal". Each year, a new *bomba* with a new name is released on the market. Each name is linked to a famous international figure with attributes of power, crime or subversion. The names collected during the fieldwork were for example: *a pall'a Maradona* (Maradonna's ball), *a bomb'a Ben Laden* (Ben Laden's bomb), *a bomb'a Sadam Hussein* (Sadam Hussein's bomb), or *a testata di Zidane* (Zidane's headbutt). Another illegal firecracker is the *mezza bomba*, which is a less powerful *bomba*.

Legal firecrackers constitute another category, corresponding to a smaller, less powerful range. The *batteria* is a battery of mid-strength firecrackers that produce a significant detonation. Batteries can reach the length of six meters.

Tracch is a very popular small battery. It is composed of a series of small firecrackers ending with one more powerful cracker called the *botta finale* (final blow). Discourses often insist on an interesting verbal depiction of the sonic sequence produced by the *tracch*. It is nearly always

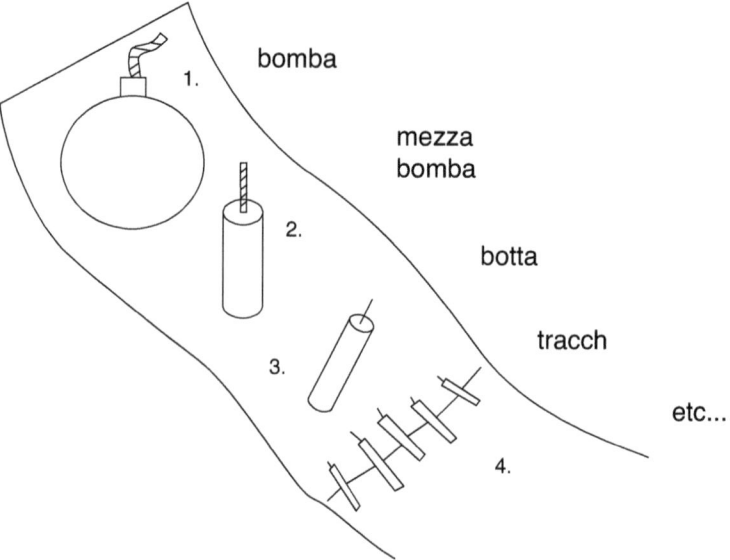

Figure 1.3 Drawing of different firecrackers' size.
Source: Olivier Féraud (2008).

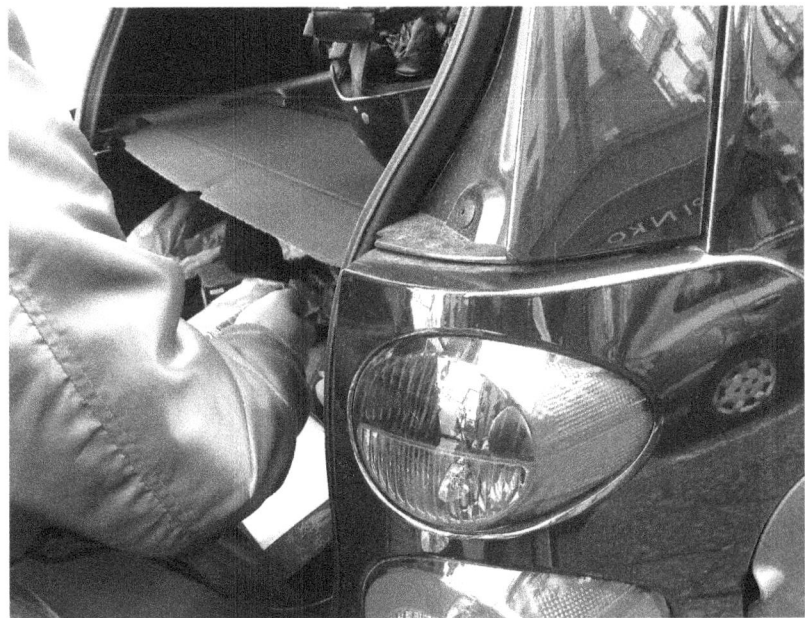

Figure 1.4 Illegal firecracker sales in the street on the day before New Year's Eve. Boys also buy black market Chinese fireworks because of the lower cost.

Photo: Olivier Féraud (2008).

the same: "PA! PA! PA! shwit! BANG!" "PA!" are the small firecracker's detonations, "shwit!" corresponds to the fuse firing, and "BANG!" is the final big firecracker's detonation.

The most powerful and illegal firecrackers are made and sold on the black market. Each user has his own vendor, a trustworthy person who can be described as a sort of firecracker dealer. Many people explain that traditionally firecrackers would be handmade at home, using paper and gunpowder.

Popular Street Pyrotechnic Practices

Firecracker and fireworks sounds occur in different contexts. The variability of use depends on the kind of relationship the user has with the act of noising. In each case, fireworks "noise" the city by investing the urban sound environment. Five occasions of using pyrotechnics can be distinguished.

New Year's Celebration

- **Document 2:** A few minutes of the Quartieri Spagnoli resounding at midnight. Olivier Féraud 2008. Some vocal reactions to firecracker's

detonations can be heard [2'26"]. Midnight is marked by a great detonation that can be heard at mark 38 second of the recording.

The New Year is a very important celebration in which fireworks are omnipresent. Pyrotechnic sounds start more than one month before. An audible
crescendo in the frequency of the detonations increases around the New
Year. The climax explodes at midnight on December 31. Fireworks and
firecrackers arise from everywhere, from the windows or the balconies. This
urban fire is experienced as a joyful war. This moment is full of both happiness and enthusiasm, although the omnipresence of explosions and rockets
render it dangerous as well. Some men, younger or older, also shoot with
guns in such a way that people never really know if bullets are real or blank
cartridges. We can thus understand why people generally advise not to go
out in the street from midnight to 1:30 a.m. Because of the great number of
accidents on New Year's Eve and the day after, authorities try to limit the
familial use of fireworks and fight against the powerful products of the black
market. Common accidents occur, for example, when children find cheap or
handmade unexploded fireworks on the streets and try to fire them. Public
awareness and police actions have contributed to diminishing private fireworks use in recent years.

Religious Occasions

Fireworks are also used during public religious processions in the streets
as a mark of joyous collective celebration. Mostly, firecrackers and batteries are used, but small rockets can also be lit in small religious contexts.
These kinds of small religious processions are organized by a local religious
association and gather local inhabitants. Firecracker batteries are lit once
in front of one of the small chapels dedicated to a saint. Using fireworks in
the daytime clearly shows that they are explicitly used for producing noise.
Also during more important religious celebrations, such as the Sant'Agata
in Catania (Sicily), the visual dimension of large luminous rockets used in
the daytime is reduced to smoke in the sky and supplanted by the impressive
sonic experience.

Celebrations

As a soundmark of celebration and collective expression of festivities, fireworks are also used for birthdays, marriage and baptism. Night and day,
family festivities are punctuated by sounds of detonations and fireworks.
Some say that the *fuocchi* phenomenon has increased in the past several
years:

> In general, if a marriage is celebrated, they do it in the square or the flat
> garden, which is also situated inside the square . . . even if it's 2:00 or

3:00 A.M., they set off fireworks . . . For the past 2 or 3 years using fire-works for any reason has become a fashion, it can be for a birthday, a marriage, a baptism, or just to celebrate some student's diploma.[11]

Fireworks are integrated in the loud sonic context of festivities such as marriage or birthdays, and even in victory celebrations of the Napoli (the famous Neapolitan football [soccer] team), in which loud popular *neom-elodico* music occupies an important place. In a popular area of the city center such as the Spanish Quarters, fireworks are fired day or night from the windows, the balcony or the street for these occasions.

The *"Malavita* Fireworks"

The other occurrences in which firework sounds can be heard but not explic-itly associated to common family celebrations or religious events can be clas-sified in a final category of unexplained detonations, a sort of "black-box" for unidentified sounds. Corroborating a contemporary urban legend, when confronted with these mysterious sounds people often evoke the Camorra. "*Malavita* fireworks" resound as an echo of gang gun-shots that sometimes resonate in district streets. Often stigmatized for the nuisance they provoke, these detonations are strangely considered as enigmatic despite the usual frequency of the fireworks phenomenon. ML reports a 3-month period when she was disturbed night and day by explosions:

> I'm convinced they were not celebrating anything because. . . if it hap-pened one or two times a week, in that case we could think they were celebrating something. . . but the fact that it occurred every evening for three months. . . but, anyway, it also happened during the winter. . .

When asked if the local inhabitants wondered about these regular explo-sions, she answered: "No, maybe people didn't want to talk about it . . . but recently, fortunately, we don't hear it anymore . . . maybe the time is gone, the euphoria . . ." she added, leaving these questions shrouded in mystery.

Globally, two distinct explanations appear in the related discourses. The first one is related to celebration: fireworks would be used to celebrate the release of a prisoner, or more precisely the return of a son from prison. Many ear witnesses tend to link these serial detonations to a reduction of sentence periods, like in 2006 and 2007, as V.[12] says: "They fired under a friend's window, in the middle of the night . . . during that period it could only be because of that . . ."

Without any visual proof, it is said that "these things are well known", and they are presented as a tradition attributed to "people like them", point-ing their supposed relation with the *malavita* underworld. In a sense, if not for the underlying motivations, this use of fireworks and crackers in this case could be considered as part of the classical celebration category.

The second explanation is more directly linked to the economy of the underworld. Setting off fireworks or crackers would constitute a system to signal the delivery of trafficked goods (such as drugs). Underlining the paradoxical nature of such a sonic and luminous signal related to a hidden traffic, V. ironically added: "by phone it would be risky; even if they used cellular . . . it's like Indians making smoke signals!" Despite this paradox, this explanation occurs more frequently than the first. Some argue that this system allows for a swifter organization, while others insist on the efficiency of such a signal to also alert all of the implicated people, including the regular customers. In any case, it is interesting that these pervasive sounds should be esteemed for their efficiency and ability to reach multitudes of people at once. This Camorra legend is a good example of noising the city: this mixture of perceptive efficiency and banality illustrates in a particularly explicit way how extensively projecting a sound in the whole sonic environment of the city can underline social strategies.

Different Dimensions of Making Noise With Fireworks

The Ritual Dimension

Globally, the New Year's celebration can be understood through three essential aspects: opulence, excess and gathering. These three aspects intervene at different fundamental levels, like food, behavior and noisy attitudes. At a symbolic level, the New Year's celebration is experienced as a ritual of conclusion and renewal, a temporal transition fixing what is considered as past and preparing what will happen in the future. The strong symbolic act of destruction of what has to be over, cancelled, forgotten or discarded is operated with happiness and emotional expression through the use of fire. The old has to be thrown away, broken and burned. In popular neighborhoods, people traditionally throw used domestic objects from the windows, such as plates of food, glass or even toilet bowls, or burn bins and garbage.

During the New Year's celebration, fire is omnipresent. Along with the symbolic dissolution of the past, the act of destruction by fire also has an apotropaic function of providing fortune. For example, A. reports that, for the New Year, his grandmother used to light only one firecracker at the window, which she released at the last moment just before the explosion in a sort of fortune-telling act: if no accident occurred, then good fortune could arise during the year.

Opulence also takes part in a game of visibility and competition. Each year, families invest a significant sum of money in fireworks, representing a large part of ordinary family earnings. A man's or a family's opulence and wealth are displayed through the amount of fireworks set off directly from the windows, as an external mark of the celebration. This social aspect of noising can also be heard on any day: some like to use fireworks just for noise as a sort of competitive game. Finding and using powerful firecrackers or long firecracker batteries in the street and lighting impressively whistling and noisy fireworks are ways for people to make their involvement in the festivity be seen and heard. Such noise competition games are also a common source of noise pollution complaints from other socioeconomic groups considering themselves as more "educated" or having a higher sense of civility.

The Social Dimension

The New Year's celebration is an intense moment for families that gather all members in a shared experience of celebration both inside and outside the home. Despite this, the celebration is not entirely family-centered: after the "interior" session (the dinner), there is a more socially oriented "exterior" session, where the city becomes the stage for celebration and inhabitants go outdoors. Around one o'clock in the morning, after having fired fireworks from the home windows, the family nucleus often divides. Parents take the younger children to see the official firework show, and the teenagers go to set off firecrackers in the streets, while grandparents stay at home. When the fireworks are being lit, the street becomes the space of the collective expression of the climax of the festivities. Although not everyone takes part in the actual lighting of fireworks, the simple fact that all come to listen to the outdoor detonations proves their involvement. Moreover, if listening may be unintentional, the loud volume of fireworks forces this aural participation. In this case of global participation, a large sonic environment is shared by all of the city's inhabitants. This is a particularly clear example of sonic immersion in that fireworks are not simply heard but are "heard in" (Ingold 2007). In that sense, popular practices of fireworks suppose a particularly expressive mode of sociability, which takes a sonic form. What can be called a soundciability here uses clear and strong media by producing powerful and impressive noise in the public space, and even more so by investing the air for a much more extensive involvement.

As noise producers, firecrackers, non-celebrational and abusive fireworks are subject to stigmatization. The strong distinction between *botti* and *fuocchi* turns into a clear sociocultural competition, in the sense that fireworks are associated to various deficiencies projected onto the Neapolitan popular context. In the critical discourses, two important arguments are observable. First, firecrackers only make noise, while fireworks are above all light, color and pleasure for the eyes (i.e., "colored lights"). Second, in addition to this gratuitous nuisance, firecrackers are dangerous and explode in the street, in the middle of what should be the public space, while fireworks explode high in the air, which is a free zone where there is no risk of accidents. A third argument is that, if firecrackers are just used to make noise and for fun, fireworks are more a matter of art, and as such require the presence of an explosives expert and are nearly always linked to official, controlled and exceptional celebrations. Firecrackers are seen as savage and uncontrolled noise, in contrast to fireworks that can be considered as domesticated or civilized noise. This can be considered as a sonic transfer of the stigmatization between middle class and popular areas of population, who are perceived as uncivilized, uneducated, dirty, speaking and shouting a rude Neapolitan language. In this socioeconomically centered system of thought, noise, dirtiness and rude behaviors are naturally associated with popular background's deficiencies in civility, economy, education and hygiene. From the firecrackers lovers' point of view, noise is not necessarily chaotic. Our observation shows that this socioeconomic model is obsolete, first because a lot of popular areas' inhabitants really do not like firecrackers, and second because many middle class boys love firecrackers.

The Emotional Dimension

Firecracker lovers show a real fascination for noise: one person may be attracted by the idea of symbolic destruction while another loves standing as close as possible to the detonations in the midst of the sulfurous smoke of firecrackers set off during the religious processions in the streets. Beyond the loud noise itself, different values, such as courage, virility and risk-taking, are associated with the search for an intense emotional experience. The search for a sentiment of power is also linked to the investing of the streets in confrontation with the urban space, based on the sentiment that loud sounds invest large spaces. By noising the city, firecracker users express a reappropriation of the street as a space of popular culture and claim a feeling of belonging to the firecracker community but also to a certain Neapolitanity.

Firecracker users' representations do not reveal as many social critiques as the middle class people showing a preference for fireworks. However, one important "soundcial" posture is the use of the street as a place for conspicuous expression. In the same way, parts of the streets are transformed into gardens or living rooms where different types of furniture are installed, such as chairs, tables, window boxes or clothes dryers, thus constituting territorial constructions that question the street as a public space. Producing loud and dangerous sounds in the street can be seen as a way of claiming the street as the space of popular everyday life. As a symbolic transposition of the traditional and hierarchical social organization, some discourses implicitly claim that firecrackers, as a traditional popular noisy expression of festivity, naturally take place down in the street to express, in a resounding way, that this is the place where the people live, while higher classes use the sky to spread their distinction in a brilliantly colorful way. These discourses are closely linked to those which criticize the structural hierarchy between rich people living in higher levels (such as upstairs in the flat or in the higher ground of Naples).[13] Loudness and dangerousness are essential parts of the firecracker's emotional expression. What is expressed is a strong and intense emotion conveying different values such as courage, virility, power and risk. These values are experienced through emotion as an exciting pleasure of being the author of potentially destructive powerful noises. F2, 22-year-old Neapolitan student, put his fascination into words:

- I have been setting off firecrackers for 20 years, I still set off crackers . . . now I'm 22 . . . since the age of 8 or 9, I fire like that, strongly, really strongly . . . I really like it, I totally love it . . . I like that . . . that something breaks . . .
- Destroying something?
- In that situation yes . . . I really like this noise . . . well, I'm not saying that I go and break . . . I like the idea . . .

In an attempt to deliver an initial conclusion about this popular firework practice, and from a communicational point of view, we can pinpoint the fact that such strong sonic actions constitute remote connections between community members, and a casting of presence, information and emotion in a much larger space than the street. In urban studies, the public nature of the street space is commonly considered as one of the higher levels of collective sharing. By thrusting informational sounds into the air, above the built space of the city, sonic actors perform at a higher level of community. They occupy and use a larger space, which is at the same time a larger perceptive space and an ecological niche (Uexküll 1934) that is not usually used by human urban inhabitants. Fireworks visually and physically propel above the level of buildings and aurally pervade above the level of the usual city's sonic environment (the urban drone). The sonic nature of the action allows one to more widely express oneself and one's message in the whole city's space.

We can now more clearly discuss how pyrotechnical sounds can build "soundcial" (socio-sonic) environments. During celebration days, these sounds are omnipresent in the daily time and space. As signs and manifestations of the presence, as well as vocal actions (Féraud 2013a), the pyrotechnical audibility shows how much the street is practiced as a social space during the day and at night, given to hear rejoicings to all ears in the district as a way of gathering others and broadcasting what is happening within this or that family. By their omnipresence, fireworks and firecrackers immerse the inhabitants into a "noisy" environment (which shows variability in its intensity). As a daily sonority, the daily life partly takes shape in the pyrotechnical sounds, incarnates the presence of others and the relations they enjoy (or not). In that sense, such sounds are a mark of the district's social life, owing to the fact that they highly contribute, as a communicative sonority, to the inter-knowledge that can be observed in popular districts. In other words, living in a place is also putting it to sound. Detonations make the places resound; they "noise" the living spaces. As a sonic occupation revealing the ways people are interconnected, fireworks and firecrackers give substance to the soundciabilities.

In conclusion, we can point out how human sonic environments are closely linked to inhabiting strategies: a mark of the ways of investing one space or another. Listening to a sonic environment with an anthropological ear requires acute attention to the inhabitant's activities, the social organization, or the type of permitted or forbidden relationship, following the daily organization, the place, the social functions or the social status of the individuals. This example of pyrotechnical practices has highlighted how studying sonic environments, ways of noising and soundciabilities can enhance our understanding of organizational, social and cultural systems from various possible standpoints, such as gender (for example women's conversational moments while hanging laundry in the late morning), age group (children shouting and playing late at night) or socioeconomic membership (discussions and chats among poor people living on ground-floor apartments, settled in the street or on doorsteps).

Notes

1 See Féraud (2013a) for a critical discussion between ethnography and perception studies concerning sonic environment.
2 See for example the World Soundscape Project (www.sfu.ca/~truax/wsp.html), which closely conserves the Schafer and Truax heritage.
3 See for example the urban ambiance studies carried out by the CRESSON laboratory (CNRS-UMR 1563 Ambiances architecturales et urbaines).
4 This aspect is the main part of my PhD research based on a fieldwork carried out in 2005–2009, dedicated to voice in public spaces. The social aspects of public voices are situated at a microsociological level, such as a piece of street and a few families, in one specific popular area called "Quartieri Spagnoli" (Féraud 2010). See also two articles (Féraud 2013a, 2013b)
5 A previous article published in French (Féraud 2009) was based on an ethnographical description. The present chapter revisits Neapolitan popular pyrotechnical practices by suggesting a new conceptual approach.
6 The urban dictionary is a participative web-based dictionary founded in 1999, originally intended as a dictionary of slang. The term "noising" can be found on this web page: www.urbandictionary.com/define.php?term=noising (accessed on June 19, 2013).
7 Critical discourses often come from musical or sound art backgrounds. For academic studies, refer for example to Chion (2007) and Schwartz (2011).
8 See for example Furtos, Joubert (2010)
9 Translation: "*Your reputation and great renown make me love you more than renown.*" *Chansonnier de Jean de Monchenu*. Paris: Éditions de la société française de musicologie, 1991.
10 In French, *feu de bengale* refers more precisely to a pyrotechnical device specifically dedicated to the production a powerful colored light. The Italian oral terminology *bengali* groups fireworks as pyrotechnical devices producing light, as opposed to firecrackers for which the interest is primarily sonic.
11 ML is a young Neapolitan student born in the outskirts of Naples (recorded in 2006).
12 V. is a history teacher at one of Naples's main universities.
13 The first floor is traditionally called *il piano nobile* ("the noble floor"). Situated just above the popular Quartieri Spagnoli, the Vomero hill is a district occupied by families with a comfortable standard of living.

References

Amphoux, Pascal. 1994. "Environnement, milieu et paysage sonore." In *Les faces cachées de l'urbain*, edited by Michel Bassand and Jean-Philippe Leresche, 159–176. Berlin: Peter Lang.

Chion, Michel. 1985. *Le son au cinéma*. Collection essais. Paris: Éditions de l'Etoile/ Cahiers du Cinéma.

———. 2007. "Pour en finir avec la notion de bruit." *L'Analyse musicale: Bruit et musique*. CAPES—Agrégation 2008 56: 7–10.

Corbin, Alain. 1994. *Les cloches de la terre: Paysage sonore et culture sensible dans les campagnes au XIXᵉ siècle*. Collection champs-Flammarion. Paris: Albin Michel.

Dauby, Yannick. 2004. *Paysages sonores partagés*. DEA Thesis, Université d'Angoulême, Angoulême.

De Certeau, Michel, Luce Giard, and Pierre Mayol. 1994. *L'invention du quotidien, 2: Habiter, cuisiner*. Paris: Gallimard.

Dubois, Danièle, Catherine Guastavino, and Manon Raimbault. 2006. "A Cognitive Approach to Soundscapes: Using Verbal Data to Access Auditory Categories." *Acta Acustica* 92 and *Acustica* 6: 865–874.

Feld, Steven. 1994. "From Ethnomusicology to Echo-Muse-Ecology: Reading R. Murray Schafer in the Papua New Guinea Rainforest." *The Soundscape Newsletter* 8. www.acousticecology.org/writings/echomuseecology.html.

Féraud, Olivier. 2009. "Une anthropologie sonore des pétards et des feux d'artifice à Naples." *Ethnographiques.org* 19. www.ethnographiques.org/2009/Feraud.

———. 2010. *Voix publiques: Environnements sonores, représentations et usages d'habitation dans un quartier populaire de Naples*. PhD Thesis, Ecole des Hautes Etudes en Sciences Sociales, Paris.

———. 2013a. "Environnements vocaux napolitains: Le paysage sonore à l'épreuve de l'anthropologie." In *Paysage sensoriels: Essai d'anthropologie de la construction et de la perception de l'environnement sonore*, edited by Joël Candau and Marie-Barbara Le Gonidec, 97–109. Paris: Comité des travaux historiques et scientifiques (CTHS).

———. 2013b. "Ethnographier les environnements sonores." In *Ethnographier les sens*, edited by Paul-Louis Colon, 117–144. Paris: Petra.

Fritz, Jean-Marie. 2000. *Paysages sonores du Moyen Âge: Le versant épistémologique*. Collection sciences, techniques et civilisations du Moyen Âge à l'aube des lumières. Paris: Champion.

Gutton, Jean-Pierre. 2000. *Bruits et sons dans notre histoire*. Paris: Presses Universitaires de France.

Howes, David. 1991. *Varieties of Sensory Experience: A Sourcebook in the Anthropology of the Senses*. Toronto: University of Toronto Press.

Ingold, Tim. 2007. "Against Soundscape." In *Autumn Leaves*, edited by A. Carlyle. Paris: Double Entendre.

Joubert, Jean and Michel Furtos. 2010. "Les troubles de voisinage sur trois villes françaises (Paris XVIIIe, Rennes, Vaulx en Velin)." In *Les troubles de voisinage: Santé mentale et régulations institutionnelles*. Proceedings of the conference organized by L'Observatoire national des pratiques en santé mentale et précarité (ONSMP-ORSPERE), under the auspices of the Direction générale de la Santé, Paris.

Oba, Teruyo. 2006. "The Sound Environmental Education Aided by Automated Bioacoustic Identification in View of Soundscape Recognition." *Journal of the Acoustical Society of America* 120 (5): 3239.

Ricci, Antonello. 1999. *Ascoltare il mondo, Antropologia dei suoni in un paese del sud d'Italia*. Roma: Il Trovatore.

Schafer, Murray. 1977. *The Soundscape: Our Sonic Environment and the Tuning of the World*. Rochester: Destiny Books.

Schwartz, Hillel. 2011. *Making Noise: From Babel to the Big Bang and Beyond*. Brooklyn: Zone Books.

Tixier, Nicolas. 2011. *L'ambiance est dans l'air: La dimension atmosphérique des ambiances architecturales et urbaines dans les approches environnementales*. Research report edited by Nicolas Tixier. Grenoble: CRESSON.

Truax, Barry. 1978. *Handbook for Acoustic Ecology: The Music of the Environment*. Vancouver: Arc publication.

Uexküll, Jakob Johann von. 2004. *Mondes animaux et monde humain, suivi de La théorie de la signification*. Translated by Philippe Müller. Paris: Pocket Collection agora. First published in 1934 with Georg Kriszat. Berlin: J. Springer.

2 Sounds of Hell and Sounds of Eden

Sonic Worlds in Ethiopia in the Catholic Missionary Context, Seventeenth and Eighteenth Centuries

Anne Damon-Guillot

Introduction

Musicologists know how difficult it is to describe sounds with words and to make them concrete for the reader. During the early modern era, Catholic missionaries faced this difficulty by reporting sounds they had heard in the extra-European countries. Whereas missionaries and natives from South America, for example, left us images, musical scores or even instruments, we have only texts for the Ethiopian case. Texts are the only memory of this sonic encounter. Thus, we have to imagine how it could sound there, through the ears and the words of clergymen who lived three or four centuries ago.

I am interested in three types of sources, established during three different periods, and that reveal three distinct positions about sound and music. The first is the text written in 1520 by the chaplain of the Portuguese Embassy to Ethiopia. The documents written by the Jesuits who were in Ethiopia in the first half of the seventeenth century form the second group of sources. Last, the report of the Franciscan Remedius Prutky, written around 1750, is the third source of the present study.

Political and ideological reasons can explain the different positions about Ethiopian and European music and sounds. Moreover, between the discovery of the so-called marvellous country of Prester John in the sixteenth century and the rejection of things Ethiopian in the eighteenth century, the way of thinking had changed: marvelling at the strange had become vulgar.[1]

The sources talk about two sonic worlds: on the one hand, the Ethiopian one, and on the other hand, the European and missionary one. The disequilibrium is obvious: the texts, when they deal with music, describe mostly the practices of the missionaries and of their entourage. And when they depict the Ethiopian music and sounds, they say more about the writers than about the depicted objects.

Consequently, we have much more information about the baroque music that was played in Ethiopia than about the music of the Ethiopian court or of the Ethiopian church. Environmental sounds are also characterized by a dichotomy. Indeed, the missionaries use powerful sounds—such as bells, voices of the preaching, fireworks—to convert the people, whereas the daily sounds of Ethiopia—like groans or weeping—are described with an eschatological vocabulary. Ambient sounds are definitely anchored in social representations.

I try to view these texts as ethnographies, considering three points:

1. All these texts were intended for the Roman authority. The missionaries wanted to show to their superiors the effectiveness of their methods, and when they failed, they attributed it to the lack of means or to the great perversion of Ethiopia, which made their task very difficult. Whereas objectivity and impartiality can never be totally respected by ethnographers, missionaries are especially partial, because they obey a religious and proselyte project.

2. Data are few. Missionaries were witnesses of an Ethiopian sonic world that is definitely gone. Thus, to read these texts as honestly as possible, to reconstitute the sonic landscape, and to understand how the network of sounds works, I have had to convoke history (in particular history of Ethiopia and of religious orders), cultural history, close reading, theology, ethnomusicology and musicology, anthropology of sound and particularly, the history of sensitivities and perceptions, whose richness and interest have been clearly shown by Jean-Pierre Gutton in *Bruits et sons dans notre histoire* (Gutton 2000).

3. Missionaries of the early modern era claim the subjectivity of their texts. The Jesuits, as well as the Franciscans, stayed a long time in Ethiopia. They tried to write exhaustive and true descriptions. Reading these texts, especially the Franciscan ones, you may be struck by their sensory aspect. They give subjective impressions about smells, about flavours, about sights, about sounds. The authenticity, the sensory approach and the subjectivity are pointed out at the beginning of the missionary reports, for example by the Franciscan Remedius Prutky who stayed in Ethiopia in the 1750s: "Everything here related the Missionary saw with his own eyes, heard with his own ears, experienced in his own person and presence, during a nine year journey; then in his own hand he wrote it down" (Prutky 1991 (1765): xxiv). Similarly, the Portuguese Francisco Alvares, who was not a missionary but the chaplain of the Portuguese Embassy to Ethiopia in 1520, wrote in his preface: "Whatever I have been able to learn I shall vouch for as something I saw if I saw it, and if it was something I heard I shall tell it as something I heard" (Alvares vol. 1 1961: 33). It is certainly a long-standing rhetorical expression, but it shows the desire for sincerity and the importance of the missionary's ear.

I shall try to answer the following questions: what do the missionary texts say about the sounds of the past? That is: what is their historical interest?

How did the missionaries talk about the sounds of the Others? How did missionaries use sounds for Romanization? There are two other main points: first, how do the missionaries hear? We have to take into account the "sonic sensitivity of their time" (*sensibilité sonore de leur époque*), as Olivier Balaÿ writes (Balaÿ 2003: 160). Then, how do missionaries write what they heard? This question has been asked by Mark M. Smith in *Listening to Nineteenth-Century America* (Smith 2001): as there are no extant sound recordings from the early-to-mid nineteenth century, Smith is thus left to examine the ways in which the nineteenth century elites wrote about sound, and in essence used sound as a metaphor. In our case, the network sound-ear-book can be read and understood in a biblical and Roman comprehension of world.

After having presented the different sources, I'll explore three points. First, I shall focus on cries, as they were believed by Europeans to be indicators of the state of a society until the nineteenth century. Then, I shall show how the sounds of Ethiopia are described as creating a sonic hell. At the opposite, the missionary sonic world sounds heavenly. All types of sounds will be taken into account, from the natural ones to the baroque musical compositions. Indeed, if the effectiveness of music in attracting new converts to Christianity has been clearly shown by experts on the Jesuits,[2] the other sounds have been less treated, although they were used for the same goal. Moreover, crossing musical and sonic data is necessary to understand the sonic worlds—of Hell or of Eden—which the texts construct.

From Curiosity to Rejection: Sources

In the first decades of the sixteenth century, the Portuguese reached Ethiopia, considered then as the kingdom of Prester John. It was the name given to a mythical Christian priest-king, whom Europeans were looking for since the Middle Ages (Hirsch 2002). The Prester John was believed to be the king of a land of plenty and a perfect Christian society. His army was supposed to help the Western Christians to fight against Islam. In 1520, Father Francisco Alvares, chaplain of the Portuguese Embassy to Ethiopia, wrote *A true relation of the lands of the Prester John* (Alvares 1961). Although the Embassy discovers step by step the heresy of Ethiopian Christianity, Francisco Alvares remained influenced by the strong myth of Prester John and tried to find in the reality what had been described for centuries. He reported diplomatic relations between the two countries that are based on mutual seduction; in this case, music appears as a tool for introducing oneself and expressing one's own identity. The following example is eloquent. On Christmas 1520, the Ethiopian Emperor (the so-called "Prester John" by Alvares) asks the Portuguese for liturgical songs. Father Alvares wants to impress the Ethiopian court:

> I took as many books as I had got, although they were nothing to do
> with the feast, but only to make up a number, because they are much

given to asking for books; and I opened them all upon the altar, and we began our matins as well as we were able, and certainly it appeared that Our Lord assisted us and gave us grace. [. . .] We prolonged these matins a good deal with proses, hymns and canticles which we introduced [. . .] and we were looking for what could be best sung or intoned.

(Alvares vol. 2 1961: 325–6)

Music appears as the best way to reach the Others. In the same way, in 1521, Ethiopians invite the Portuguese for the consecration of a church:

They performed a great rite, with singing, and playing instruments, and dancing, and leaping. When a great part of the rite had been performed, the Prester sent to ask what we thought of it [. . .] we answered that God would be served in many ways, and that this rite seemed to us good, and that also ours seemed to us good, because all was for God.

(Alvares vol. 2 1961: 360)

The tolerant tone and the sincere curiosity for the musical and liturgical practices of the Ethiopians are not shared by the Portuguese Jesuits some years later, in the first half of the seventeenth century. In the Jesuit political and religious project, music and sounds are used for the Romanization of the Ethiopian people, as can be noticed in the letters, reports, diaries of the journey and erudite summa they wrote. The Jesuit mission was ordered by the Portuguese sovereign Joâo III in 1550, but the Jesuits were present in Ethiopia only from 1607, with a climax in proselytism from 1620 to 1630. The aim was to transform Ethiopia into a Catholic kingdom, in order to have a precious ally in this part of the world (Pennec 2003). However, Ethiopia was already Christian, since the fourth century, but its Christianity was judged heretical by Rome. The Ethiopian mission was a difficult one; Jesuits encountered a great deal of resistance, especially from the Ethiopian clergy. However, the Ethiopian Emperor Susneyos converted to the Roman faith in 1621. But Jesuits were expelled in 1633, and Ethiopia returned to its previous faith. Ethiopia blotted the Jesuit episode out. Catholic churches were destroyed, and no trace of this period was kept.

Last, the very personal text of the Franciscan Remedius Prutky (Prutky 1991 (1765)), written around 1750, describes a deleterious situation. Indeed, after the expulsion of the Jesuits in 1633, three Franciscans went to Ethiopia in the first half of the eighteenth century; they were assassinated, only some years before Prutky's coming. Moreover, the country suffered in this time from deep poverty. Now, the missionary music can neither be used for seduction nor for evangelism; it is reduced to a protective role, as Prutky's harp helps him in difficult situations. Otherwise, in the Franciscan text, sounds are both described in the Ethiopian context and also used in a symbolic way, in a rhetorical construction against the Ethiopian people.

This paper only takes into account the missionary texts—not the one from the Portuguese Embassy of the sixteenth century. The descriptions of Ethiopia that these texts offer are different from one mission to another. There are several authors for the Jesuit texts, but only one, Remedius Prutky, for the Franciscan text, which is more subjective. The Jesuits had the time to try out their methods of conversion, and their texts talk about their use of music, sounds, and arts for the Romanization of the population. On the other hand, Prutky had no time enough to really put in place methods of conversion; so, his text is more a description of Ethiopia in 1752.

Cries and Sonic Identity

In *Les Voix de Paris; Essai d'une histoire littéraire et musicale des cris populaires de la capitale depuis le Moyen Âge jusqu'à nos jours* (1857), Georges Kastner defines the cry as the "masses' language". According to him, cry "is in a manner the speech itself and replaces it every time when the collective life wants to express."[3] Moreover, he writes that

> the big cities have a language; they have even, if I can use this expression, a sort of proper music that expresses at all hours the movement and the evolutions of the happy or sad life, laborious or quiet, that they host. Paris, for example, has a strong voice, and anyone who heard its murmurs in riot days, even anyone who lent an ear in the most peaceful times to the thousand clamours that are mixing in the streets, this one will never forget what is characteristic in the Parisian sonic chaos.[4]
>
> (Kastner 1857)

This interesting essay, which deals with Paris as a "sonic city", follows some eighteenth-century theories about the origins of music by quoting at its very beginning the French composer Jean-Philippe Rameau (1683–1764): "Listen to people who *sing* how they *shout* in the streets . . ." (Rameau, *Code de musique pratique* [1760]).[5] Thus, cries reveal who people are, what they experience and what they want, and they draw a sonic identity of a place.

The Franciscan Remedius Prutky tells about the cries of the Ethiopian people in the *Itinerarium* that he finished writing in the 1760s, at the time of Rameau's theories. In a fascinating text, he explains how shouting was a way for people to catch the Emperor's attention.

> At times, when more pressing business is afoot, the more reliable ministers are summoned together before the last door to receive the Emperor's replies, and especially when the people are making an outcry in the hills and are gathered together too close to the palace, shouting endlessly for their Emperor with the words *Jan Hui Jan Hui,* that is, Your Majesty, continually repeated. This is the custom that obtains among this people in all case of need, of calling upon their emperor [. . .]; in case

of oppression they have no recourse save to appeal to the Emperor for help and to cry interminably Jan hui: until he sends one of his servants to ask what their demand is. Outcries like this are heard almost every day, a second beginning when the first ceases, monks crying out Jan hui equally with the laity [. . .] Often even nightfall puts no end to the horrible clamour, which is kept up continually though transferred from one place to another, and, unless force be used, they do not cease. [. . .] and however much the Emperor hates the daily and nightly noise, he has not the power to repress or quieten it.

(Prutky 1991 (1765): 160)

This type of precise description is historically precious, showing the relation between sound and power, and it contributed to the construction of the orientalist knowledge. We know that this sonic practice—that is, a sort of sonic torture!—remained. Indeed, we have early nineteenth-century accounts of this long-enduring custom with the texts of Pearce (Pearce 1831) and of Johnston (Johnston 1844). Beyond the historical interest of the information given by the missionaries, we have to ask the following questions: what kind of account of Ethiopian soundscapes did the missionaries leave us? How did they hear, how did they listen?

Sounds of Hell

Even if the sounds that missionaries chose to describe are mostly negative, I will quote first an extract written by the Franciscan Remedius Prutky, in which he depicts a heavenly Ethiopian nature. All the sounds in this excerpt show the perfect harmony between animals and humans:

a remarkable bird especial to Africa [. . .] is claimed by the Ethiopians to act as their pointer to game and guide to the huntsman, and to possess almost supernatural powers: its [. . .] name is *Fonton.* [. . .] as soon as it sees in the forest a gazelle, or snake, or a bee's nest, or a wild beast, or anything either useful or harmful, it flies around the huntsman and everywhere pursues him, urging him by cry and by song to approach the prey. As soon as the Ethiopians recognise him they follow his flight, with the words *Fenton Kere*: as they follow him the Fonton advances and cries out in front of the huntsman, until he finds the prey. [. . .] as a signal that the prey has been reached the bird changes its note, and the Ethiopians search diligently and easily find the honey, of which they always leave a portion for the bird. [. . .] I could truly call Ethiopia a land flowing in honey, butter and milk, were the populace not so idle.

(Prutky 1991 (1765): 201)

Here is the point. Ethiopia could be a country where birds and humans could share the same language. But Ethiopia is a lost heaven, and it resounds with weeping.

All the human sonic expressions, musical or not, are judged negatively. The Franciscan Remedius Prutky criticizes the vulgarity of the imperial banquet by insisting on its tumult. For Prutky, this noise is the proof of the incivility of the assembly: "The crowd of people behaved as in a European tavern: offensive gestures, quarrels, noisy separations, coarse laughter, beast-like belches" (Prutky 1991 (1765): 169).

The comparison with the sounds of animals is used to describe the Ethiopian music too. For example, Prutky writes these words to characterize the music at the Emperor's court: "a noise like the caterwauling of a hundred cats" (Prutky 1991 (1765): 167)—he is talking about a polyphony of string instruments.

Beyond the coarseness and the animality of the Ethiopian sounds as depicted by the missionaries, we can notice that in the Jesuit texts, like in the Franciscan one, the authors insist on the sounds of misfortune. Thus, all dwell on funerary lamentations. A Jesuit called Almeida, and also, later, the Franciscan Prutky,[6] describe the performance of the mourners from Abyssinia,[7] for example: "lamenting loudly [. . .] to the sound of the drum, striking together the palms of their hands, beating their breasts" (Almeida 1954: 66).

In the same way, Prutky devotes long passages to the wails of the starving: "they continually assail the ears of the passers-by with *raven raven*, hunger hunger; at the doors of death they redouble their groans, we are dying, dying, they cry; seldom are their cries heard" (Prutky 1991 (1765): 270).

The image of an impoverished Ethiopia is constructed also by the evocation of natural disasters that invade the country. These disasters are described in their visual and sonic dimension, in striking descriptions: for example, the clouds of noisy and swarming insects that destroy the cultivated lands or the roars of the wild, dangerous beasts.

Actually, missionaries construct in their texts an Ethiopia that sounds as if it was struck by malediction. This malediction justifies the Catholic mission: this is a country so poor that you have to save it; at the same time, this malediction is used as an excuse for the failure of the mission (!): Ethiopia, cursed by God, is definitely lost, and nothing else can be done for it. Then, Remedius Prutky insists on the dereliction of Ethiopia, in order to show to Rome how his missionary task is difficult and always hindered. In this way, it is interesting to read how he interprets the sound of the thunder during the rainy season, in opposition to the autochthonous reaction:[8]

> Then, quite unexpectedly, a great flash of lightning, a roll of thunder in the heavens whose reverberations were everywhere, and the day of judgement seemed upon us, with a continuous noise in the sky as of roaring lions, so that we thought that the heavens were falling: and this is the Abyssinian winter, no day without rain. Foreigners and strangers are struck with some fear by this commotion, but the natives ignore it, and I at every moment pictured ruin and unimaginable horror.
>
> (Prutky 1991 (1765): 186)

For Prutky, Ethiopia is on the brink of its always imminent destruction. Its present-day suffering is only the foreshadowing of its coming suffering in hell. Thus, the poor's wails prefigure the cries that they will emit in hell. This conviction is based on a passage of the gospel according to saint Matthew, that Prutky quotes: "Blind and miserable people, luckless in this world, even more unfortunate in the world to come [. . .] where *there will be wailing and gnashing of teeth* (Matthew xiii. 42, 50)" (Prutky 1991 (1765): 270).

In the sonic portrait of Ethiopia that the missionaries draw, the notion of lie is recurrent, with the idea that what we hear is wrong. For the missionaries, lie is present both in the hypocrisy of the Ethiopian people and in their heresy. First, there is a gap between the faith claimed by the Ethiopians and the faith that they really feel. That is what Prutky writes:

> The Christian faith is full of impurities, professed in the mouth rather than felt in the heart, by words rather than deeds [. . .]. I can exclaim with Isaiah: *I am a man of unclean lips, and I dwell in the midst of a people of unclean lips.* [. . .] As the holy Apostles wrote of old *This people honours me with their lips, but their heart is far from me.* [. . .] professing one way with his lips and another with his life, one thing in private and another in public.
>
> (Prutky 1991 (1765): 224–5)

In the same way, missionaries consider that the Ethiopian Christian rite is only lie, because its sonic manifestations are heretical. On this point, Jesuits and Franciscans are unanimous, and they list what they call the mistakes of the Ethiopian Church. According to them, the formulation—what is *said*—of the sacraments is wrong and the church services are incorrect in their sonic form itself. Prutky writes:

> In the more important festivals some of the congregation applaud with their hands, in obedience to the command of David *Clap your hands together all ye people* [Psalm 47 (46), 2], and others beat time with sistra and drums, like bacchanals, and are so delighted with the noise that no music would seem sweeter.
>
> (Prutky 1991 (1765): 231)

Beyond the negative judgement on this practice described as "noise", this short passage contains two interesting pieces of information. On the one hand, it attests to the existence, in 1752, of an instrumental practice that is still current in the liturgical context of today's Ethiopian church. This practice is called *'aqʷaqʷam*, and I was able to observe it many times in Ethiopia (Damon-Guillot 2007). On the other hand, this short description includes two analogies: the performance of the cantors follows the David's biblical summons, and it has aspects in common with Bacchanalia. The reference to antiquity links the sonic practice of the Ethiopian church to paganism, while the quotation of David's psalm links it to Judaism. Thus, for missionaries, Ethiopian rites are said to be Christian, but actually, they are not. Therefore, what is at stake is the true and right way to express the Christian faith aloud—by words, by music and by other sounds. The Catholic way appears as the right one.

Sounds of Eden

The missionaries describe their own sonic practices, which can be musical or not musical: there are the sounds of Rome, opposed to the sounds of Ethiopia. The aim of some of their sound practices is to change the sonic milieu of the Ethiopians, in order to change their mind and to convert them.

The use of sounds as a way of conversion is well known by the Jesuits (Damon-Guillot 2009). It joins in a massive sensory program that aims to move and touch the Ethiopian people, as the verbs used by the Jesuits show: the missionaries want to make the Ethiopians cry, to make them laugh, to make them happy, to satisfy them, to fill them with wonder, to surprise, to disturb and to captivate (*rapire*). To reach their goal, they use different means: the distribution of devotion's objects (rosaries, crosses, images), the reconstruction of religious scenes (the Christmas crib, for example), the stage performance (*Ecce Homo*), the execution of musical pieces (song of the Mass, of the Passion for example) . . . and bangers, bells and ringing clocks. Missionaries import new sounds, which accompany some spectacular events, but which interfere in the daily life of the people too. By these sonic means, missionaries take possession of the territory and of the souls.

The Catholic mission in Ethiopia does not really rest on the Christianization of the population, as it was evangelized from the fourth century, but on its Romanization. The question of religious authority is thus central. To come to power, one needs to appropriate the sonic space. In order to occupy the territory and to show the missionary presence, rockets (*raggi*), bangers (*mortaletti*) and others fireworks (*lauori di poluere arteficiata, fuochi lauorati*) are used, as attested by this text of the Jesuit Alfonso Mendes:

> For Vespers on the 10th of May, the Saturday before the Sunday of the Good Shepherd, many rockets were fired, and bangers, and many fireworks were constructed; everyone enjoyed the display, but more especially the Emperor; late in the night, he went out of his residence by the light of the torches and even climbed onto the church's terrace, from where fireworks were lit to be admired at everyone's pleasure.[9]
>
> (Alfonso Mendes and Gasparo Paës 1628)

The use of these pyrotechnic displays goes further than the wonder that they can arouse. Olivier Féraud, in his paper "Une anthropologie sonore des pétards et des feux d'artifice à Naples", writes about the Neapolitan detonations that such sounds force all the people to hear them; he adds that these sounds "through a sensory dimension that is intentionally impressive and sometimes violent, [. . .] convey sense, cultural values, emotional charge or even information."[10]

Fireworks don't strictly speaking convey a religious message—although they appear, in the Jesuit excerpt quoted above, in a para-liturgical context; their sumptuous sparkle, visual and sonic, is rather a manifestation of power intended for the Ethiopian government.

Sounds of bells and clocks reveal more complex stakes, as they impose a Roman perception of time. In a description of the catholic church *Gännätä 'Iyäsus* ("Paradise of Jesus"), constructed in an Ethiopian place called Azäzo in 1621, the Father Jesuit Almeida mentions the "torre de sinos" (Almeida 1907: 388), literally "tower of bells". The bells of the Catholic churches in Ethiopia are a new sound for the Ethiopian ears. Loud bells impose a Catholic presence on those who hear them. As the French historian Alain Corbin showed in another context, bells construct a "territorial identity" (*identité territoriale*) as far as their "sonic ray" (*rayon sonore*) spreads (Corbin 1994: 98). In the missionary context, the peal of bells takes possession of the land. As it was shown by Corbin for the French rural areas of the nineteenth century (Corbin 1994: 79) and by Antonello Ricci for villages of Calabria (Italy) during the twentieth century (Ricci 1996), the sound of bells has a community role. Indeed, when the Father Jesuit Gasparo Paës arrived in Ethiopia in 1624 and went for the first time in the Jesuit residence of Gorgora, he was welcomed by "the sound of bells (*campane*) and a polyphonic *benedictus*" (Mendes and Paës 1628: 47). So, these sounds—bells and liturgical music— connect the members of a same religious community together. According to Corbin, the bell "allows the individual to feel more easily the identity of the group to which he belongs."[11] The terms employed—*campane, sinos* ("bells", plural form in Italian and in Portuguese[12]) and *torre* ("tower")— lead us to think that the several bells were kept in an independent building like a *campanile*. This type of building, which had a great success in Jesuit missions in Bolivia,[13] gathers many big bells together, increasing the sound intensity[14] and the polyphonic possibilities. Last but not least, the bell modifies time perception, as it organizes the day according to the Roman religious services. About the importance of bells in European time perception and time construction, Steven Feld writes the following lines:

> After twenty-five years of recording rainforest soundscapes in Papua New Guinea, I've started to listen to Europe. I'm struck by a sonic resemblance: bells stand to European time as birds do to rainforest time. Daily time, seasonal time, work time, ritual time, social time, collective time, cosmological time—all have their parallels, with rainforest birds sounding as quotidian clocks and spirit voices, and European bells heralding civil and religious time.

> (Feld 2004)

Jesuits imported clocks to Ethiopia in the 1620s. For example, Father Barnetto had a small clock—"horioletto" (Mendes and Paës 1628: 48)—that filled the Emperor with wonder because it had an automatic ringing. Clocks imported by Jesuits are more than sonic gadgets as, like bells, they cut the time in a different way as the one then used in Ethiopia. Clockwork generally takes part in the Jesuit programme of Christianization. For example, in 1601, when the famous Jesuit Matteo Ricci arrived at the imperial court of Peking, he offered a spinet, a map of the world and . . . two ringing clocks. Catherine Pagani, a specialist of Jesuit clockwork, explains:

> By the time of Ricci's arrival in the Far East, clocks and clockmakers had been used in Europe as a metaphor for God and the creation; for the Jesuits, the clock went beyond its role as a technological artefact and represented the higher beliefs they hoped to instil in the Chinese.
>
> (Pagani 2006: 659)

The Jesuits had a great belief in the power of sounds and of music to lead the Ethiopian heretics to the truth (i.e., that of Catholicism).

It is not my point here to talk about the role of music in evangelism, although missionaries used it a lot to touch the heart of the population. However, I would like to give just one example. The Jesuit Father Lobo relates a scene that occurred around 1625: some Jesuits were in the kingdom of Dancali—which was under the Ethiopian emperor's authority—and the situation was tense because the king did not want the missionaries to go further in the country without paying. Missionaries gave presents, but it was not enough. Then, a violinist played pieces that eased the atmosphere:

> One of the pieces imitated the bray of a donkey in a such realistic way that they [the autochthonous] recognized it immediately with great applause without anybody having said them what it was about, because it was something completely familiar and frequent in their daily life.
>
> (Lobo 1984: 127)

In this example,[15] ambient sounds invade the music. People of Dancali may have not appreciated the baroque music in its more usual forms, as they had of course no code for understanding it, but the sounds of nature played on the little violin created a common reference that made people laugh together. Music and sounds of nature, when they are imitated, allow people to go beyond words. As the relationships became better after this musical piece, the Jesuits showed that music and sounds won where words had failed.

The problem is the symbolic deafness of Ethiopia pointed out by missionaries. Ethiopia was not able to hear the words and the sounds of the Catholic mission, because of its perversion. That is what Prutky explains, a century after the expulsion of Jesuits:

> There was a time when Ethiopia had been prosperous, and Catholic: now she is wretched and heretical, pagan, idolatrous, Mahometan, Judaist. Once she was worthy of every praise, now she is worthy of none, for of the Ethiopians of today, *Eyes have they but they see not, they have ears and hear not* Psalms cxv. 5, 6.
>
> (Prutky 1991 (1765): 141)

As Ethiopia is both dissonant and deaf, it remains unsaved and far from Eden.

Melothesia Aethiopica: An Example of Ideal Missionary Music

I would like to end this paper with an excerpt from the *Musurgia Universalis* (1650) by Athanasius Kircher (Kircher 1650).[16]

Kircher was a Jesuit, expert in oriental languages and a great scholar. The above text deals with Ethiopian liturgical music, although Kircher never went to Ethiopia. The tone, the content and the aim of this text differ substantially from the reports of the Jesuits who went on the Ethiopian field.

Kircher set up in his *Musurgia* a vast system of composition of verses, rhythms and melodies. In a universalist vision of music, harmony and the world, he developed a theory based on the harmony of the spheres and numbers, related to religion. After having collected some data on different musical traditions, he used them to compose songs following his own system. Thus, in the part of his book devoted to Ethiopian music, he wrote a text in Ge'ez[17]—probably based on the Ethiopian liturgy—and put it together with a melody and a rhythmic pattern, with the help of large combinatorial arrays presented in his *Musurgia*. Kircher wrote that this "recipe" could be used by missionaries in Ethiopia, in order to compose Ethiopian songs . . . that have finally nothing in common with the Ethiopian ones! Indeed, the above text does not exist in the Ethiopian liturgy; moreover it contains spelling and grammar mistakes, and the melody is far from the real Ethiopian liturgical songs. The Ethiopian liturgical music is (and was) monodic. Kircher offers a four-part harmonization, composing a perfect tonal music. About the conception of polyphony and counterpoint in the missionary context, I would like to quote David Irving:

> To early modern Europeans, counterpoint represented a means by which sound and society could be rationalized, and in this sense it became a formidable agent of colonialism. Europeans also deliberatly used counterpoint as a self-conscious cultural emblem to emphasize their difference from the non-European Other: one of the principal ways they could maintain a sense of musical "uniqueness" and "superiority" was

to point to the apparent absence of counterpoint elsewhere, thereby increasing intercultural difference.

(Irving 2010: 3)

In his idealistic project, Kircher does not consider the musical practices with contempt but wants them to be a part of a wide logical system: a catholic

Figure 2.1 Athanasius Kircher, *Musurgia universalis sive ars magna consoni et dissoni*, tomus 2, liber VIII: 235 (Kircher 1650). Bibliothèque numérique patrimoniale du Service Commun de la Documentation de l'Université de Strasbourg.

system, in the "universal" meaning of the word. Thus, the musical system that he developed had to be understandable by everybody and easily applicable. That is why he composed an Ethiopian music acceptable for European ears. We are beyond the hostile sounds of Ethiopia, and in a universalist vision of music. From the *strange*, which had been a synonym of danger for the missionaries in Ethiopia, Kircher brings us to the *known*.

Conclusion

Missionaries consider European music "rational, contained by language, and subject to rules and meters" (Rath 2003: 150), while they define Ethiopian music as noise. Like this nonsensical music, the other Ethiopian sounds are depicted as lacking rules. As such, the missionaries insist on vocal nonverbal sounds—wails, weeping—that are also outside of language. There is an underlying opposition here between wild and civilized, animal and human, nature and culture. Moreover, the opposition between the missionaries and the "others", between the two worlds, is obvious for those who experience the encounter on the field, whereas the original Catholic project, here reminded by Kircher, wants to unite the worlds into one. The lines written by Florent Coste in a paper called "Philippe Descola en Brocéliande" (Coste 2010) are appropriate. Coste describes medieval Catholicism from the angle of analogism ("analogisme"), one of the four ontologies defined by the anthropologist Philippe Descola (Descola 2005). This "long Middle Ages" ("long Moyen Âge"), which goes until the seventeenth century according to Coste, sees the world as a "multitude of beings [that] derive from the One that covers them from on high."[18] This double Catholic ambition, both unitary and missionary—and mission experiences the diversity of the world—can be read in the texts about Ethiopia of the seventeenth century: thoughts and acts try to bring the multitude of voices and sounds into a unique system.

Notes

1 See the notions of "the enlightenment and the anti-marvellous" in Lorraine Daston and Katharine Park. 2001. *Wonders and the order of nature, 1150–1750* (New York: Zone Books), 329.
2 For example, about Goa, see Victor Anand Coelho. 2006. "Music in new worlds", in *The Cambridge History of Seventeenth-Century Music*, ed. T. Carter and J. Butt (Cambridge: Cambridge University Press), 88–110.
3 Georges Kastner (1857). *Les Voix de Paris; Essai d'une histoire littéraire et musicale des cris populaires de la capitale depuis le Moyen Âge jusqu'à nos jours précédé de considérations sur l'origine et le caractère du cri en général et suivi de* Les Cris de Paris *Grande Symphonie humoristique vocale et instrumentale*: 3. Paris, Brandus: *langage des masses; est en quelque sorte la parole même, et la remplace dans toutes les occasions où la vie collective chercher à s'exprimer*. (My own translation).
4 Kastner, *Les Voix de Paris*, V: "Les grandes cités ont un langage; elles ont même, qu'on nous passe l'expression, une sorte de musique propre qui exprime à toutes

les heures du jour le mouvement et les évolutions de la vie joyeuse ou sombre, laborieuse ou paisible, dont elles sont le foyer. Paris, par exemple, a une voix puissante, et quiconque en a entendu les frémissements aux jours d'émeute, quiconque même a prêté l'oreille dans les temps les plus pacifiques aux mille clameurs qui se croisent dans ses rues, celui-là n'oubliera jamais ce qu'il y a de caractéristique dans le chaos sonore [. . .] parisien". (My own translation).

5 Kastner, *Les Voix de Paris*, title page: "Écoutez les gens qui *chantent* ce qu'ils *crient* dans les rues . . . " (Rameau, *Code de musique pratique*)" (My own translation).

6 Remedius Prutky 1991 (1765). *Prutky's travels in Ethiopia and other countries*, trans. J. H. Arrowsmith-Brown (London: The Hakluyt Society), 248: "with loud lamentations".

7 Abyssinia refers exactly to a geographical area that the present-day northern half of Ethiopia and Eritrea covers.

8 In his book *How early America sounded*—"a contribution to the history of the senses" (p. 2)—Richard Cullen Rath devotes a chapter to thunders and roarings: "The idea of thunder as the voice of a deity, so common in the seventeenth-century European American soundscape, does not emerge from the seventeenth-century Native American historical record. The combination of the incomprehensibility and animacy of natural sounds was not limited to thunder." Richard Cullen Rath. 2003. *How early America sounded* (Ithaca: Cornell University Press), 36.

9 Alfonso Mendes and Gasparo Paës. 1628. *Lettere annue di Ethiopia. Del 1624. 1625. e 1626. Scritta al M.R.P. Mutio Vitelleschi Generale della Compagnia di Giesu* (Roma: Per l'Herede di Bartolomeo Zannetti), 69: "Nel Vespro, che fù alli 10. di Maggio, Sabbato innanzi alla Domenica *Pastor bonus*; si gittarono molti raggi, si spararono molti mortaletti, si fabricorono molti lauori di poluere arteficiata, che furono festeggiati singolarmente dall'Imperatore; il qual'vci di casa a molte hore di notte a lume di torcie, e sali sopra la solana della Chiesa, d'onde s'auuentauano i fuochi lauorati, per mirarli più a suo gusto" (My own translation).

10 Olivier Féraud. 2009. "Une anthropologie sonore des pétards et des feux d'artifice à Naples", *ethnographiques.org* 19. www.ethnographiques.org/2009/Feraud: "à travers une dimension sensible qui se veut imposante et parfois violente, [. . .] sont porteuses de sens, de valeurs culturelles, d'une charge émotive ou même d'informations" (My own translation).

11 Alain Corbin. 1994. *Les Cloches de la terre; Paysage sonore et culture sensible dans les campagnes au XIXe siècle* (Paris: Flammarion), 154: "permet à l'individu de ressentir plus aisément l'identité du groupe auquel il appartient" (My own translation).

12 The Portuguese Jesuits used to write either in Portuguese or in Italian.

13 See the campanile in the Jesuit missions of Santa Cruz in Bolivia (middle of the eighteenth century). Cf. Alain Pacquier. 1996. *Les Chemins du baroque dans le Nouveau Monde; De la Terre de Feu à l'embouchure du Saint-Laurent* (Paris: Fayard).

14 About sound intensity and sensory fascination created by bells, see. Christine Guillebaud. 2009. "Musique mécanique et temple hindou: histoire controversée d'un dispositif visuel et sonore", *Terrain. Revue d'Ethnologie de l'Europe* 53: 98–113.

15 Imitative repertoire was appreciated in this time. See. the *Capriccio stravagante* composed by the Italian Carlo Farina between 1625 and 1630, at the same time as Lobo was in Ethiopia. As in the text of Lobo, the violin has the main role and imitates animals' noises.

16 It was digitized by the University of Strasbourg (Service Commun de la Documentation de l'Université de Strasbourg, France): http://docnum.u-strasbg.fr/

cdm/compoundobject/collection/coll10/id/1768/rec/5. Listen to the musical piece *Melothesia Aethiopica* by "Le Baroque Nomade," directed by J.-C. Frisch (2010).
17 Ge'ez is the liturgical language of the Ethiopian Church.
18 Florent Coste. 2010. "Philippe Descola en Brocéliande", *L'Atelier du Centre de recherches historiques* 6, http://acrh.revues.org/1969; doi: 10.4000/acrh.1969: "la multitude des êtres dérive de l'Un qui les surplombe" (My own translation).

References

Alvares, Francisco. 1961. *The Prester John of the Indies: A True Relation of the Lands of the Prester John, Being the Narrative of the Portuguese Embassy to Ethiopia in 1520 Written by Father Francisco Alvares*. 2 vols. Translated by Lord Stanley of Alderley, revised and edited with additional material by C. F. Beckingham and G. W. Huntingford. Cambridge: The Hakluyt Society. Translation originally published in 1881.

Balaÿ, Olivier. 2003. "Les chorographies de l'urbanité sonore." *Géocarrefour* 2: 159–167.

Coelho, Victor Anand. 2006. "Music in New Worlds." In *The Cambridge History of Seventeenth-Century Music*, edited by T. Carter and J. Butt, 88–110. Cambridge: Cambridge University Press.

Corbin, Alain. 1994. *Les Cloches de la terre: Paysage sonore et culture sensible dans les campagnes au XIXe siècle*. Paris: Flammarion.

Coste, Florent. 2010. "Philippe Descola en Brocéliande." *L'Atelier du Centre de recherches historiques* 6. http://acrh.revues.org/1969. doi:10.4000/acrh.1969.

d'Almeida, Emmanuelis. 1907. *Historia Aethiopiae*. Vol. 6. Edited by C. Beccari (R.AE. S.O.I, V and VI). Rome: C. de Luigi.

Damon-Guillot, Anne. 2007. *La Liturgie en mouvements: 'aqʷaqʷam, réalisation chantée, gestuelle et instrumentale du texte liturgique dans l'Eglise chrétienne orthodoxe unifiée d'Ethiopie*. PhD diss., Université Jean Monnet de Saint-Etienne, Saint-Etienne.

———. 2009. "Toucher le coeur des schismatiques. Stratégies sonores et musicales des jésuites en Ethiopie, 1620–1630." *Le Jardin de musique* 6 (1): 65–99.

Daphné sur les ailes du vent (Baroque around the world). 2010. XVIII-21 Le Baroque Nomade, dir. Music director J.-C. Frisch. 2 CD Arion ARN268810.

Daston, Lorraine and Katharine Park. 2001. *Wonders and the Order of Nature, 1150–1750*. New York: Zone Books.

de Almeida, Manoel. 1954. *Some Records of Ethiopia, 1593–1646: Being Extracts from the History of High Ethiopia or Abassia by Manoel de Almeida: Together with Bahrey's History of the Galla*. Translated and edited by C. F. Beckingham and G.W.B. Huntingford. London: The Hakluyt Society.

Descola, Philippe. 2005. *Par-delà Nature et Culture*. Paris: Gallimard.

Feld, Steven. 2004. Liner notes to the CD. *The Time of Bells*, 1. VoxLox 63447 9827815.

Féraud, Olivier. 2009. "Une anthropologie sonore des pétards et des feux d'artifice à Naples." *Ethnographiques.org* 19. www.ethnographiques.org/2009/Feraud.

Guillebaud, Christine. 2009. "Musique mécanique et temple hindou: Histoire controversée d'un dispositif visuel et sonore." *Terrain: Revue d'Ethnologie de l'Europe* 53: 98–113.

Gutton, Jean-Pierre. 2000. *Bruits et sons dans notre histoire: Essai sur la reconstitution du paysage sonore*. Paris: Presses Universitaires de France.

Hirsch, Bertrand. 2002. "A l'origine de la reine de Saba et du Prêtre Jean." *Histoire du christianisme* 9: 54–57.

Irving, David R. M. 2010. *Colonial Counterpoint*. Oxford: Oxford University Press.

Johnston, Charles. 1844. *Travels in Southern Abyssinia*. London: Madden.

Kastner, Georges. 1857. *Les Voix de Paris: Essai d'une histoire littéraire et musicale des cris populaires de la capitale depuis le Moyen Âge jusqu'à nos jours précédé de considérations sur l'origine et le caractère du cri en général et suivi de* Les Cris de Paris *Grande Symphonie humoristique vocale et instrumentale*. Paris: Brandus.

Kircher, Athanasius. 1650. *Musurgia universalis sive ars magna consoni et dissoni*. 2 vols. Romae: Typis Ludovici Grignani.

Lobo, Jerónimo. 1984. *The "Itinerário" of Jerónimo Lobo*. Translated from Portuguese by Donald M. Lockhart. London: The Hakluyt Society.

Mendes, Alfonso and Gasparo Paës. 1628. *Lettere annue di Ethiopia. Del 1624, 1625, e 1626. Scritta al M.R.P. Mutio Vitelleschi Generale della Compagnia di Giesu*. Rome: Per l'Herede di Bartolomeo Zannetti.

Pacquier, Alain. 1996. *Les Chemins du baroque dans le Nouveau Monde: De la Terre de Feu à l'embouchure du Saint-Laurent*. Paris: Fayard.

Pagani, Catherine. 2006. "Clockwork and the Jesuit Mission in China." In *The Jesuits II: Cultures, Sciences and the Arts, 1540–1773*, edited by J. W. O'Malley, G. A. Bailey, S. J. Harris, and T. F. Kennedy, 658–678. Toronto: University of Toronto Press.

Pearce, Nathaniel. 1831. *The Life and Adventures of Nathaniel Pearce*. London: Henry Colburn and Richard Bentley.

Pennec, Hervé. 2003. *Des jésuites au royaume du Prêtre Jean*. Paris: Centre culturel Calouste Gulbenkian.

Prutky, Remedius. 1991 (1765). *Prutky's Travels in Ethiopia and Other Countries*. Translated and edited by J. H. Arrowsmith-Brown and annotated by Richard Pankhurst. London: The Hakluyt Society.

Rath, Richard Cullen. 2003. *How Early America Sounded*. Ithaca: Cornell University Press.

Ricci, Antonello, ed. 1996. *Mesoraca: Vie musicale d'un village en Calabre*. CD VDE-GALLO 872 (collection AIMP XLII).

Smith, Mark M. 2001. *Listening to Nineteenth-Century America*. Chapel Hill: University of North Carolina Press.

3 An "Obscene" Calling

Emotionality in/of Marginalized Spaces: A Listening of/into "Abusive" Women in Govindpuri (Delhi)

Tripta Chandola

The Calling

And thus does Zizek (2006) expound on the "traumatic dimension of voice" by focusing on *The Exorcist* in *The Perverts' Guide to Cinema*:

> Voice is not an organic part of the human body. It is coming from somewhere in between your body. Whenever we talk to another person there is always this minimum of ventriloquist affect, as if some foreign power took possession. Remember [speaking over the clip from the film, *The Exorcist*, where the girl is possessed] that at the beginning of the film this was a beautiful, young girl. How did she become a *monster* [emphasis added] that we see? By being possessed, but who possessed her? A voice. *A voice in its obscene dimensions.*
>
> [emphasis added]

This is an obscene chapter. It deals with obscenity as a particular and peculiar "traumatic dimension of voice" performed by women onto other women in the traumatized space of a specific slum in the city of Delhi, India's capital city. However, it is not only its subject matter that lends this chapter its character. It is also in the liberties it takes to obscenely identify in these performances the potential to displace patriarchal-spatial hierarchies; an exhibitionist display of emotionality; and a well-articulated desire for love, not only as an esoteric experience but also a condensed social, sexual reality. Since at the core of every trauma lies (unfolds) a violent social, moral, physical event, the ruminations in this chapter constantly concern themselves with identifying these sites of violence the obscene performances not only claim, but also create, on its Self and on the Others.

Women spewing sexually explicit and violent abuses (in this context, in Hindi), toward the female body, which are traditionally reckoned to be the classic masculine expression to reiterate the hierarchy, as the particular instance of obscene "traumatic dimension of voice", is the focus of this chapter. Whilst the chapter acknowledges the broader materiality of gendered obscene-sonic exchange in the slums, this chapter focuses on the particular and peculiar economy of this exchange when the obscenities are not only claimed by but are also exclusively directed at women by *other* women. By implicating themselves in the violence directed toward the 'real' and 'imagined' body of the Self (and thus taking 'charge' of that violence, at least rhetorically), the women create a disruptive and volatile space where gendered spaces, roles, and identities necessitate reframing. The evocation of these abuses, I argue, is a strategic act of subversion and circumvention of the *patriarchal* hierarchies. The landscape of patriarchal hierarchies is not an exclusive domain of masculine presence(s) and reiterations; and more often than not, it is the performance of *masculinities*—by both men and women— which accord it its particular characteristic. In that sense, while this chapter acknowledges that the cartographic, emotional and social imaginations of the patriarchal landscapes are devised by the dominant sensibilities, women often assume a *masculine* persona to institute these imaginations, especially when the exchange does not involve gendered interactions but unfolds in an apparently gender 'neutral' setting exclusively between women.

It is within this framing that the evocations—obscenities by women directed at women—are affectively employed toward several agendas: social, cultural, spatial and political. However, in this chapter I explore the evocation of these abuses to map the cartographic and cathartic experience and experiencing of 'love' in, and within, the slums of Govindpuri (hereafter "GP"). The chapter then dwells upon the agency and extent of strategy available to the marginalized—here, women in an essentially patriarchal setting, and slums within the broader materiality of the city—to affect the designed subversion and circumvention to complicate the reckoning of the Self deflected through the prism of sonic performances, emotions, identity and violence. In that, this chapter, even though romantically inclined, refuses to romanticize violence by engaging with its perverse everydayness. In the discussions that follow, it is a matter of deliberation to not highlight the particular social and political considerations and consequences of "voice" and "sonic performativity" as agency in the given context. The intent is not to collapse these distinct categories. Instead it aims to unfold these obscene evocations as a complex and nuanced negotiation between the two to high-light the ruptures, continuations and displacements between different kinds of sonic permissibility available to a certain group and the resounding impact it can have.

Baby and Bitiya, two formidable women in GP, who not only allowed me to experience their experiencing of love within this schematic, but who also agreed to have their narratives exploited for broader extrapolations, are the punctuations—not as objectified entities, but as necessary instruments (in all their sensuousness)—carrying these explorations further. I, as a bearer of the feminine form, and an interlocutor-in-charge, insert myself in the text, not with a self-indulgent agenda, but to highlight the anxieties of the encounter of the obscene sorts, across myriad considerations, especially of class distinctions.

Obscenely, Yours

Beginning at the basics: the self, before I venture into the Self of the Others. I grew up in a setting reeking of colonial and real hangovers. Both my parents were in the Indian army; my father was part of the elite, combative commando forces and my mother a dentist in its medical forces. Over the weekends we had croquet games, long-drawn bridge games and lots of gin. We, the children, did not partake in the latter though. We grew up with smatterings of grammatically incorrect English, and our parents—mostly, fathers—exclaiming, "bloody hell", "God damn you", and "bastard". That was the extent of obscene exclamations I grew up with. I never heard them swear in Hindi, but as I grew older, I got to know of abuses in Hindi: *maader-chod* (mother-fucker), *behen-chod* (sister-fucker), *chutiya* (cunt). However, it was only when I had left the security of parental nesting, acquired half-baked degrees, romanced with revolutionary ideas, drank enough dark rum and reckoned myself to be truly "liberal" that I started using these expletives as punctuations as the men around us did. I was not alone. I was part of a cohort who had grown up with socialist realities and leftist ambitions while assuming neo-liberal sensibilities. We, of course, like them (the men) did not mean them literally; the violence was truly displaced, or so we thought. The beginning was hesitant though, but once realizing the currency the utterance of these expletives carried in sustaining a "moral and social" shock, it was incorporated as part of everyday emotional and intellectual expression. Men who found it deplorable did not see us beyond the main door. The exchange—social, intellectual and sexual—was thus mediated by a highly sexualized, violent vocabulary. This exchange, in all its liberal pretensions, not only displaced the body and site of the violence, but violence itself. However, all said and done, we never lost our moral-virginal hymens.

The liminal space we had managed to carve out through these obscene performances allowed us to transgress across conflicting social-moral landscapes. I had reckoned that I was thus truly liberated from "middle-class" sexual mores and moral prejudices. However when entering yet another liminal space, I was compelled to renegotiate the social-sexual-moral economies I was convinced I had claimed.

In 2003, I was appointed to assist Dr. Jo Tacchi in a Department for International Development (DFID) funded research on "Role of Information and Communication Technologies (ICTs) in Poverty Alleviation". A prominent slum settlement in Delhi, India's capital city, was one of the identified research sites. Until then, even though I had lived in Delhi for almost a decade, my experience of and exposure to the slums in Delhi was through a primarily middle-class, educated, urban lens. This implied that, while I was aware of the rhetoric of displacement and resettlement vis-à-vis the slums in popular mainstream media and academic discourse, I had never experienced the space firsthand. Though conscious of the discursive practices that "othered" the slums and slum-dwellers, I was still reluctant and hesitant when it came to setting my terms of engagement, primarily because of my limited knowledge of the space. The narratives highlighting the everyday violence, displacement and marginalization of the slums also—often, subconsciously and insidiously (as fine subtext)—included testimonies of the social, moral and sexual conducts in these spaces. These, the narratives emphasized, were *different*, and this difference lay in the distance from the middle-class-ness of these practices.

And thus I ventured into the slums of GP, hesitant and reclaiming the middle-class-ness I had spent years to shed off. Or at least I reckoned. At the most fundamental level, this was obvious in the deliberation of attire I chose to present myself in the slums. It was not the "Westernized" appearance I usually donned—T-shirt and jeans—but a more staid one reflective of the 'indigenous' culture—*salwaar-kurtas*[1]—with, of course, a perfectly draped *duppatta*.[2] However the deception went deeper and further: a heavy smoker, I did not dare light up in GP; a drinker of some merit, I refused to claim this indulgence; romantically and sexually adventurous, I definitely did not acknowledge these encounters, or even their possibilities. However, pertinent to the context of this chapter, the most dramatic shift was in the presentation and performance of my *sonic* self in the space of the slums. The language of communication and conversation in GP was Hindi—that in itself was a shift, as I inhabited spaces where Indian-English was the *de facto* language. Moreover, the iteration of Hindi I chose as my *sonic* identity within the materiality of GP was chaste and definitely devoid of the obscenities, which otherwise were part of my everyday vocabulary.

It has been ten years since those early days of hesitant, deceptive encounters in GP. Following the DFID research project, I undertook to pursue my doctoral research focusing on politics of production and articulation of sound as an interface to interrogate the everyday interactions between the residents of the GP and their middle-class neighbors (Chandola 2010). The anxiety of leading an almost schizophrenic identity as a researcher overwhelmed me, and I invested in intellectual and methodological inquisitions to resolve the sites from where these split-sonic performances emanated. Not without its distressing emotional, intellectual and theoretical reckonings, I came upon the realization that central to the assumed sonic performance in GP was the internalization of the logic the testimonies (insidiously in academic texts and overtly in mainstream media) sustained: the otherness of the slums, and its residents, and this difference arising out of the distance from middle-class sensibilities. The pathology of assuming the deceptive, chaste sonic identity was premised not in witnessing the transgressive spaces women claimed in the slums (as we—the middle-class counterparts—aspired for in our contexts) by obscene utterances, but in the danger imagined in the identification of the self with that of the Others. The "Self" of the Others was thus not only systematically absented from the discursive space(s), but it was also strategically demonized by affecting a distance through assumed sonic identities to assert an embryonic distance.

Figure 3.1 Surface smiles: Govindpuri is a highly gendered space where the mobility of women comes under close scrutiny by both the immediate family and the extended social network.

Photo: Tripta Chandola (2012).

Once arrived at these deliberations, I agreed to put myself into as much scrutiny and observation as I took the liberties of the "Self" of the Others. Thus we—the women and I in GP—smoke, drink, discuss our affairs and political positions (with liberal smatterings of *obscenities*, which we any-way employ as punctuations) with truthfulness, which does not necessarily obliterate the class distinctions, but it surely does not deliberately perpetu-ate or deflect it. However, most significantly, we collectively acknowledge the currency of sonic-obscene performances in claiming spaces, though not without their violence, in our specific contexts, even though we necessarily do not perform them together.

Shutting Anyone's "Speakers"

Bitiya is a feisty young woman. By her own admission, she has done it all: got married at the age of 16 to her lover against her parents' will; had a daughter by 18; left her abusive, alcoholic husband at 19; had a raging affair with a neighbor's relative; supported her family, including getting her two sisters married off, by taking up sex trade; had a live-in lover for seven years; and presently is readying to bring up his child after they had a volatile and violent breakup. She is a force to reckon with: "I have done things on my own terms and I have borne the consequences as well. No one in the locality can say anything to me. *I can shut anyone's speakers.*"

It was not long before I witnessed her "shutting the speakers." She was in the middle of a heated argument with one of her neighbors—a young woman—when I arrived. The context or the cause of the altercation was lost to me, and I did not dare interrupt the exchange. Even though this exchange was liberally doused with obscene expletives, they were restricted to the normalized *behen-chod, maadar-chod* variety, but soon the argument picked up momentum, and so did the nature of the obscenities. They became increasingly violent and sexual. By now Bitiya was dominating this sonic exchange. The choice of her expletives insinuated violence onto the feminine body, which included, but was not limited to, "shoving things in her cunt; getting the neighbor raped by her uncles; her [the neighbor's] incestuous sexual encounters with her brother, father and any stranger who would have her; and the ultimate evocation of the sexualized violence of the neighbor's enjoying being raped."

The young woman was thus silenced, and she agreed to take down the garland of worn-out shoes she had hung facing Bitiya's house as an insult to the latter's family.

I was not unaffected by this highly violent and sexualized exchange of obscenities between the two women, even though I had witnessed similar exchanges earlier. Noticing my unease, Bitiya offered the following explanation: "Here, the only way to shut people up is by spewing more *gannd* [filth] than they can. That is the only way anyone's *speakers* can be silenced." The explanation offered by Bitiya was not without its Zizek-ian evocations. By identifying the sonic performativities of another in terms of a technological-mediated object—the speakers—Bitiya in fact arrived at a proposition similar to that of Zizek's that the voice in fact can be "coming from somewhere in between your body." Also in this evocation, the metaphor of speakers, which can be turned off, is particularly telling, as it poignantly sums up the spaces of dominance—social and cultural spaces—the obscene-sonic performances permit. Thus in this specific performance the sonic space is dominated by the one who can silence or shut the speakers.

However, silence—both performed (being silent) and imposed (being silenced)—is not a static category of sonic being and cannot be contained within the singularity of a listening position within a specific context. Being *silent* and being *silenced* can rupture, intersect and interlude the soundscapes in a context in similar manifestations. But the resounding impact of the particular performances more often than not emanates from the spatial, social and political positionality the *performer* occupies. In the Indian context, the negotiations between being silent and being silenced is strongly situated within its historical, religious and political epistemologies. And these manifest themselves thus: the silence demanded of the lower-caste/classes vis-à-vis

Figure 3.2 Sonic performances: The women are often required to perform silence, without talking too loudly, to strangers and more. However, the women continually perform sonic digressions, like hurling abuses at the groom as a traditional practice in this pre-wedding ritual.

Photo: Tripta Chandola (2012).

the upper-caste/classes both in their everyday, immediate encounters but also as agents of knowledge production; the deliberate silencing of the subaltern as a political category, and the exalted 'silence' of the men of cloth.

Vocal Digressions: The Cartography of Abusing and Loving

The narratives of Baby and Bitiya I discuss in this chapter concern themselves with some of these negotiations: sonic dominance, silencing and displacement of spatial-patriarchal hierarchies. But they also venture into the geographies of emotionality of the "Self" of the Other as articulated through the experiencing of love. GP is a highly gendered space, where the mobility of women comes under close scrutiny by both the immediate family and the extended social network. Here, it is the feminine body on which the otherness is doubly inscribed, both of the structural and everyday violence. This otherness is inscribed by limiting the performances the feminine "self" is capable of—bodily, sonically, sexually and emotionally. The "being" and "becoming" of the feminine self is situated within a hetero-normative narrative with subservience and compliance as its core ethos; digressions from this normative narrative are closely monitored—mostly by the older women—and invite social and cultural disapproval; and in extreme cases ostracization often also resulting in physical violence.

In this section I will emphasize the manner in which instances where sonic and emotional digressions by the feminine 'self' disrupt and displace the registered hetero-normative narratives, though not without its violences and violations—to the "Self" and "Others".

Both Bitiya and Baby are single parents. However, that is not the only thing the two have in common. They both left their marital homes to escape abusive husbands and since then have been the arbiters of their respective families. On different occasions and in varying circumstances, both of them have earned a decent living through sex work. Over the years both of them had several "love" affairs outside of both their Muslim and slum community. Most of them have been clandestine, but in their cases 'a' love affair stands out as the ultimate experience: relationship with Dimpy in the case of Bitiya, and Baby's affair with Chand. They conducted these respective relationships openly, challenged the communal order, and had live-in relationships.

Here it might be worthwhile to highlight (especially as regards responding to the issue of the encounter of the researcher's *self* with the researched's) that these confidences by both Bitiya and Baby were not revealed in a "research" encounter but were shared over a period of few years during which I, as a researcher, was in turns an object of inquisition and research to which I responded with as much *truthful integrity* as I expected from the *researched*. Over the years we transcended the sonic distance and displaced sonic performances of identities to arrive at *sonic* intersections whilst acknowledging the class distance, allowed "us"—I shared this relationship with most of the residents of GP, especially women—to share collective *sonicities*. The shared collective sonicities across class and spatial considerations within the broader materiality and imagination of the city are not without their negotiations, and often lend themselves to varying practices of *silencing* (Chandola 2012).

Bitiya and Baby's romantic undertakings allow situating the intersection of these two digressions—sonic and emotional—within the specific materiality of GP, whilst complicating the position of slums in the broader imagination of the city as spaces capable of *emotionality*. Bitiya's relationship with Dimpy and Baby's with Chand came to stormy endings. The deliberation toward the final closure of the respective relationships involved public fights, loud *obscene and abusive* exchanges and physical violence. During and after the end of the relationships, Bitiya and Baby, casual acquaintances until then, found in each other unusual allies. Their open defiance of social-moral-sexual norms meant that when the said relationships ended, they could not seek out the social support networks available to, for instance, a recently widowed or a married woman abandoned by her husband, or one who returned to her parental home on account of consistent abuse, predominantly physical. Even though in the case of both Bitiya and Baby, abuse—both physical and emotional—along with abandonment were central to their narrative and experience of an essentially patriarchal relationship, they were not extended the concessions on account of the arrogant identification of "love" as the determining rationale for the said relationships.

Herein unfolds the intersections of the sonic, sexual and romantic digressions. Bitiya and Baby were incensed by their partners' new romantic involvements, but also for not being able to receive any social and cultural validation for their experience of "love". They both agreed upon a retaliatory strategy. The "anger" they felt on account of the displacement was, however, not directed at their former partners, but their present lovers. And thus they decided to "teach" them a lesson by publicly shaming them, by *shutting their speakers*. The negotiations for arriving at this confrontation are uncannily similar in both the instances. Both Bitiya and Baby set out to establish the everyday routines about the *other* woman in question, they gathered as many details about their histories and present preoccupations and the geographies of "love" they were claiming with their ex-lovers.

One afternoon Baby was informed that her ex-lover, Chand, and his present romantic interest were spotted at a public park not very far from GP. The moment seemed opportune, and the two allies—Bitiya and Baby—set out to *shut the speakers*. Once the two of them were spotted in the park, Baby took to abusing the romantic interest in question, whilst completely ignoring the ex-lover, in highly sexualized and violent obscenities. The *obscenities* in themselves demand an intellectual inquisition to locate the violence—real and imagined—articulated by them; however, the concern of this chapter is in the very performance of these *obscenities* rather than the cultural modalities of their production. These *obscenities* were marked by two prominent sets of rhetoric: first, to establish her prowess as a sexual subject by claiming the very real and imagined violation of and violence toward the feminine body inherent to these obscenities. These included evocations to the effect, "my cunt can hold as many cocks as I want, if you had the same capacity you would not steal my boyfriend"; "I can accommodate different cocks in different orifices at the same time"; and "it is my cunt, what I do with it is my business . . ." But the effectiveness of the *obscene* performance as a retaliatory strategy lay in disenfranchising the *other*—Chand's present romantic interest—of exactly the same sexual subjectivity and control over it as Baby claimed for herself. These included calling her a *randi* (a whore), and projecting on to her feminine body violence of a highly sexualized nature, "you will be gang raped" and "hope you are fucked by your whole clan, but even that won't satisfy you," and "obviously you are insatiable, that is why after being fucked by everyone in your neighborhood and family, you use your cunt to attract other men."

The woman in question—Chand's romantic interest—was taken aback, especially since Baby had Bitiya to reiterate, almost perform the function of an echo, in this obscene performance just extending the space and scope of sonic colonization. Soon a group of onlookers gathered about. Some men, including Chand, tried to intervene. However, at that moment Baby started tearing off her clothes and threatening that if anyone interfered she would file a suit of "section 376" against them. Under Indian Penal Code, 1860, Section 376 is reserved to report and charge the accused for attempting or having committed rape. If reported, the police have to take action against the accused, and it remains as a recorded criminal case against the identified perpetrator until proven innocent.

If Baby's retaliatory strategy relied upon making a distinct demarcation between sexual subjectivities as claimed by the sonic performances, Bitiya's strategic intervention to encounter the *other* collapsed these demarcations by sustaining a narrative in which the *other's* corporeality was held as vulnerable to the real sexual and physical violence she had encountered in her relationship. Indeed this was also a publicly performed *obscene* sonic moment. She, along with Baby, made an unannounced visit to Dimpy's present lover's house. Bitiya then proceeded to narrate in some detail the sexual violence— both real and rhetorical—she had endured. She evoked her body as a *piece of meat* that Dimpy devoured as and when he wanted; he treated her like a *randi,* often physically and verbally abusing her. She made a plea to the *other* to reject Dimpy on account of the shared violation of the feminine body. The climactic moment of this obscene sonic performance was inscribing the script of an imagined violence onto the *other's* body: "he will *fuck* you as he wants; if you don't agree to what he desires, he will not shy away from *raping* you and talking *filth* about you to his friends." Her ultimate threat to disrupt the romantic adventures was to file a complaint against Dimpy under Section 376, especially as by then she was carrying his child.

Silencing the Lover's Speakers: Muting the "Self" of the "Other"

If indeed "voice" is to be considered as something "coming from somewhere in between your body", then it is also laden with the potentiality of occupying other "in-between-nesses": spatially, socially, politically and culturally. "Voice" as a simple act of speech and its rhetorical capacity to evoke a collective reaction (for instance, political and religious congregations, among others) is at once grounded and displaced. "Voice" emanates from "a" time-space continuum, but it reverberates across multitudinous, intersecting temporal and spatial realities resonating a reiteration of the "voice", intended or otherwise. This potentiality of "voice" to literally, metaphorically and rhetorically extend one's domain of "being" is well acknowledged in GP. And thus the women are required to perform silence of sorts: *don't talk too loudly; don't talk to strangers; don't retaliate; don't talk back.*

The women however continually perform the sonic digressions. They challenge, subvert and circumvent these hierarchies by claiming the sonic space, by performing obscenities of the nature discussed in the earlier section. However, at this juncture it is pertinent to establish that not all sexualized obscenities are registered as digressions. Some of them like *maader-chod* (mother fucker), *behen-chod* (sister fucker), *chutiya* (cunt) are normalized in the given context, and are used by both men and women as interjections and punctuations, both jocularly and in slight altercations. These obscenities are not absent of the *imagined* sexualized violence. However the site of the violence—the body of a mother or a sister—is still claimed (or in fact un-claimed) in its abstractions, steadfastly located within the familial and social order wherein the figures of the mother and the daughter are revered and respected, and thus beyond the realm of the 'real' violence these imaginations contain.

The sexual and social freedoms claimed and exercised by Bitiya and Baby are in no way singular instances of challenging the hetero-normative, masculine cartographies in GP. However what sets aside the narrative of these two women are the significant overlaps in their experiences—social, cultural and romantic; but also the particular manner in which both of them assumed a certain *masculinity* in claiming these spaces. The instance of Bitiya "shutting anyone's speaker" is but an assertion of it. They are both constantly approached by neighbors, relatives and friends to "deal" and "negotiate" situations, especially involving local cops, goons and matters of "fights" in their respective streets; one of the reasons why both women enjoy this "privileged" position is on account of their ability to spew *filth* and *shut anyone's speakers*. As mentioned earlier, GP is a highly gendered space where the mobilities and performances of women—social, sexual and sonic—are highly restricted. The "obscene" sonic performances of Bitiya and Baby disrupt the established hierarchies. The men—often amused—find it disconcerting because of its emasculating potential to displace them from their claimed space. The women—especially those at whom these "obscenities" are directed—are further disenfranchised by the peculiar encounter of gendered violence (however rhetorical and free of *real* violence) by other women. However, Bitiya and Baby, though performing this violence and claiming the masculine space, are not subtracted from the rhetorical and violence onto the feminine self inflicted by these "sonic-obscenities". The only recourse available to them to claim the masculine spaces, as women who are *besharam* [shameless] enough to spew the obscenities, is to expose their own cartographic, emotional, sexual and sonic selves to the very violence they intend to inflict, and thus displace.

If women spewing sexualized, violent abuses are the ultimate sonic digression, the declaration of "love"—as an experience and desire—by them is its emotional equivalent. "Love" and its "declaration" threaten to disrupt the precariously sustained order of normative social, moral and sexual values, especially in regard to containing and controlling the feminine "self". The obscenities performed by women, which do indeed register as sonic digressions and affectively disrupt the spatial-patriarchal-sonic hierarchies, are the ones in which the women directly implicate themselves and other women in the violence directed toward the "real" and "imagined" feminine self.

The Danger of the *Other's* Love

"Love" is dangerous. It resounds with social, sexual and moral possibilities and digressions. However, the pathological dread of declaration of "love"—especially by women—is the exhibitionist display of the "self" vis-à-vis an identified "other". In the concluding discussion to this chapter, I will situate this pathological dread of "love" as a peculiar instance of perverse masculinities in a marginalized setting of the slums. I shall also highlight the manner in which this *perversity*, and thus its depravity, of slums often evoked by the state, middle-class retort, and in cultural representation of slums is a justification to maintain a distance from these "spaces" and displace them. A paternalistic disciplining agenda is inherent to these narratives, which is symptomatic of the broader anxiety of the dominant structures and narratives to allow for an emotionality, and thus an identification of a well-defined and claimed sense of "self" to the marginalized spaces and communities.

As discussed in the previous section, Bitiya and Baby found solace in each other to articulate their experience, anxiety and trauma of "love" within these negotiated cartographies. It was only within the shared experience of displaced "selves" that the two of them could rehabilitate their individual "self", especially since they lacked any other narrative spaces to claim it. The end of their respective relationships was articulated by both of them (in collective and independent conversations where I was inadvertently present)—in different terms—as a significant moment of rupture to the projected and imagined sense of "self", as within weeks of the break-up both Dimpy and Chand had assumed new "romantic" relationships. Socially, culturally, sonically and sexually lacking the space to locate the "love" as a valid category of experience within the "real" materiality of GP, the displacement from an "imagined" site—however displaced—where this experience was validated by the presence of a responsive "other"; both Bitiya and Baby encountered the ultimate displacement of being absented from this collective, fantastical realm by the insertion of an another—sexually active and sonically performative "self". The *voice* of the "other" (Dimpy's and Chand's newly acquired romantic interests), muting their own, compelled them into undertaking matters, into *shutting the other's speakers*—even whilst sharing an intimate, immediate and violent identification with the *other* as always occupying the space of the Other within the hegemonic, masculine performativities and spaces.

Emotionality in Marginalized Spaces: The "Self" of the Other

Slums are heterotopic spaces in the city. They are both dreaded and desired, the former for its "potential" to disrupt the fundamental core of social-moral values owing to the imaginations it evokes on account of its density, dirt and digressions—social, cultural and moral. Within this dreaded potentiality for

Figure 3.3 Power structures: Political hoardings, some of them communal, smile down upon their hardly affluent votebanks in Govindpuri.

Photo: Tripta Chandola (2012).

digressions lies its perverse desire. However, this desire rarely translates into a direct engagement with the space, but manifests itself in the hyperbolic interest in situating the position of the slums in the "present" of the city. This tension is especially exaggerated in a city like Delhi, which has ambitions to transform itself into a "world-class, clean, green" city.[3] Moreover this transformation, essentially structural, also relies on the readily available, cheap manual labor from these marginalized spaces and communities. This ambition draws inspiration from following the Singaporean model, which prides itself in transforming itself into a "world-class city" under Lee Kuwan Yew in a very short period of time (Ghani 2011). In fact, Sheila Dixit, Delhi's chief minister in her third term, got a special mention in *LKY Cities in Transformation Award*[4] for her efforts to improve the city's environmental, civic and urban planning.

With "Delhi as Singapore", Sheila Dixit extended to the burgeoning middle-class in Delhi a model that immensely appealed to their "aspirational" ambitions of what Slavoj Zizek identifies as "capitalism with Asian values".[5] The scope of this text does not allow to engage at length with the problematic and politics of employing "Delhi as Singapore" model as strategic rhetorical tool, which was affectively employed to justify violence—by the way of demolitions, displacement and resettlement—on marginalized spaces and communities (namely, slum dwellers, homeless people and migrant labor) in the city. However, it allows to explore the particular reckoning of the "self" as a modern, disciplined and self-governing individuated entity which has insidiously found its way into urban planning discourse as well mainstream, cultural representations. It is within this particular notionality of the "self" that I complicate the position of "slums" in the broader imagination of urban materiality by focusing on its "emotionality" with "love" as a key concern in GP.

The Oxford English Dictionary defines "emotions" (n.) as "a strong feeling deriving from one's circumstances, mood, or relationships with *others*" [emphasis added], and "emotional" and "emotionality" are defined as the states that express this "strong feeling". Central to this definition of emotions extending to its performance, emotionality, is a strong sense of "self" and the relationship of this self with an identified "other". Slums are strategically denied a "self" as it allows to accommodate the anxiety about their "otherness" across political, intellectual, social, cultural and indeed, emotional manifestations. In its most fundamental aspect, it completely disenfranchises slums of any "identity" and thus its assertion. It systematically limits their "right to the city". This fundamental disenfranchisement further extends into *denying* the slums and its residents the possibility to imagine an- (or any) *other*. The denial of the "self" of the slums in discursive spaces, middle-class imagination and mainstream representation is then logically extended to acknowledging any "emotional" capacity or its performance, *emotionality*.

This double denial, first of the "self" of the slums and then the possibility of "othering" by the Other, translates not only in immediate disenfranchisement, but also significantly allows for the displacement of the marginalized both in the historical and futuristic imagination of the urban. The peculiarity of the suspended displacement in the imagination of the state is not incidental but strategic. Owing to this suspension, the demolition, displacement or violence inflicted on the slums finds justification as it is understood that they neither have any historicity nor any future claims to the memory and culture of the space they inhabit—that until "re-settled" by the state, they exist in a void. And thus the ruthlessness of the violence inflicted is often masked within the rhetoric of "benevolence"; in that they are in fact being extended "legitimate" claims to history, memory and culture. The lack of acknowledgment to their "emotionality" is yet another strategy (though seemingly insidious and instinctive) to perpetuate their violence. For, if the residents of the slums were indeed identified as 'emotionally' capable, they would have to be acknowledged to have capabilities of "individual" expression, which would then extend to acknowledging their "collective" identities as well.

However, this denial of emotionality does not imply that their "performance" or "expression of self" in the public, or for that matter in their private spaces is not *not*-acknowledged. In fact the performance is constantly scrutinized; however it is not engaged within the framework of expression of "self" but as a gross deviance from the "modern, disciplined and self-governed" self that is acquiring a currency within the cultures of urban transformation in Delhi. And this imagination of the "self", drawing from the Singaporean model, has been affectively consolidated in the popular, middle-class aspirations, which then find resonance in urban planning projects, several of which—including the *Bhagidhari* system[6]—were recognized as exemplary efforts by Sheila Dixit in the special mention she received in *LKY's Cities in Transformation Awards.*

Love in the Times of Othering: Muting the "Self" of the Other

At the outset this chapter announced its obscene intent. And here, in the conclusion, wherein the narrative structure demands a closure and neatly folded resolutions, the chapter performs its hyperbolic obscenity by its refusal to succumb to these compulsions in that it does not arrive at a logical culmination of the conversations initiated, but aims to leave with provocations both for the author and its reader.

The deliberation to listen into the obscene sonic performances of women in GP, the identification of "self", emotionality and moments of disruption of sonic-spatial and patriarchal negotiations was not a cheap attempt toward sensationalization. Instead by undertaking these listenings—not without their violence, both real and imagined—it was to precisely highlight the perversity of the available moments of encounters between the 'mainstream' and the "marginalized" to recognize these pathologies: of the "self" of the *other.*

Women spewing the highly sexualized and violent abuses in GP are a perverse titillation to the dominant agents (here, men) and narratives in its "real" encounter with this body but also in situating these bodies as sexual subjects within the broader cartographic imagination of self and emotions. If the women are indeed articulate and claim these violence(s), it is because they desire them. But also the vocalization of this "desire"—a performance of the "self", so to say—necessitates the imperative to discipline them. And thus the space and scope available to women to express them-"selves" is limited to obscene performances and encounters, which are fundamentally recognized as "offensive or disgusting by accepted standards of morality and decency". Even "love", an otherwise exalted and celebrated emotion of being within the "mainstream" hegemonic discourse, is only allowed to be actualized and articulated within the discussed obscene performances of and by the women in GP.

Thus love as an expression of self and emotionality is denied legitimacy to the women in GP, operable only in its hyperbolic manifestations. This particular predicament of women in GP is not only representative of the sustained marginalization they encounter as the "other" within its dominant, patriarchal context but also symptomatic of the othering slums (as a space) encounter within the broader urban imagination. Essential to sustain the *othering*—inscribed on the women in the localized context of GP, and slums as a space in its generalized projection—is then to deny them a well-articulated sense of "self" by dismissing their emotionality.

However, emotions *indeed do* abound in marginalized spaces. But making this *seemingly* commonsensical assertion demands qualification, and more importantly, quantification. Within the very tapestry of this necessity to qualify are woven the questions which have preoccupied philosophers, scholars across disciplines and artists: the construction of the "self", the position of the individual and the intimate relationship between the "self" and the state, which then raises further issues of citizenship and the spaces available to different and diverse "selves" to enact it in its complete capacity. However significant these questions are, here it is important to attempt to unveil not only whether emotions abound in marginalized spaces (in fact I begin with that assertion), but to further understand the politics of denial of emotionality in these spaces. The recognition of the emotional of the Other is also plagued with a fundamental methodological and philosophical paradox. Indeed, here lies an inherent dilemma because in recognizing the emotional of the other, one also acknowledges the 'self' of the other (and in fact engages with it).

And Thus the Savage Is a Savage, and Remains a Savage

Perhaps we need to take a step back, and before pondering on the denial of emotionality and its politics, perhaps it is pertinent to wonder why the denial in the first place. Of course, there is the entire contestation of the Self-Other as discussed in the earlier section, and indeed inherent to this denial is a strategic disciplining agenda. However, we, as human beings, are instinctively and intuitively aware of "emotions"; we know they are important and that they shape our lives in ways sometimes even beyond our imagination. We all have succumbed to them: love, jealousy, loneliness, betrayal, anger, angst, hurt . . . this landscape abounds in its wilderness. And only while taking a walk amid this wilderness of emotional possibilities, especially while reflecting on the Self-Other constitutions in this landscape, does it becomes evident that the Other after all is not denied all emotionality. The emotions associated with the Other, which find credence, and even sympathy, are of anger, rage and betrayal (though only if it is against the "system"). There is sometimes even space for the performance of these emotions by the Others; though it is only recognized in its collective manifestations justified, celebrated, sympathized or dreaded within the rhetoric of the subaltern, finally rising in the long-awaited revolution.

In *Don't Ask Me for That Love Again*, one of the greatest poets from South Asia and a committed communist, Faiz Ahmed Faiz, while celebrating his lover's beauty, evokes most poignant imagery to justify his forsaking the love for a cause thus: "There are other sorrows in this world/comforts other than love/ Don't ask me, my love, for that love again." Here, the *sorrows* are not of a personal nature, but a response to the plight of the poor in society whose ". . . bodies [are] plastered with ash, bathed in blood" to serve the rich who have "cast their spell on history."

Romantic love is not for the revolutionary, perhaps an impediment to the Revolution itself? But why is love an anathema to revolution? And if the revolutionary herself cannot claim love, what about those—the *Others*—for whom the revolutionary renounces her love?

The cathartic moment in the compulsion to choose or renounce *love* in one's commitment to the "self" or the "Other" lies in the very individuated and involved articulation of love as an experience, process and practice. Love as a concern for philosophers, scholars, mainstream media and popular culture remains the epitome of the celebration of the "self": in the surrendering, suffering, exhilaration and complete indulgence it demands. It is indeed almost a narcissistic indulgence. It has capacity to completely obliterate the Other. When the poet, in the throes of his melancholia, announces to his lover that romantic love is not an indulgence he can afford, the loved—the *Other*—is completely absented. The pathos and the pain of the loved are irrelevant, and it is the lover's discourse that dominates.

It is this dread of the Other as an individuated entity with the capacity to not only experience but also articulate a plethora of intense *emotions* with the potential to absent and obliterate the *Other* of the other that propels the hegemonic imagination into catatonic paralysis to acknowledge love as a valid category of emotionality of the marginalized. And thus only spaces available to the "self" of the *Other* to claim sonic and emotional territories is through either an *obscene* or a *hysterical* performance. This hyperbolic rhetoric is then strategically evoked to deny an acknowledgment of their "Self" within broader, structural discursive spaces.

Notes

1 A type of suit with loose trousers and long shirt. It is a common, everyday attire for most young women in Asia.

2 A long scarf worn with the *salwaar-kurtas;* in most instances it is considered essential, and not wearing it is often seen as a sign of indecency.

3 See: Delhi, India: Among the Greenest Capitals in the World, http://delhi.gov. in/wps/wcm/connect/bd5bc9804eff00e9885bacb60aeecb21/Delhi_Booklet. pdf?MOD=AJPERES&lmod=1202017102&CACHEID=bd5bc9804eff00e 9885bacb60aeecb21 and "Towards a clean and green Delhi", http://delhi. gov.in/wps/wcm/connect/Common/common/chief+ministers+office/bhagidari/ achievements+of+environment [Both items accessed on 15 December, 2013]

4 See: www.leekuanyewworldcityprize.com.sg/publication.htm, and www. leekuanyewworldcityprize.com.sg/mentions_sheila.htm [Both accessed on 15th December, 2013].

5 In this reckoning of "Capitalism with Asian Values" Zizek has recognized LKY as signaling a new phase in global capitalism not only in the Asian context, but with implications globally, wherein the "logical" connections between Capitalist regimes sustaining democracy have been seriously severed. The reckoning is that while this particular encounter has facilitated a hyperbolic culture of capitalist

consumption, it is no longer reliant, nor does it pretends to be, on notions of democracy, long argued by liberals, to sustain it. See: www.newstatesman.com/ideas/2009/10/today-interview-capitalism, and www.foreignpolicy.com/articles/2012/10/08/capitalism#sthash.ZtHwOIgO.dpb.

6 The premise of the *Bhagidari* System (literally translated as "participatory system") is to involve "citizens" in the processes of governance so as to make it effective, transparent and collaborative. However, the only citizen groups that are presently involved in the *Bhagidari* System are the Resident Welfare Association (RWAs) of middle-class, often gated settlements and market traders'associations (MTAs) (Chandola 2012).

References

Chandola, Tripta. 2010. *Listening into Others: In-between Noise and Silence.* PhD Thesis, Queensland University of Technology, Brisbane.

———. 2012. "Listening into Others: Moralising the Soundscapes in Delhi." *International Development Planning Review* 34 (4): 391–408.

Ghani, A. 2011. "A Recipe for Success: How Singapore Hawker Centres Came to Be." *Institute of Policy Studies Update*, May 2011. http://lkyspp.nus.edu.sg/ips/wp-content/uploads/sites/2/2013/04/AG_history-of-hawkers_010511.pdf.

Filmography

Zizek, S. perf. 2006. *The Pervert's Guide to Cinema.* Dir. Sophie Fiennes. P. Guide Ltd.

Part II

Sound Displays and Social Effects

4   Standing Out From the Crowd

Vocal and Sound Techniques for Catching People's Attention in an Indian Bus Stand

Christine Guillebaud

With their unclear boundaries, Indian cities are often perceived as places where the observer can quickly become disoriented. Indeed, the limits between public and private activities are often difficult to discern (Appadurai 1987), the boundaries between street and sidewalk are porous with dense circulation both on the roads and in the crowds, and a constant stream of the most heterogenous daily activities (Gandhi and Lotte 2012). Many anthropologists have underlined the elusive nature of this urban space, particularly that of the old cities "where the vast majority of Indians still lived were simply seen as unhygienic, opaque, and dangerous" (Gandhi 2011: 206). The sound space does not escape this chaotic representation. Indian megacities are among the "noisiest" in the world. There, as elsewhere, decibel readings are scrupulously carried out according to regional, national, and international standards. Even though the notion of "pollution" may seem legitimate in a public health perspective and for the improvement of the quality of city dwellers' daily lives, for the anthropological study at hand, it presents some problems. On the local level, a physical decibel reading carried out at a traffic intersection, a hospital, or at a school hardly reveals anything about the way in which inhabitants and users listen to or use these spaces. It also fails in fully revealing the ways in which ambient sounds are perceived, or about how to evaluate and appreciate the sensory environment. The notion of "pollution" arbitrarily places thousands of daily commercial and ritual activities on a same level of acoustic reality, although their sound characteristics are difficult to compare. Our research consists of observing (and recording) these fragments of daily life in different public spaces (markets, temples, train/bus stations). In focusing on their sensory dimensions, listening to and observing these places *in situ* is one of the goals that this study aims to reinstate.[1] Different vocal and sound techniques are produced in these spaces to create effects that are perceived by the inhabitants, clients, and passers-by or generally to attract their attention; or even to shape "ambiances"[2] that impose specific listening postures on these same listeners. The present chapter focuses on the example of a bus station, considering it as a relatively autonomous *milieu*. By *milieu*, we mean a composite world made up of sounds produced, perceived, and listened to, both intentionally and otherwise. This simple definition—centered on the idea that experienced "sound worlds"[3] exist—is also inscribed in a wider anthropological undertaking. We indeed consider the bus station as a site for what is commonly referred to as everyday public interactions (Goffman 1973 [1959]), which involves different procedures for sound perception as well as singular ways to divide space. I have chosen to focus on the example of the Saktan Tampuran Bus Stand[4] located to the north of Trichur, a city of the southern Indian state of Kerala. The choice of this particular station is primarily due to the fact that I have been there many times and have traveled to, from, and through there for many years.[5] But also, as a "bus station", this place seemed relatively typical, in the sense that its architectural, human, and acoustic characteristics are commonly found in most of the stations throughout the country. I consider this site as an exemplary case of a sound *milieu* and not as a culturally isolated space.

The Bus Station: A Sound Space and Its Listening Scales

At the bus station, as a space of mobility and circulation, travellers find themselves immediately thrust into a dense sound environment. The multiple events occurring at once give the impression of a vast chaos of sound. The observer is struck by the amount of (sound) events and the resulting saturation, even moreso because the spatial configuration of the station seems to be on the contrary particularly well defined.

- **Document 1:** A morning at Saktan Tampuran Bus Stand (Trichur, Kerala). Video [04'53"]. Image: Christine Guillebaud, 2008.

Following the stream of passengers, a central platform can be seen along which several dozen buses are parked awaiting their departure. These vehicles are not parked there randomly, but have each taken a space reserved for each one of the destinations. Among them is the town of Guruvayur, a holy place with its celebrated Krishna temple, Guruvayurappan, a very sought-after destination notably during the festival periods that rhythm the Hindu calendar. There is also Shoranur, a town where many transfers are made to northern districts. And Kuntakulam, the urban center with its different traditional factories. Many workers go there every day. In the Saktan Tampuran station, there are also many permanently installed small businesses, teashops, and groceries aligned in the middle of the platform. They mark the circulation space of travellers moving along in two opposite directions. The platform functions as an intermediary space reserved for passengers waiting to board.

The video montage shown here reunites different shots. I had the chance to film different areas of the platform: within a stream of pedestrians moving or among a group standing, sometimes focusing on certain interactions, notably involving ticket collectors stationed at the back of the vehicles. To my surprise, the image reveals little about the extreme sound saturation that characterizes the place. The sound space is a concentration of sounds of traffic,

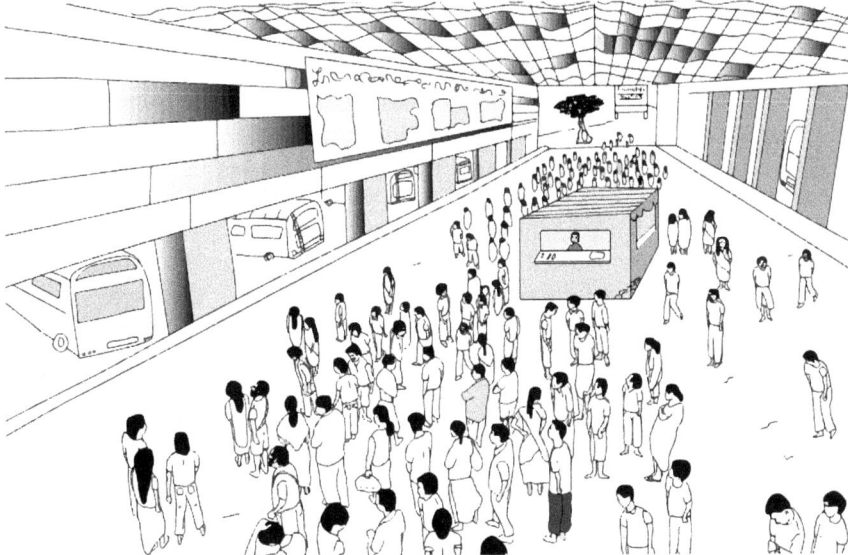

Figure 4.1 Saktan Tampuran Bus Stand (Trichur, Kerala, India). Digital tablet drawing based on field video (Ch. Guillebaud).

Artist: Inès Dobelle.

motors, and the multiple harangues of the ticket collectors. The first impression of this sound space is one of extreme discord between the stream of passengers and the different recorded sound actions. There is no coordinated and global logic of the sound space here but rather different listening scales that are mainly organized around the ticket collectors. Each of these "criers" stands at the foot of his bus. This outwardly oriented posture precisely favors communication interaction with the out-bound pedestrians. The ticket collector's function is to first attract and invite the travellers to take their place on the bus. It is only once the bus is full that this ticket collector may proceed to selling the tickets on the bus by moving about in the aisles.

The Crier: The Man Who Captures More Than He Informs

Upon listening to these cries for the first time, one might think that these criers' calls are informative; in other words, that they are simple announcements. In this way, their function would be similar to that of the vocal announcements diffused via microphone and loudspeakers (or pre-recorded announcements) as is the case in many bus and railway stations around the world. However, here nothing else is associated to these voices. There are no display boards, no timetables, and no space centralizing information. There are as many criers as there are destinations and just as many buses ready to depart. These differences are essential: the entirely acoustic nature of the announcements and the multiplicity of the sound sources imply equally multiple perception modalities and localization of these voices.

From a semantic point of view, the voices of these criers always indicate the destination—the name of a town. However, the striking feature of these calls is more the sound form rather than their statement itself. It is not surprising then that there is quite a variety in the ways to call and harangue and the acoustic choices used individually by the criers. They set themselves apart in this sound *milieu* marked by high intensity and saturation. Rather than choosing semantic clarity, articulation, and intelligibility, these criers voluntarily shorten the names of the towns and cities. The holy city of "Guruvayur" becomes "Guruyur", Kuntakulam is heard as "Kulam", and the city of Trichur becomes "Chur". The contraction of these terms is combined with a prosodic principle of constant repetition and a melodic and tonal coloration that amplifies the phenomenon of personalization. Due to the simultaneous cries of the collectors and therefore the extreme multiplicity, words' meaning is somewhat blurred in favor of specific sound effects.

With this type of sound production, one could wonder whether the term "announcement" is truly relevant as each crier must produce his own singular way to capture the attention of the clients. If the collectors reasoned in terms of announcements, there would be no need to make any public call as the geographic placement of their bus already indicates the destination of big cities, as well as the sign on the vehicles. Also, an "announcement" implies a certain element of schedule and time; it indicates the time of departure and generally the place where the passengers should go to take the bus. This previsional nature would generally favor the punctuality of the departure. In many countries, one sole and unique loudly broadcast voice (when this voice is diffused uniformly in a same space) is often used for this purpose. This voice relates information expressed in a future tense—the train or bus "will leave" at such a time from such a platform; it coordinates pre-scheduled actions to which travellers are invited to comply. In an Indian bus station, on the contrary, time is conjugated in the present. Time is *immediate*. Voice information is transmitted when passengers are already on the move; it is indeed not used to invite the passengers to move. Also, the acoustic propagation of these voices can only be heard in a limited area (they are not amplified) and in a dense sound space where they do not monopolize the full attention of the passengers. With his call, the crier condenses three types of information at the same time. He indicates *in situ* 1) the destination (semantically identifiable), 2) the bus's location (by the fact that he is next to his vehicle), and 3) the imminent departure (by capturing the attention of the potential client).

The criers cannot be considered as guides who indicate the itinerary or help pedestrians in moving about the station, as each destination has its limited zone within the station. This partly explains why the criers remain close to their buses. As soon as the passengers hear and follow the crier's call,

Figure 4.2 Ticket collectors. Saktan Tampuran Bus Stand (Trichur, Kerala, India). Digital tablet drawing based on field video (Ch. Guillebaud).

Artist: Inès Dobelle.

they penetrate into his acoustic sphere and have only but a few steps to take before boarding the bus. The collector's task is therefore not to give general and programmed information, but to capture the clients' attention within a very short lapse of time, a sort of *sound-action instant* before boarding.

The collectors also combine characteristic gestures with these calls. With their arm raised in the air and their hand cupped inward toward the bus, they call the travellers to come toward *their* bus rather than to the neighboring buses. The goal here is to fill the vehicle, as it will leave only as soon as it is full.

Passengers' Perception Modalities

Now, if we consider the point of view of the client (the listener), the general organization of the bus station is well known. Each space in the station is dedicated to a particular destination and because this placement is rarely

Figure 4.3 Bus departing. Saktan Tampuran Bus Stand (Trichur, Kerala, India). Digital Tablet drawing based on field video (Ch. Guillebaud).

Artist: Inès Dobelle.

Figure 4.3 (Continued)

modified, travel habits become ingrained. If everyone knows the destinations and the corresponding platforms, one could wonder why the collectors need to harangue the passengers in such an active fashion. Their action coincides with a very precise moment of the passengers' attention: the moment when passengers visually perceive the collector (lateral vision) and acoustically distinguish his projected voice—that is, just before they get on the bus. The collector thus focuses all of his action on the furtive glance and the attention that the pedestrian pays (or not) to his sound call. Informal interviews that I was able to conduct with collectors confirmed this observation. For the most part, the call is nothing other than a way to make a "time announcement", an expression said in English[6] by the collectors to describe their work. Contrary to a call that would be performed in a less marked sound environment, such as that of a street vendor in a residential neighborhood (Guillebaud 2011), there is no factor of surprise behind the call of the station crier, but rather a dual principle of attraction and recognition. In this context, the client is literally immersed in multiple sound spheres, which impel him to listen in certain ways. The multiple sound projection acts upon his perceptive sphere and drives him almost simultaneously toward one vehicle or another.

The principle of a multitude of *salient voices*, rather than a sole announcement, leads to a great variety of *in situ* negotiations. This principle finds an echo in the visual logic of the buses. The colors, motifs, drawings of deities, and ornaments all distinguish each vehicle and contribute to a certain visual competition (See Video 1: time code 03'30"). The fact that the voices are precisely not organized according to a monopolistic principle allows us to grasp the fragmented organization of the sound space that is not governed randomly but rather according to the logic of *multiple attraction*.

The Crowd: Flow and Positions

The spatial element of attraction can be observed in the criers' use of their bodies. Even though they stand at the back of the bus, they are always placed omnidirectionally (they pivot), whereas the pedestrians follow the progression determined by the structure of the central platform. Rarely do these pedestrians turn around, nor do they change direction or itinerary once in the station. In reality, there is little hesitation, and the waiting time for the passengers is often short, limiting stationary postures. The teashops and the grocers are the only spaces on the platform where individuals can be observed waiting. In the same way, the passengers who travel in small groups (families, work colleagues, students, etc.) have a tendency to stop more readily, but this time remains very limited. A continuous flow is customary. It is indeed the station's architectural and acoustic organization that conditions this mobility.

Another important element linked to this must be taken into account. There is no space reserved for queuing or for passenger order. The stops in the station are temporary and the ways to get on the bus subject to few rules. The passengers get on board when they present themselves before the bus, and the departures happen as the vehicles fill. It is often common to think that great affluence could be seen as an inextricable source of waiting, or even delay for passengers, but in the situation described above there is another logic at hand; the continuous flow of departures and the competition between the buses favor a certain fluidity in the crowds. In this perspective, the sonorous and antimonopolistic way to manage the affluence here makes observing this place through organized figures less effective. For example, if waiting lines were imposed in such an acoustic economy, the sought-after fluidity would be hampered. In a recent article on "The Culture of the Queue in India", Ajay Gandhi summarizes the queue's defining feature:

> It is a teleological and universal form; requires bodily self-containment; demands synchronicity with others; and inculcates a detached, disciplinary sense of place.
>
> (Gandhi 2013: 5)

The author justly underlines the quasi-emblematic nature of the queue in contemporary Indian institutions, as a manner to "normalize" crowds (and their bodies). The "massified queues" imposed for example in the metro of the Indian capital city of New Delhi exemplifies the way in which public authorities impress their "institutional authority, such as that of the state, moulds public sociality into passive seriality" (Gandhi 2013: 3).

The absence of waiting lines in the bus station strongly contrasts with the example of the above-mentioned metro. It is clearly characteristic of the private management methods of the bus companies that operate here.

Here, the daily road traffic linked to this public place is not predominantly managed by the State. The business competition here imposes a decentralized management of the crowd. However, the absence of synchronicity and apparent discipline (to use the terms in the definition presented above) does not equate with chaos and confusion. The logics that we have identified thus far appear here in all their singularity:

1) Acoustic salience of the voices
2) Triple semanticism (destination, localization, departure)
3) Multiple attraction
4) Sound-action instants
5) Principle of flows

An Auto-Regulated Sound Space?

While the specific and private economic framework sheds light on these sound practices, it is not sufficient to simply explicate them. Indeed, as we have mentioned, the sound space of the bus station is not conceived of as a global entity. Rather, it unfolds in a multitude of listening scales centered around individuals and their mutual interactions. In this way, our example falls within the scope of modes of collective coordination and what is commonly called "theories of emergence". In a remarkable study of the figures of road traffic at an "intersection without stoplights" in Bombay, Emmanuel Grimaud (2013) recalls the analytical relevancy of this notion:

> Generally designating the appearance of new characteristics and behaviors beyond a certain degree of complexity, the notion of *emergence* has acquired varied meanings and has given rise to very different uses, whether in physics, biology, artificial intelligence, or in philosophy. [. . .] it has engendered research in each of these domains that can lead to a different consideration of the articulation between the individual and the collective, the creativity of the interactions as well as the manner in which the complexity is envisaged. Approaching things from the point of view of emergence means insisting upon the self-organized nature of the figures of traffic and questioning modalities and (driving) behavior that emerge to a certain degree from the density and the heterogeneity which would not appear if the drivers had been confronted with more homogeneous conditions.
>
> (Grimaud 2010: 3)

It is interesting to point out the discrepancy between the collective forms of auto-regulation and those which, on the contrary, are conditioned by a very significant regulation or homogenization of behavior. If the question of

passenger flow is considered, the example of the Delhi metro illustrates yet
again an obvious contrast with road traffic. Certain authors, such as Rashmi
Sadana, see in the metro the archetype of "modern disciplinary institu-
tion" (Sadana 2013: 81). It implies material barriers (security check, ticket
booth, and automated entry), explicit rules and reglementations (displays
for users), modes of management of bodies (waiting lines), encompassing
new forms of sensory and spatial experience (with air-conditioned comfort
and automated hi-tech surveillance), which are associated with values of
safety and order (Sadana 2013: 81). Concerning bus transport, this same
author writes:

> Similar codes of behaviour can be found on the city buses, but the feel
> of them is quite different; they are more intimate in a physical sense, the
> space is more constricted, and people routinely speak to one another,
> often to cajole, scold, harass, or flirt. The key figure on the bus is the
> ticket collector. He does not only take money, give out tickets, and return
> change; he manages the crowd, and with a slap of his hand on the side
> of the bus he cues the driver on when to start moving. He shouts at
> people, telling them what to do, and how to behave, admonishing them
> for "acting like children" or "holding everyone up". He both surveys
> and manages the crowd. And at the bus stops other riders give you infor-
> mation about which lines go where and which are good lines; there is
> a continual sharing of information and advice, a well as collective grief
> over late buses or non-existent ones.
>
> (Sadana 2013: 82)

The description is centered on the managerial function of the ticket collector and pinpoints the underlying common public opinion that the crowd is
by nature undisciplined and in order to be ordered would need an outside
agent responsible for its organization and management (here the ticket collector) or specific technical arrangements (as for the metro). In order to
fully capture the relevance of this idea, one significant dimension remains
to be considered: the eminent sensorial nature of the interactions (not only
concerning language). As we have tried to show, vocal calls are central to
the function of the ticket collector. From the strict acoustic perspective, they
also contribute to the emergence of complex sound forms that go beyond the
individual action of the collector and do not result from the simple addition
of individual interventions of several criers. In this way, they make the sound
space emerge with its organization that is for the most part auto-regulated. It
would be false to consider these criers as simple "conductors" (in the orches-
tral sense) of the sound space acting in an isolated and independent manner
from the others. The principle of competition implies collective coordination
and ensures the fluidity of the crowd's movements. The comparison of flows

of people within the bus station and in the metro does remain useful for us here. It seems that the first presents a double singularity. On the one hand, it relies upon the "nothing automatic" and the "everything humanly vocalized",[7] and on the other hand, it presents the agents as demonstrating their capacity to regulate the crowd flows *in situ*, without explicitly announced rules, nor those interiorized by all. Their action is fundamentally inscribed within the implicit that is proper to acoustic perception. Finally, this management capacity operates itself at different levels (between different criers, between one crier and a passenger, between different criers and several passengers), which can generate a certain complexity in the sound organization that should not be hastily reduced to chaos. In the sound *milieu* of the station, the individual and the collective sometimes adjust to one another and at other times ignore each other, making the voices an element that marks the space in an ever partial way.

About the Voices in the Station: Many Ways to Attract Attention

Up until this point, I have shown that the competitive logic is the motor behind the vocal performance of the criers: the more prominent the voice within this environment, the more the crier exercises attraction. It seems that many commercial activities in the station operate according to a similar logic. Although independent from the transport activity, the lottery booths installed in a quasi-permanent way in and around the station share the same sound space. Let us now use the following video excerpt to analyze this activity.

The Lottery Business

- **Document 2:** The Lottery car. Saktan Tampuran Bus Stand (Trichur, Kerala, India). Video [03.'16"]. Image: Christine Guillebaud, 2008.

The lottery at the Saktan station is set up in an old Ambassador (a particular type of car best known because it has been traditionally used in India as a taxi). Permanently parked just a few meters from the particularly noisy platform, in addition to being used by another business, the car also contributes to the sound environment thanks to an amplification system of very basic technology. A radio-cassette player is linked to a speaker placed on the roof of the car. The sound installation requires sustained efforts on the part of the lottery salesman. Sitting in the backseat of the car, the salesman ensures the continuous broadcast by flipping the tape, as the cassette format obliges, every 30 minutes (See Video at 2'01"). But what type of sounds is he broadcasting? The lottery announcements are entirely vocal but differ considerably from the bus stand criers' calls, mainly due to the way in which

they are produced. To distinguish them in the public space, the announcements are prerecorded and then systematically accelerated. This work is done
beforehand, by an engineer locally known as "Mister John", a Christian[8]
who resides a few kilometers from the Saktan Tampuran Bus Stand. His
work consists in pre-recording the announcements, modifying the speed,
then copying them onto cassettes. These are then distributed throughout
the lottery network in the main towns of the state. As the sole supplier
for the voice of the lottery, he has the monopoly on the Kerala regional state
lottery market.

In this type of centralized production, the voice is also prepared according
to pre-defined acoustic parameters and identically reproduced at every selling point. In accelerating the ordinary voice, Mr. John draws the listeners'
attention to the high-frequency spectrum, but does not alter the intelligibility of the announcement itself. In other words, the announcement conserves
its initial semantic content. The technical procedure is combined with other
parameters previously defined in the vocal announcement. The speaker uses
a particular prosody, based on the repetition of certain key words (such as
"the luck for ten rupees, *go, go go!*") inciting potential players to step up
and take their chance. As I observed and experienced on site as well as in the
laboratory, this unusual enunciation also modifies the daily listening posture
of the passers-by.

Little Laboratory for Acceleration

What does the acceleration of such a statement imply? For Mr. John, with
whom I spoke, the "artificial touch" or "technical touch" added to the
announcement is an effective way to capture the attention of the passers-by. In
general, in our cultural environment, we are used to different types of acoustic
accelerations to which, each at different levels, we attribute meaning or even
different emotions. However, as for the most part of the sounds we hear daily,
we rarely pay attention to the effects that these produce on our perception. In
order to analyze this point, we have undertaken an experiment (in collaboration with Vincent Rioux),[9] in order to determine the precise acceleration level
used by Mr. John. Thanks to the Supercollider program,[10] we have attempted
to artificially detect the parameters of the lottery voice by inverting the work
initially done by the sound engineer. From the lottery sound recording, here
are the deceleration-reacceleration stages that we have traced.

- **Document 3:** Successive stages of deceleration and reacceleration based
  on the lottery sound recording [01'21"].

The pattern underlines the four main stages of the experiment: 1) a progres-
sive deceleration until a very slow speed (that is, below the recorded speed);
2) a reacceleration until the level that we estimated as that of the original

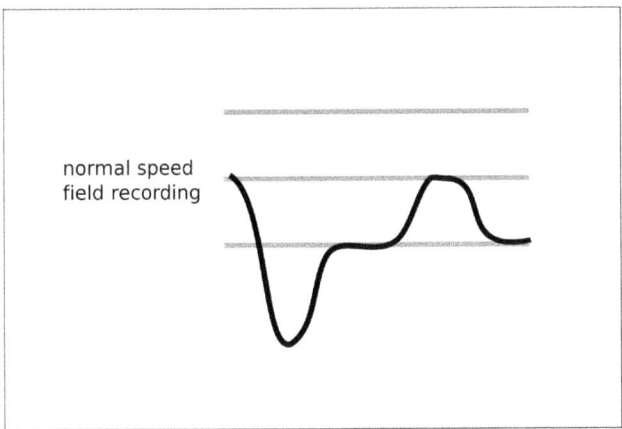

normal speed
field recording

Figure 4.4 The Lottery Voice. Definition of three thresholds of elocution speed: High, "normal", low (Experiment 1).

elocution (that of the speaker at a natural speed), 3) a reacceleration until a reference level (that of the initial recording), 4) a deceleration until a level identified in stage 2 (the speaker at his natural speed).

This simple experiment reveals the supposed "original" vocal speed that Mr. John had accelerated up to 20 percent. The engineer had indeed precisely chosen a level that ensured the listeners' complete understanding of the message (the semantic value is therefore one of the retained criteria). This experiment also unveiled the play on perspective of two sound strata: the sounds surrounding the car on the one hand, and the artificial voice on the other. They force the listener to double his/her aural attention. To understand this play on perspective, a very brief allusion to the cinema will be of use. Scientific accelerations are indeed very common when filming natural phenomena that occur over a span of time. Accelerated images of germination or plant development come to mind, which enable us to perceive natural phenomena that partially elude human observation. In these types of films, it is necessary to adapt our "human" perception of time to the movement of the plants and to accelerate the images. Everyone can recall that in this type of cinema, such a temporal change also transforms the elements perceived in the images. Observing the accelerated germination of a plant also implies that the nearby environment—the insects, birds, mammals, etc.—radically disappears from our field of vision. Pursuing the comparison with the acoustic realm, it is thus very likely that the perception of a voice on two sound layers (time dimensions) also relies on the same paradox. Even if we have not obtained the explicit confirmation from Mr. John, it seems that the use of acceleration aims to provoke such an effect on auditory perception.

His choice to accelerate the recording by 20 percent is also essential. This is obviously controlled by the engineer: the voice must be clear, intelligible, and devoid of any other component that could appear "artificial", as he indeed expressed. We know that, depending on the acceleration level, our interpretation of a statement can considerably vary due to the emotional tone that we attribute to it. It is common to associate an average level of acceleration to a comic tone, as is the case, for example, with cartoons that often use this effect.

- **Document 4:** Extract from a "Work Song" from *Cinderella*, Walt Disney. Video [01'21"].

In this excerpt, Cinderella's mice friends are hastily preparing the dress that the heroine will wear to the ball. If these little characters seem affectionate and funny, it is because their accelerated voices contribute to the sought-after comic effect.

If we now consider the upper acceleration level, the voice loses its intelligibility, and the comic effect is also affected. The "fast-forward" technique is an exemplary case. It is generally used by sound engineers to locate sound pieces or cuts in long recordings. We have also applied this to the lottery voice recordings for the purposes of demonstration.

- **Document 5:** Accelerated voice with "comic" effect followed by the "fast-forward" technique, experiment based on the lottery sound recording [00'47"].

Following the same stages found in Document 3, but this time starting with the acceleration, it is clear that there is a loss of complete intelligibility

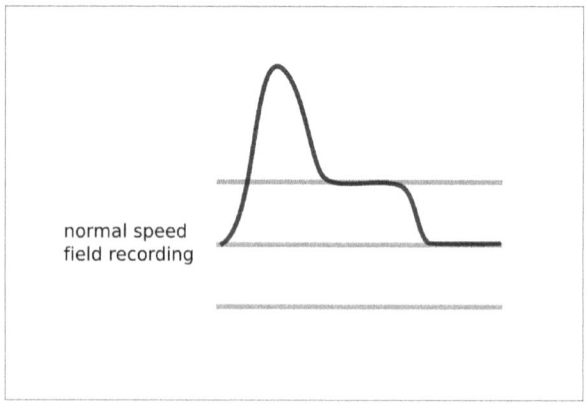

Figure 4.5 The Lottery Voice. Definition of three thresholds of elocution speed: High, "normal", low (Experiment 2).

and that this leads to "segmented" perception: the listener only distinguishes silences or the variations creating blocks of sound. In contrast with the preceding accelerations, we attribute but little meaning (or emotion) to extreme acceleration most likely because the initial vocal character is no longer recognizable.

Testing Mr. John's vocal arrangement, first by slowing it down and then by speeding it up, shows that this specialist's work is at an intermediary level between the comic and the outrageous. Accelerating the segment creates a tonal effect at the limit of the human voice (the "artificial" effect), which remains nevertheless recognizable for the listeners in the sense that it preserves the semantic content of the statement.

A final element must be taken into account to describe the lottery voice. It was remarkable to us that Mr. John insisted upon the "technical" dimension of this voice, rendering the effect almost un-"natural" in the process. When comparing this to the use of other public voices in the world, such as announcements broadcast in stations or other public transport hubs, the same argument for "artificiality" is put forth to describe the recorded voices. However, in most cases this carries a negative connotation. This is particularly the case with transport announcements in France, such as in the railway stations (SNCF) or in the Parisian metro network (RATP).[11] Quick referral to the press releases indeed reveals a completely different point of view.

Artificial Versus Natural Voices

* **Document 6:** Excerpt from a radio broadcast (France Info).

At the SNCF, for example, a feminine voice, that of former radio hostess Simone Hérault, has dominated the French rail network for thirty years. In the past, these announcements were entirely recorded in a studio. Today, they are made using a computer program that composes announcements with words and phrases that were pre-recorded by the speaker using different intonations. Despite using a "natural" voice, this technical development has given way to a parallel debate on the "human" nature of the announcements within the transport network and their effect on the users, or even on their travel experience. Appreciations and comments about the vocal quality of Simone Herault's voice can be read and heard:

> Among the best-known off-voices of France, there is one that is never off track. For 30 years, Simone Hérault has been informing travellers from all over. Announcements with a sweet-sounding, almost motherly voice.
> (*France info*)

"My voice is the sound logo of the SNCF" she likes to say. With 40 days of recording a year, this former FIP radio hostess has brought change to these messages "by removing the railway jargon" and at the request of the stations or the region, by making the announcements "more user-friendly" or more personal:

> [. . .] I mainly record words digitally, town names and timetables using ascending and descending intonations that technicians at the SNCF's audiovisual center later put together according to the requests and needs of the different train stations [. . .]. The travellers could have a thousand reasons to hate me when I announce delays or cancellations, so I always try to have a smile in my voice and to send out positive vibes!
>
> (*Le Parisien* Jan. 25, 2014)

> Simone Hérault seems nice. She is! . . . her hostess voice really fits her. "My voice is naturally cheerful and reassuring", she says.
>
> (*Sud-Ouest*)

From these different excerpts emerges a similar theme: her capacity to soothe and to foster a certain friendliness in the travelling experience. In this way it is not surprising that in the digital production process a "naturally" recorded feminine voice was retained. The Parisian metro network has also pursued such quality where the above mentioned descriptors converge with those previously described. According to Song Phanekham, head of Visual and Sound Identity for the RATP:

> Just like with colors, each line has its voice. [. . .] The system is put into place with the renewal of the trains [. . .] The voices must be calm, soothing and articulate.
>
> (*Metronews*)

Other press reviews insist more readily upon the fundamentally "human" quality of the voice, which legitimates the transporters' choice to de-automatize the public announcements and to thus reduce their "artificiality". The musician-composer, Rodolphe Burger, in charge of the project of the vocal announcements broadcast in the Parisian tram explains:

> In the stations, it will be more about landscape, or what we call sound-scape. For the tram announcements, we are intervening on something that already exists but which is uniquely functional. But now, we are replacing robotized voices with the voices of the users.

But what are human voices supposed to convey that simple automated announcements could not? The inherent diversity of the natural voice, which appears as a basic principle of the sound composition, provides a first element of response to this question:

> Beyond the music, the innovativeness of the project lies in the information for passengers. Indeed, the names of the stops are not always

pronounced by the same voice, but by several! While respecting the sound design adopted by the RATP, voice "couples" are used for each station. These voices are those of common people. It is a way to pay homage to the people who live in the city. From 7 to 77 years of age, unknown or famous, feminine or masculine, with or without an accent . . .

(ratp.fr)

This search for the common is also expressed in a similar way by the composer of the tram announcements:

I wanted all sorts of voices. Sound images of the population—explained the musician. Men, women, young people, old people, unknown people and famous people. And all sorts of accents.

(20 minutes journal)

Second, a collective dimension is attributed to the dailiness of the voices (and their inherent diversity), that of the "urban community":

Beyond a musical jingle, Rodolphe Burger aimed to mark a difference from the habitual monotonous tone of the RATP: "The voice that we will hear is not the voice of an administrative authority delivering information or a signal at a technical level. It is the voice of the people, the common voice."

(quoi.info)

This is cancelled by the technocratic approach to information transmission. The disembodied voices that are generally used cause the "aura", or the breathing, of the names to disappear. When "real" voices are used, the point to which the aura of the name comes back and resonates and how this changes the horizon of the "urban community" are striking.

(vacarme.org)

Finally, the collective imagination of the voice is reinforced by the principle of sound territorialization put into place according to the neighborhoods the line runs through. Once again, Rodolphe Burger has stated:

In Montreuil,[12] along the tramline, there is a significant Malian population. I recorded several of the inhabitants' voices, but also tourists from around the globe.

(vacarme.org 20 minutes journal)

A similar example, that of the announcement broadcast in the "Ella Fitzgerald" station, confirms this care to adequate linguistic origin and territorial imagination.

- **Document 7:** Parisian Tram announcement (Line 3b). "Ella Fitzgerald—Grands Moulins de Pantin" Station.

Recited by the singer Jane Birkin, the announcement was also recorded using a male voice with a British accent.

> It provokes a deflecting effect, a tiny invitation to dream and travel. The usual approach to sound signaling in public places, which is generally purely functional, is reversed. Here, the effect of the "real voices" is striking: the stations sound like places, and the litany of the stations becomes the text of the city. Moreover, the random variation of the different voices makes each journey unique (one can never, in the strictest sense, take the same trip).
>
> (*vacarme.org*)

Conclusion

The ethnography of the sound space of the Indian station first illustrates that in a competitive context it is finally the contrasted occupation of the different strata of the sound spectrum that effectively creates social interaction. The examples of the criers' voices as well as the voice of the lottery are to be seen as complex practices of sound manipulation where the desire for prominence is not only operated through parameters of intensity but rather of tone, prosody, and time structure. In this sound environment that is so distinctively unique in density, the acoustic events are organized at different scales, while relying on auditive acuity serving economic stakes and allowing efficient management of the crowd on a daily basis. By comparing these public voices in their temporality and their spatiality, we have remarked that sound does not create anything in and of itself (ontologically) but rather has the potential to generate action and co-action that sets apart the experience of the travelers. The approach that we have used is therefore in line with the present efforts of social science researchers to address the perception/action dyad in particular through the category of affordance (Thibaud 2010, 2011, Pecqueux 2012).[13]

> speaking "of affordance of events", implies not only situating oneself within a general frame where perception means situated accomplishment—veritable action—but more so measuring how certain events do much more than simply attract our attention. Indeed, they impose themselves on our present activities, that is, provoke a reorganization of our activity from the avoidance of an obstacle (such as after hearing a horn) to more subtle and less mechanical reorganizations.
>
> (Pecqueux 2012: 222)

The example of the sound environment of the Indian bus station can be easily placed among the "less mechanical" forms of action (and reaction). It relies upon multiple forms of attention on the part of the travelers and weaves together perceptive focals that are produced both by the sounds and reconfigured according to the effects of the different events. There is nonetheless one additional dimension that seems to escape the category of affordance: the auto-generated nature of the sound productions (that we have identified in this chapter thanks to the notion of emergence). The sound forms regulate themselves *in situ* beyond the sole and individual intervention of each producer of sound, and yet, do not result from the simple addition of these.

At this stage of the analysis, we would like to suggest that it is necessary to identify at least two types of affordance: the first, that we shall call "simple", is of a monopolistic order, as is the case with voices in centralized stations; the second, that we shall call "complex", unfurls itself according to diverse and yet simultaneous channels and is in part auto-generated.

It is likely that new ethnographies should be carried out in other public spaces in order to hone the criteria of this distinction between "simple" and "complex" affordance (see Table 4.1); or even to open the way toward the consideration of other types of affordance. In the meantime, the study of the Indian bus station furnishes a wider empirical foundation for future work that will focus more generally on the modalities of daily attention in what is today commonly called "city mobility-places" (Hennion 2012).[14] Finally, with the central place that this study gives to vocal production (and creation), it should also spark larger diversification in fieldwork conducted classically by vocal anthropology (Feld *et al.* 2004, Le Breton 2011). If the intrinsically emotional dimension of the voice justly deserves targeted studies in the artistic and ritual spheres, daily city life remains a topic to be explored, in the sense that natural and artificial voices contribute differently to our ordinary ways to interact, to behave in a crowd or even to appropriate territories.

Table 4.1 Two types of affordances.

Simple Affordance	Complex Affordance
Acoustic Salience: monopolistic	Acoustic Salience: multiple
Univocal Sound Layers	Sound layers in perspective
Individual focalization	(cf. Lottery voice)
	Auto-generated collective forms

Notes

1 This research has been developed through the MILSON program (Pour une anthropologie des MILieux SONores/For an anthropology of sound environments) that I have had the honor of directing since 2011 with the support of the

Fyssen Foundation. For further information, see the program website: http://milson.fr, and Guillebaud (2012).

2 For an archeology of the notion, see notably Thibaud (2012).

3 "Sound worlds" is a more specific ethnomusicological expression used by Canzio (1992).

4 Ancient ruler of the kingdom of Cochin (eighteenth century).

5 Ethnomusicologist by training, I have conducted research in this region of India for nearly two decades.

6 Malayalam is the language spoken in Kerala. However, in everyday life, a certain number of expressions are specifically said in English, generally when the speakers wish to convey a certain element of modernity linked to what they are saying (as is the case here) or when it carries a certain emotional charge.

7 If the two means of transport cohabitate in the city, the way in which they respectively manage crowds does not result simply from a technological development but rather according to very distinct modus operandi.

8 The population of the state of Kerala is composed of about 55 percent Hindu, 26,5 percent Muslim, and 18,5 percent Christian. *Census of India*, 2011. http://www.census2011.co.in/data/religion/state/32-kerala.html

9 Acoustician and computer scientist, member of the research group, and also a contributor to the present volume.

10 About this language and its use in other contexts, refer to Vincent Rioux's contribution in this volume.

11 I have chosen these French examples because they are from the country where I live.

12 Town located east of Paris in the Seine-St-Denis department.

13 Term initially forged in psychology of visual perception by James J. Gibson (1979). For a synthesis of the notion and an analysis of its relevancy for sound events, see Thibaud (2010) and Pecqueux (2012: 215–21).

14 Places defined as "habitual, regular, central, dense, integrated in the urban rhythm of work and leisure; they are incorporated in an ordinary mobility space (even if bustled)" (Hennion 2012: 175).

References

Appadurai, Arjun. 1987. "Street Culture." *India Magazine* 8 (1): 2–23.

Canzio, Ricardo. 1992. "Mode de fonctionnement rituel et production musicale chez les Bororo du Mato Grosso." *Cahiers de Musiques Traditionnelles (Cahiers d'ethnomusicologie)* 5: 71–96.

Feld, Steven, Aaron Fox, Thomas Porcello, and David Samuels. 2004. "Vocal Anthropology: From the Music of Language to the Language of Song." In *A Companion to Linguistic Anthropology*, edited by Alessandro Duranti, 321–345. Blackwell Companions to Anthropology. Oxford: Wiley-Blackwell.

Gandhi, Ajay. 2011. "Crowds, Congestion, Conviviality: The Enduring Life of the Old City." In *A Companion to the Anthropology of India*, edited by Isabelle Clark-Decès, 202–222. Blackwell Companions to Anthropology 8. Oxford: Wiley-Blackwell.

———. 2013. "Standing Still and Cutting in Line." *South Asia Multidisciplinary Academic Journal*. http://samaj.revues.org/3519.

Gandhi, Ajay and Lotte Hoek. 2012. "Introduction to Crowds and Conviviality: Ethnographies of the South Asian City." *Ethnography* 13 (1): 3–11.

Gibson, James J. 1986 [1979]. *The Ecological Approach to Visual Perception*. Hillsdale: Lawrence.

Goffman, Erving. 1973 [1959]. *La mise en scène de la vie quotidienne*. Vol. 2. *Les relations en public*. Paris: Éditions de Minuit.

Grimaud, Emmanuel. 2010. "Figures du trafic. Ethnographie cinétique d'un carrefour sans feux." *Tracés: Revue de Sciences humaines* 18: 23–44.

Guillebaud, Christine. 2011. "Vocal interactions in urban soundscapes: An Indian example." Paper delivered at the *41th International Council for Traditional Music World Conference* (ICTM, 13–19 July). St John's: Memorial University.

———. 2012. "Towards an Anthropology of Sound *Milieux*: Perspectives from India." In *Ambiances in Action/ambiances en actes: International Congress on Ambiances, Montreal, Sept 2012*, edited by Jean-Paul Thibaud and Daniel Siret, 317–322. Grenoble: International Ambiances Network.

Hennion, Antoine. 2012. "La gare en action. Hautes turbulences et attentions basses." *Communications* 90: 175–195. Paris: Éditions du Seuil.

Le Breton, David. 2011. *Éclats de voix. Une anthropologie des voix*. Paris: Éditions Métaillié. Coll. Traversées.

Maunier, René. 2014 [1941]. "Groupe et durée. La queue comme groupe social." *Terrain* 63: 12–21.

Pecqueux, Anthony. 2012. "Les affordances des évènements; des sons aux évènements urbains." *Communications* 90: 215–227. Paris: Éditions du Seuil.

Sadana, Rashmi. 2013. "On the Delhi Metro: An Ethnographic View." *Economic & Political Weekly* 45 (46): 77–83.

Thibaud, Jean-Paul. 2010. "Towards a Praxiology of Sound Environment." *Sensory Studies—Sensorial Investigations* 2010: 1–7.

———. 2011. "The Sensory Fabric of Urban Ambiances." *Senses and Society* 6 (2): 203–215.

———. 2012. "Petite archéologie de la notion d'ambiance." *Communications* 90: 155–174.

5 Melodic Refrains in Japanese Train Stations

The Management of Passenger Behavior Through the Use of Electric Bells

Pierre Manea

Trains are a major means of public transportation in Japan. In 2000, 59 million passengers rode trains, a mode of transport representing 27 percent of passenger traffic.[1] Urban adherence[2] to trains is higher in Tokyo than in most Western cities, and history holds the explanation. When the United States Navy's Commodore Perry forced Japan to open its border in 1868, it had no railways at all. Only ten years later, four large-scale public railway lines were opening service. Starting in 1881, the country underwent several euphoric periods of railway construction that broke the territory up into several rail networks. In addition, Tokyo experienced large-scale destruction with the Great Kanto Earthquake of 1923, which destroyed 44 percent of the urban area. This further hastened the urbanization of the suburbs, the population of which tripled between 1913 and 1924, jumping from 0.7 to nearly 2 million inhabitants (Aveline 2003: 46), and led to the diffusion of Tokyo's center. This growth was an opportunity for transport operators. Several private railway companies were created, and by 1928 the network had expanded 16-fold from its 1913 scale, multiplying the number of passengers carried daily by a factor of 21 (6.6 million). Regulation-wise, railway companies had a free hand in using the space around their stations, where they would develop many residential areas and secure a return on property investments in the railroads themselves. The city spread around stations and along their lines. Railways helped create these "quite integrated urban structures" (Aveline 2003: 65), and the dialectic between urban development and demand for transport also transformed the nature of the train, securing its position as a daily feature of city life.

After World War Two, Japan experienced a period of rapid economic growth, with the development of heavy industry in the Tokyo area. This led to dramatic employment and population growth, and hence to an increase in demand for transportation that put the existing network under great strain. Railway companies responded by doubling railroad tracks, allowing both local trains and rapid service trains on the same lines, connected their networks to subways, and improving trains' reliability, among other things. Although Edo (Tokyo's name until 1868) could be crossed by a man on foot in a day, throughout the twentieth century railways greatly contributed to shaping and expanding the megalopolis, inexorably connected to the train. What happened in these trains and stations was likely to have an effect on imaginaries, attitudes, and habits, and they were quite likely to be scenes where issues relevant to public life played out. This is what I hope to demonstrate, by focusing on the railway system's sound environment. I will discuss the formation of certain sound practices taking place on station platforms throughout the twentieth century that would lay the groundwork for much sound information use today, looking especially at departure melodies. This will shed light on some of today's informational practices, which will be described in the last part of this paper.[3]

I.   From the Bell to the Station Melody: The Mandate for Rationalization and Management

As long as there have been trains, there has been a need to inform users of their impending departure. On many departure platforms, whistles or bells were commonly chosen as signals due to their remarkable sonic features (their range and ability to concentrate sound on narrow frequencies). But the sheer size of the Japanese railway network, as described above, made room for a specific use of sound as a way to handle passengers.

The Electric Bell in the Hands of Platform Agents

From 1945 onward, "departure bells" (a form of electric bells) came to be used in all Japanese National Railways (JNR) stations (Yoshimura 1992: 52). These bells were famous for the clanging, metallic sound of their ring, which could last from a few seconds to over a minute. Along with the distorted voice of the platform agent (ekiin), this loud, irritating signal could "stir hysteria" (Shiozuka 2013: 13) and transform crowded platforms' sound environments into "wrestling rings" (Ide 2009: 10).

These bells served as tools in platform agents' hands. First, they were used to manage boarding and disembarkation procedures. Bells helped highlight or clarify the unfolding of events framing the passengers' "active window"— the time slot during which they are to act. This is the semantic content or intention of the electric bell (what Latour [1992: 157] called the "encoded prescriptions" of a mechanism). Second, and as a consequence of the first point, bells have been used to rationalize the flow of passengers.[4] This was achieved by taking advantage of the highly textured quality of their sound, designed to induce tension and draw attention by being loud and stress provoking (Yamaha 1988). The signal's acoustic container, a rapid, repetitive ringing, was indeed suitable for producing a sense of urgency, as with many alarm sounds (Leroux 1991: 9).

I will now describe the social negotiation between train companies and passengers that led to the approval of bells as behavior management tools.

1.   Overcrowded Trains and Deviant Behaviors

In 1950, Tokyo passenger train occupancy averaged 200 percent of capacity, with some lines as high as 340 percent. In 1960, the average was 300 percent. In 2000, rush-hour occupancy was still at 244 percent on busy lines like the Yamanote line (Aveline 2003: 35). Bearing in mind that over 250 percent, bodies are so compressed that it is impossible to move, and above 300 percent passengers' health is at stake, it is easy to understand how terrible commuting was during what was unsurprisingly called the "hellfire of transportation" (koutsuu jigoku). No wonder Japan became famous for its "push-men," hired to (com)press bodies through closing doors as trains prepared to leave the station.

Japanese railways companies' attempts to lower the occupancy rate included increasing the number and speed of trains running on each line, limiting friction points in stations (simplifying their architecture, installing automatic ticket turnstiles, equipping trains with automatic doors), encouraging the use of train passes instead of simple-use tickets, and so on.

Such technological improvements and practical arrangements were implemented systematically throughout the twentieth century. Nevertheless, technological enhancements were often limited, and progress was severely slowed by passenger behavior. To increase the overall number of trains, the duration of stops at each station had to be addressed; companies therefore consistently made a point of adapting "the man to the machine" to reduce boarding and disembarkation time and targeted improper boarding habits.

2.   Deviance in Boarding Procedures and Its Management

Exercises were held in 1926 to find the fastest possible boarding time for a very crowded train (Arasui 1959). A simple twofold conclusion was drawn: both agents and passengers needed training and consciousness-raising to shorten the process.

A)   TRAINING AGENTS

First, railway agents working on platforms and in trains were trained to eliminate any delay due to their "discipline being lax": a 1902 Railroad News Letter identified agents' attitudes as being behind delays of "three minutes" at Shinjuku Station and "two minutes" at Kokubunji (West Tokyo) station, for example (Takemura 2001: 52). Although these delays would not prompt complaints in many countries even today, expectations of punctuality were already running high, especially as the public assumed that delays came with flagging attention to danger and risks, which was intolerable. The 1900s were a period of great social change, and the establishment of punctuality was a major feature of this development that was introduced alongside modern modes of production and work. New generations of workers were taught to respect working hours (Mito 2002: 99), and trains had to support this economic and generational change.

B) TRAINING PASSENGERS

If demand for punctuality triggered public criticism of the quality of the National Railways' (NRs) service, it would in turn justify large-scale disciplinary strategies for the passengers themselves. Thus began a passenger "management" period, during which companies tried to get them to assimilate "boarding techniques" (Mito 2002: 99, 101). Most delays were due to passenger behaviors that prevented trains from leaving stations on time. They were primarily concerned with saving their own time (Konwa 2001: 68), even if it necessitated deviant acts in contradiction of the NRs' security and efficiency objectives. Passengers boarded trains as they used to board the tramway, habits that were indeed appropriate to tramways' slower pace— passengers would dash to catch trains, or even hang on to the outside of the car to avoid the (long) wait for the next one. Likewise, tramway conductors' habits mirrored these practices; as part of their service, they often waited to let dashing people board (2011). I will not detail the various informational and standardizing campaigns of the first third of the twentieth century, but generally speaking they were normatively phrased and fostered the development of manners: "man" had to become a "more noble person," by accepting "new knowledge" and "gradually learn[ing] new habits" appropriate to the railway environment (Yamamoto 1935: 2). The objective was to shape correct behaviors and boarding routines suited to trains and train stations as public spaces.

To do so, the NR provided passengers with an overarching view of railway traffic, to raise awareness of traffic flow as a whole (Tanaka 2005: 187); in other words, passengers were introduced to the fluid mechanics at work in the railway network, where one's train is inevitably connected to all the others. On a practical level, agents were trying to get passengers to "go into the train after those coming out had [gotten] off" (Mito 2002: 102) and to discourage troublesome and disruptive boarding acts like dashing onto the train (Tanaka 2005: 195), not waiting for the train to stop before boarding or leaving it, or trying to board an obviously overcrowded train (Honda 1927: 252). Coordinating the entry and departure of passengers, achieved by lining up on platforms in front of the doors, patiently awaiting their turn to board, etc., was a constant concern, since management of these procedures was closely linked to punctuality. Both passengers and companies sought punctual trains (Ito 1930), and passengers were constantly encouraged to follow the guidance offered by the agents overseeing platforms.

These efforts succeeded: in 1915, the average duration of train stops was one or two minutes for major stations, and 30 seconds for minor ones; but in 1926, with the exception of one major line, it could be reduced to

20 seconds in every station when necessary (Mito 2002: 101). First of all, this highlights the high-speed pace of movement between stations: agents were counting boarding time to the second. It also shows the integration of normative discourses on the "global flow of trains," the understanding that following agents' guidance indeed sets the pace of train traffic and individuals' travel conditions. It thus reveals passengers' incorporation of boarding techniques (i.e., "orderly, in single file", Mito 2002: 101) that were ceaselessly repeated in vocal announcements, and their acceptance of guidance that was understood as the answer to their demand for reliable, efficient, and superior service.[5]

Technological advancements, passenger behavior, agent guidance, and the relationship between them: a whole context shifted, in that the nature, position, and interactions of each actor in the railroad environment, understood as a network (in the Latourian sense; see Callon 1986), made punctuality possible. The transportation performance promised by the company ("we will take you to your destination on time") wasn't only "coupled with technical advancements or embedded in automatic procedures," it also required "human guidance" (Joseph 2004: 12). Habituation to the train as a new mode of transport, and to the guidance in smoothing out passenger and train flow in particular, was not achieved by top-down enforcement, but through a mutual agreement that answered both the passengers' request for speed and

Figure 5.1 A platform agent about to trigger the departure melody in Shinjuku Station.

Photo: Pierre Manea (2013).

the NR's obligation of efficiency. In their constant efforts to increase speed, agents strove to maintain the strict rhythm of boarding and disembarking (Ito 1930). In this article, I claim that this mutual agreement achieved progressively through various educational strategies allowed railway agents to experiment with departure bells and open a period of diverse and highly developed sound information practices. Due to the aforementioned network shift, agents came to be seen as "authorized representatives" when they used their "skeptron" (Bourdieu 2002: 140) and rang electric bells. The success in reducing the duration of train stops shows that passengers trusted the railway companies to improve efficiency. From this responsibility for performing punctuality came recognition of agents' authority as expressed through their announcements and use of sound signals.[6] With acquisition of this "mandate," the practice of sound information enters a phase of generalization, which I will describe next.

II.   Managing Boarding and Disembarking Processes: The Electric Bell

This long historical journey to the origins of sound informational practices highlighted the social construction of departure bells taken as a technological system (Bijker 1993). It is helpful for understanding how sounds are actively used in trains and stations today. Yet the above considerations prove to be useful in contextualizing the various uses of a single sonic tool, the bell, and especially Japanese stations' sonic signature, the departure bell. I will thus briefly describe its multiple uses throughout the second half of the twentieth century, and show how it laid the basis for today's informational signals.

Electric Bells in Action: Four Patterns

I identified four patterns of bell use and organized them in chronological order of appearance during the boarding process (see Figure 5.2). The descriptive method employed is derived from the phenomenological attention to the sonic detail structures of subway stations and subways in movement developed in Masson's dissertation, *La Perception embarquée* ("Perception Aboard", Masson 2009). I initially discretized sound signals using Schaeffer's "reduced listening" (1966).[7] Following Masson's method, I next produced "sample scores" of the analyzed samples (see Figure 5.1). This method enables the identification of phenomenological links, or "sonic adjustments" (Masson 2009: 234), between sound signals. Then, building on these sets of links (or adjustments) more complex patterns, "sonic referents," are identified (Masson 2009: 246).

In the example below, as the subway moves on to the next station, a referent, the "sonic wave," is produced by the occurrence of the following signals and their co-occurring sonic effects (see Augoyard and Torgue

Figure 5.2 Passengers rushing onto a train, Shinjuku Station.
Photo: Pierre Manea (2013).

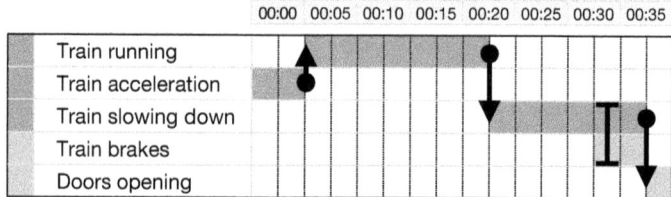

Figure 5.3 A sample score, with the signals of the train's movements and their respective adjustments (arrows: succession; line with limits: co-occurrence).

2005): "acceleration" (crescendo), "running" (sonic drone, reverberation, sometimes resonance), and "slowing down" (decrescendo). All these signals are successively adjusted to one another (see below).

Building on this descriptive method, I analyzed live recordings of platform sound environments dating from 1955 to 1975 (see Ishidzuka 2011). Listening to the boarding procedure unfold from the passenger's perspective, I not only examined the esthetic dimension of the sound environment but tried to connect the explicit signals[8] (informational sounds), aimed at passengers and expressing an intention, with those produced as a consequence of activities, movements, and/or actions—implicit signals. I would like to show how these years of experimentation with sounds, before today's era of automation-punctuated train trips, exemplify both an awareness of a mandate to rationalize behaviors through sound and the concretization of events through sonic signals.

Patterns that withstood the test of time became part of agents' sound and informational practices, some of which will be detailed later.

The Boarding Process and Sound-Effect Signals

1. The Approach Bell

In most cases, the approach bell lasts as long as the announcement itself (up to 20 seconds). It re-enforces the content of the announcement with extra-linguistic information, but it has another phenomenological value, since its purpose is to induce stress and force people to pay attention (Yamaha 1988). Less frequently, the ring may be rather brief and precede the agent's announcement. In either case, the approach bell bursts into the calm auditory space, functioning as a short jingle, an "introduction sound" (Yoshimura 1992: 49) that orients attention to the content of the announcement.

From the passengers' perspective, this signal is qualified by a "sonic incursion": it "not only interrupts the present state, but also dictates new behavior for a given moment" (Augoyard and Torgue 2005: 65). This sonic effect is emphasized by the intensity gap between the station's background noise (composed mainly of human interactions) and the loudness of the bell itself, or by agents' habits, as they sometimes ring the bell repeatedly, demanding the attention of those who are indeed waiting for the train. The bell hence tends to produce a synecdoche effect, an "overvaluation" of the signal (Masson 2009: 299), as "any situation of waiting or vigilance favors [the] emergence" of this sonic effect (Augoyard and Torgue 2005: 126).

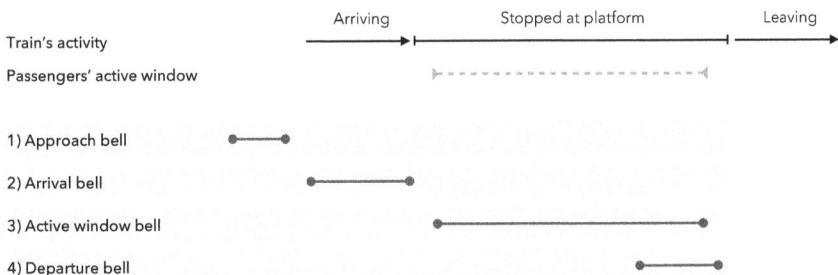

Figure 5.4 Four different uses of the electric bell: The approach bell rings before any sound from the train can be heard from the platform; the arrival bell is triggered with the actual arrival of the train; the active window bell signifies the time during which passengers are to act; and the departure bell is triggered before the doors close, and might continue a few seconds after.

It is close to a "modal" signal, in the sense that it aspires to force a particular interaction with the new reality that it itself dictates, by temporarily making non-boarding-related activities irrelevant.

- **Document 1:** "An approach Bell at Kouchi Station" (1955–1975). Source: Ima Yomigaeru Kokutetsu, 2010, Columbia Music Entertainment. CD 3, Track 19. ASIN: B003800360. EAN: 4988001300908.[9]

2.   *Arrival Bell*

Contrary to the approach bell, the arrival bell is co-present with the sonic signals of the approaching train. Without it, the evolution of the ambiance would be rather slow as the sounds produced by the train approach the audible range, but the bell transforms the sound environment more suddenly.

Like all electric bells, this signal is a "sonic line" (Masson 2009: 235), albeit this time simultaneous with the train's gradual appearance. Yet where sound is concerned, it is clearly optional when a train arrives: if sound is "a consequence of the activity" (Masson 2009: 213, 244), then the train's own sonic productions are sufficient testimony to its arrival and presence; it is already making noise. In all sound scores made using Masson's methodology, the train's arrival is unmistakably recognized by a fundamental form, the end of the "sonic wave". The result is that the arrival bell qualifies or characterizes the period of deceleration (the descelerando, the increase of engine intensity as it approaches a listener's ears, etc.). It is therefore the arrival itself that is emphasized by the signal.

Such use of the arrival bell shows what I call a sound-effect signal: it functions by imposing a particular meaning on the timeframe it spans. In movies, sound effects are artificially made to go with the action on the screen, producing enough "fakeness" to sound "real" according to the "Platonician theory of simulacrum" (Leroux 1989: 95). As isomorphic indices (Chion 1994: 121), sound effects hence not only "ring true," their sound "is true" (Chion 1994: 107). Additionally, a sound effect is tightly controlled: its placement in time and space can be adapted to follow the on-screen action as closely as possible. As a result, it is a materializing sound index (Chion 1994: 114), and it contributes to the action's rhythm, putting it in a spatial context and "localiz[ing it] in a concrete space" (Chion 1994: 117).

In contrast, a sound-effect signal is not an isomorphic index: it is indeed a signal that functions comparably to a sound effect in the staging of everyday activities. When used as a "sonic line" alongside a train's arrival, it represents a controlled encoding of the event, and becomes a way of qualifying the environment by providing meaning. As shown earlier, a train's arrival in a station already produces many sounds. But platform agents control neither the meanings passengers give to these sounds (or their subsequent actions), nor the movement of the train itself, its pace, its halt. Here, the electric bell provides a way to take back that control, as it is layered over the sound environment already transforming with the train's entry into the aural space. Hence, in applying the concept of sound-effect signal, I highlight the meanings that sound signals give to an action, a situation, a process in progress, or a state of being. Put in terms of materializing sound indices, the sound-effect signal gives form to the meaning passengers ought to give to the train's arrival. It eliminates potential "momentary discord" (Chion 1994: 37) between what is seen and what is heard. At the same time, it reveals the "director's" prior judgment (that of the agent or company) of how the train's arrival should be understood. In the case of the station, layering a ready-made reading of "when you hear this, you should understand that" over the train's arrival refers to the agents' mandate: the quest for a rationalized passenger flow, with behaviors suited to various travel situations. In this sense, too, this signal aspires to a performative dimension, dictating a meaning onto the situation and thereby emphasizing a range of appropriate behaviors.

- **Document 2:** "An Arrival Bell at Fukui Station" (1955–1975). Source: Ima Yomigaeru Kokutetsu, 2011, Columbia Music Entertainment. CD 6, Track 3. ASIN: B004WLXTZQ. EAN: 4988001475200.

3. *Active Window Bell*

The active window bell rings approximately from the opening of the doors to their closing. If the train stop is brief, it will also be brief and quite similar to the departure bell (see below), but in most cases it rings from 30 to 60 seconds. Opening and closing doors are connected by this sound, which fills the active window interval, thus making it made clear, since the bell continuously declares, "It's time to act!" But as a continuous drone, without rhythmic, tonic, or melodic variation, it indicates little about the progress of the event under way. At best, this uniform bell tone is an echo signaling the static presence of the train. Rushing passengers cannot rely on it to indicate if the doors are about to close or not, and must find another way for figuring it out (visually, or through vocal announcements). Informationally weak, this bell's use is also variable. This contributes to undermining its value: triggered manually, it may be stopped a few seconds before or after the actual departure . . . From the passengers' point of view, this lack of synchrony makes it an unreliable and inaccurate basis for action, while the trains' implicit sounds are likely to be adequate for initiating boarding, as with the start of the drone of "ventilation equipment and compressors in a factory or [. . .] on a building site play a role of sound punctuation of working rhythms, even for people who do not directly depend on their functioning" (Augoyard and Torgue 2005: 41, see also Thibaud 1987: 49). Therefore, the margin created by its temporally floating boundaries does not secure a consistent, invariable equivalence between what is heard and what is happening. Its performative potential is thus limited to what has already been identified: mobilizing and focusing passengers' actions through a stressful, strident, metallic sound. Through this sound practice, the need for punctuating signals that clearly indicate the end of the boarding time-frame becomes clearer, and horns, whistles, announcements, and ultimately departure bells will be used to compensate for the limited informative qualities of this monotonous active-window bell.

From a sonic perspective, the sound of the electric bell was sometimes put in the background (although this is a contradiction for a signal, which should be in the foreground) by the masking effects (Augoyard and Torgue 2005: 66) produced by trains' powerful, wide-spectrum sounds (fans, engine). To the contrary, when its volume is turned up, its intensity hinders understanding of agents' announcements and whistles, obliging them to perform niche effects in pitch and intensity (Augoyard and Torgue 2005: 78) to gain prominence and ensure the correct transmission of messages or signals.

- **Document 3:** "An Active Window Bell at Yonezawa Station" (1955–1975). Source: Kokutetsu, Furusato no Eki, 1999, Pony Canyon. CD 1, Track 26. ASIN: B00005FR22. EAN: 4988013000506.

4.   Departure Bell

The departure bell is the use of electric bells that most closely resembles the train chime practices more familiar in Euro-American settings: a signal sounded before the doors close, also called a "barrier sound" (Grosjean 1988). Yet this departure bell is different, because its semantic intention, or "functional requirement," is not to "fractionalize the passengers' flow" (Grosjean 1988: 46), as is indeed the case for the majority of barrier sounds found in France or elsewhere in Europe (see Masson 2007). From the rail company's point of view, the barrier sound has two simultaneous roles: it signals the end of the boarding process, and it manifests a regulation by sanctioning the agents' right to close the doors; thereafter, further attempts to enter the train would be "at the risk of one's safety" (Grosjean 1988: 45). Accordingly, while this "warning signal" possesses a "regulatory value" representing potential proof that the company did its best to avoid injuries, it also denotes a vision of the passenger as a potential deviant. Its encoded prescription shouts, "Stop!" at the daring passenger.

In Japan, the departure bell differs from European use of barrier sound on both functional and pragmatic levels. Functionally, it is not intended to bar access to the train, exposing potential deviance. There are still practically no barrier sounds in Japan.[10] The departure bell instead points to the timeframe during which boarding can be performed; as a signal, it is the expression of a social norm ("it is appropriate to board now"), whereas the barrier sound is the expression of a social control ("don't board anymore"). In this sense, the departure bell embodies the educational objectives of the various normative campaigns described earlier and gives value to public space as a place where normative training can be provided. Passengers are to master and perform boarding techniques during the timeframe that the departure bell is sounding. Second, on a pragmatic level, Japanese departure bells focus attention on the impending departure of the train, not the imminent closing of its doors, and they do not try to stop passengers from boarding, whereas this is the semantic intention of the barrier sound. The social control of potential deviance and the role of issuing warnings have been given to human agents, and are performed through verbal announcements. There is a clear "distribution of competences" (Latour 1992: 158) between sounds signals and vocal information in that regard.[11]

- **Document 4:** "A Departure Bell at Ryougoku Station" (1955–1975). Source: Ima Yomigaeru Kokutetsu, 2010, Columbia Music Entertainment. CD 2, Track 1. ASIN: B003800360. EAN: 4988001300908.

III.   The Departure Melody

This analysis provides several perspectives on the socio-historical background of what may be heard in Tokyo train stations today, and pinpoints some factors that shaped the contemporary trend to announce any and all events involving passengers. The patterns identified above became widespread thanks to an important agreement between railway companies' on-site representatives (the agents) and the passengers. But the polysemic use of the electric bell was mainly due to the limitations of the tool itself, as there was no control over the sound it produced (tone, granularity, and in many cases intensity). So, while polysemic in purpose, the reality of the boarding scene was marked by repeated use of the same signal, as agents reacted to the situation on the platform, triggering the same bell at several occasions during the period framing boarding. The coexistence of many possible meanings for that one sound gave it a deictic dimension (that is, context-dependent), which was both contradictory and problematic, for it could not be instantaneously understood and required at very least a second verification (i.e., visual confirmation). This problem was indirectly addressed by the transformation of the previously described patterns (approaching bell, arrival bell, and departure bell) into recognizable and distinct types of melodic chimes.[12] The signals that fill today's stations are those that withstood the test of time and proved to be valuable management tools for railway companies.

Consequently, today's sound practices are in many cases continuations of developments that took place over the last century. Such is the case for the lyrically rich departure melody, which is a refinement of the uniform, monotonous departure bell. Many stations, and usually each track at each station, now have their own melodies. In JR East (Tokyo's main network), for instance, these melodies are complete jingles composed by musicians specialized in radio work, and they are so numerous that several CD compilations have already been released (often selling out quickly). Since they still indicate a timeframe for boarding, their format is tightly controlled to match their function: they feature a wide frequency spectrum to preserve primacy, and are highly compressed to remain audible in various environments and on a variety of station loudspeaker systems. From a sonic perspective, although electric bells' tonal monotony and their stressful and irritating traits were indeed addressed, station sound environments are now generally dissonant because departure melodies are rarely tuned to one another. From a socio-cultural perspective, the departure melody is also the object of community reappropriation.

- **Document 5:** "Ue Wo Muite Arukou: an Arrival Melody at Kawasaki Station" (2008). The song, translated "Sukiyaki" in the US, was major hit in Japan as well as American pop chart. Its author, artist Sakamoto Kyu, was born in Kawasaki. Source: Keikyu Eki Merodi Original (Japanese), 2009, USM Japan. CD 1, Track 6. ASIN: B001PBQLHY. EAN: 498805551146. An excerpt of a live recording can be found on YouTube.

Local commercial associations often foster the use of local departure melodies—that is, short versions of songs of famous singers from the area instead of original jingle compositions. As this phenomenon enriches the station with socio-cultural echoes, it localizes it in the socio-geographical realm (what could be called a symbolic adherence to local culture). But at the same time, it also changes the role of the departure signal: as it dissociates its acoustic container from its semantic content or intention, it gives it some functions that are not strictly related to the management of passengers.

Sound-Effect Signals Carry On

At the same time, many of today's sound signals may also represent the expansion or broadening of previous sound practices. In opening this conclusion, I would like to provide some examples of what I have designated as a sound-effect signal.

In the Seibu network (East, North East of Tokyo), approach signals are replacing the function of both approach and arrival bells. They, too, have a sound-effect signal dimension, but take the logic even further. They are no longer broadcast from platform speakers, but from speakers located in the rail bed that are oriented toward the platform. As with the numerous trains that are equipped with speakers to provide automated warnings to those standing nearby, the approach signal now resonates from the specific area concerned. The location of the sound signal and the location of the physical event are equivalent. The signal is even more relevant as a materializing index here because it specifies where attention should be focused for the next event. In the Keikyû Network (South-South East of Tokyo) local approach

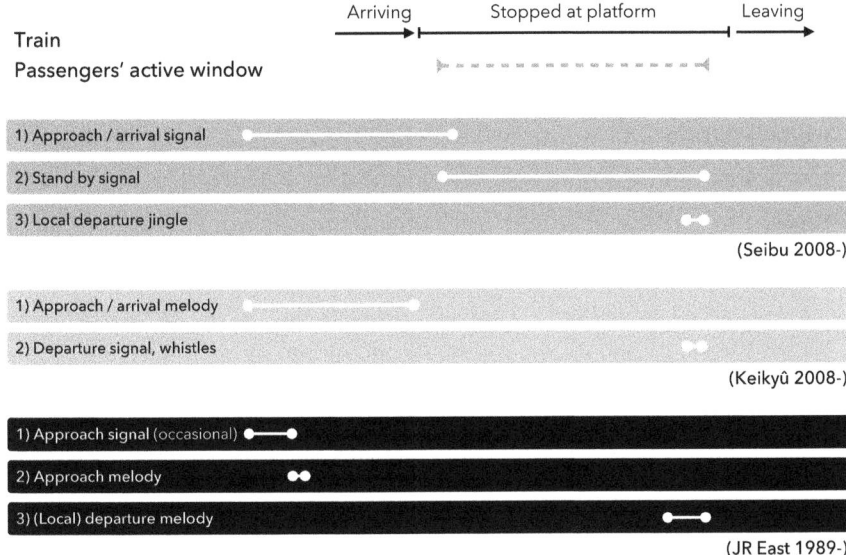

Figure 5.5 Signals and melodic chimes in three modern networks.

melodies play the same role, as their 25-second jingles may be repeated up to six times until the train reaches the platform. It literally stages or enchants (Bull 2000: 183–4) the arrival of the train in music, providing an emotional layer to the passive state experienced by passengers waiting for the train.

Another implementation of a sound-effect signal is the doors opening/closing signal. The opening (and closing) of doors is accompanied by a sound-effect signal: a soft, two-note signal, repeated twice. Once again, it is not a barrier sound, but a signal expressing the action (doors opening) to which it corresponds. This sound-effect signal doesn't provide more potential for action; it merely parallels a set of mechanical sounds (hydraulic mechanisms triggering the opening) that, along with the visual confirmation of the doors being opened or closed, would be sufficient to prompt passengers to react accordingly. It does, however, eliminate any doubt from interpretation. This sound is unquestionably linked to the actions of the doors, especially as this signal is now widely used by all rail companies.

The last example that I would like to provide is the stand-by signal. While train doors are open, many trains emit a one-second, gentle, single note stand-by signal, repeated every 5 seconds. The signal itself clearly emanates from the vicinity of the doors but is heard throughout the car. In addition to manifesting the open state of the doors, it also gives a pace to the state of waiting endured by passive passengers (while waiting in a local train being passed by one or more express trains, for example). Although this stand-by state is already clearly characterized by a sonic referent, the "widening of the acoustic envelope" (the sonic space literally opens along with the doors, enlarging the car's sonic dimensions; see Masson 2009: 237) that is easily perceived and clearly understood as proof of the train being stopped, the situation is still layered with this signal, whose encoded prescription states "we are waiting . . ."

Notes

1 In France, for instance, this rate is 5.6 percent, and it is 0.6 percent in the United States (See *Domestic Transportation Statistics Handbook* 2000).
2 Or the degree to which it corresponds, or "adheres," to the city's morphology (Amar 1993).
3 While important, the cognitive dimension of passenger reception of sounds, how they listen, and their physical actions in relation to the train and station sonic environment will not be discussed in this paper, as I chose to focus on developing the historical and social construction of sound signals as behavior management tools.
4 Platforms are overflowing with automated visual information today: how many doors per car and cars per train, the arrival times and platform numbers, the distance between the train and the station, etc. This clearly illustrates the gradual development of visual display, a subject that deserves attention, but this paper primarily focuses on the sonic dimension of this rationalization. It should also be mentioned that visual information was and still is frequently both *offered* and *used* as a way for passengers to confirm and control their timing, rather than as a means of social control over him; indeed this is, generally speaking, the main role of sound use in Japanese society (see Bayley 1991: 43–5, for a comparison of Japanese policemen's use of sound and American policemen's use of light in confronting social deviance), and especially so in trains (see Nakamura 2002).
5 Mito (*Ibid.*) and Tanaka (2005) provide detailed accounts of how the discourse on manners and boarding etiquette was incarnated in new behaviors.
6 The social control of deviance through micro-interactions between passengers should also be mentioned, which also played an important role in the gradual regulation of behaviors through time.
7 As a generic expression, a "sound signal" indicates any sonic phenomenon that could be identified as a discrete unit (Masson 2009: 289). It may be composed of several other sonic components. For example, "train slowing down" is obviously a signal referring to at least two elements: the decrescendo of the slowing train and the decrease of the sonic intensity of the movement itself.
8 Following Grosjean's functional distinction (1988: 45).
9 All the following recordings were made between 1955 and 1975, and unfortunately the documentation available does not allow to be more specific.
10 In the past few years a few subway lines have introduced them.
11 Station agents (as opposed to bells) warn of the imminent closing of the doors after the departure bell has stopped, reacting to passengers' behavior. An announcement might say: "The doors will close when the departure bell stops ringing." Agents may even stigmatize the deviant, repeatedly saying: "Please do not rush onto the train!" with an increasingly forceful voice. This repetition may attract the attention of other passengers, triggering a shift in their listening mode from floating to attentive. Awareness is raised, and the deviant, now identified, is more likely to be the object of informal social control—a powerful means of constraint in Japanese society—through micro-social interactions. In addition, once the train

has left the station, an agent on the train may add another element of formal social control through the train loudspeakers, by, for instance, addressing the deviant now onboard: "To the passenger who rushed into the train, we ask you to refrain from doing this. Rushing into a train can cause delays and accidents."

12 This happened during the transformation of the JNR's public image after its semi-privatization (around 1987), in answer to complaints about these bells' irritating noise.

References

Amar, Georges. 1993. "Pour une écologie urbaine des transports." *Les Annales de la Recherche Urbaine* 59/60: 140–151.

Arasui, Shigeo. 1959. *Kokutetsu Densha Hattatsushi*. Tokyo: Denki Kenkyukai.

Augoyard, Jean-François and Henry Torgue, eds. 2005. *Sonic Experience: A Guide to Everyday Sounds*. Translated by Andra McCartney and David Paquette. Montreal: McGill-Queen's University Press.

Aveline, Natacha. 2003. *La ville et le rail au Japon: L'expansion des groupes ferroviaires privés à Tokyo et Ôsaka*. Paris: CNRS Éditions.

Bayley, David. 1991. *Forces of Order: Policing Modern Japan*. Berkeley: University of California Press.

Bijker, Wiebe E., Thomas P. Hughes, and Trevor F. Pinch, eds. 1993. *The Social Construction of Technological Systems: New Directions in the Sociology and History of Technology*. Cambridge: MIT Press.

Bourdieu, Pierre. 2002. *Questions de sociologie*. Paris: Les Éditions de Minuit.

Bull, Michael. 2000. *Sounding Out the City: Personal Stereos and the Management of Everyday Life*. Oxford: Berg Publishers.

Callon, Michel. 1986. "Some Elements of a Sociology of Translation: Domestication of the Scallops and the Fishermen of St Brieuc Bay." In *Power, Action, and Belief: A New Sociology of Knowledge*, edited by John Law, 196–233. New York: Routledge.

Chion, Michel. 1994. *Audio-Vision: Sound on Screen*. Translated and edited by Claudia Gorbman. New York: Columbia University Press.

Domestic Transportation Statistics Handbook: Fiscal 2000. 2002. Tokyo: Japanese Ministry of Land, Infrastructure and Transport.

Grosjean, Michèle. 1988. *Métro: Espace sonore*. Paris: RATP, Département Développement Prospective.

Honda, Tomoshiru. 1927. *Densha Jikoron*. Tokyo: Toyo Shoseki Shuppan Kyokai.

Ide, Hiroaki. 2009. *Mienai Dezain*. Tokyo: Yamaha Music Media.

Ishidzuka, Junitsu. 2011. Liner notes to, and editor of the CD *Ima, Yomigaeru Kokutetsu. Oto no Tabi ("Bring JNR Back to life. Sonic Travel")*. Columbia Japan CD COCX-36804–36806.

Ito, Yoshitomo. 1930. "Magoto ni Supiido Jidai!" *Sandee Mainichi* 21: 32.

Joseph, Isaac. 2004. *Météor, les métamorphoses du métro*. Paris: Economica.

Konwa, Jiro, ed. 2001. *Shimpan Dai Tokyo Annnai*. Tokyo: Chikumagaku Geibunko.

Latour, Bruno. 1992. "Where Are the Missing Masses? The Sociology of a Few Mundane Artifacts." In *Shaping Technology/Building Society: Studies in Sociotechnical Change*, edited by Bijker Wiebe and John Law, 151–180. Cambridge: MIT Press.

Leroux, Martine, ed. 1989. *Les Faiseurs de bruit*. Grenoble: CRESSON.

————, ed. 1991. *Les Facteurs sonores du sentiment d'insécurité*. Grenoble: CRESSON.

Masson, Damien. 2007. *La perception embarquée: Analyse sensible des voyages urbains*. PhD diss., Pierre Mendès-France Université, Grenoble.

————. 2009. "Métronomes métropolitains. La dynamique sonore des voyages urbains." In *Variations d'ambiance. Processus et modalités d'émergence des ambiances urbaines*, edited by Jean-Paul Thibaud, 229–310. Grenoble: CRESSON.

Mito, Yuko. 2002. *Teikoku Hassha*. Tokyo: Kotsu Shimbunsha.

Nakamura, Naofumi. 2002. "Railway Systems and Time Consciousness in Modern Japan." *Japan Review* 14: 13–38.

Schaeffer, Pierre. 1966. *Traité des objects musicaux*. Paris: Seuil.

Shiozuka, Hiroshi. 2013. *Eki Mero*. Tokyo: Fusosha.

Takemura, Tamio. 2001. "1920 Nendai ni okeru Tetsudo no Jikan Kakumei." In *Chikoku no Tanjo*, edited by Hashimoto Takehiko, 47–75. Tokyo: Sangensha.

Tanaka, Daisuke. 2005. "Tsukin Tsugaki suru Shintai no Keisei." *Sociologos* 29: 180–198.

Thibaud, Jean-Paul. 1987. *Culture sonore en chantier, le chantier comme milieu révélateur des modes de professionnalisation*. Grenoble: CRESSON.

Yamaha. 1988. "JR Higashi Nihon, Shinjuku Eki. Hoso Setsubi Kaishu Keikakuan." In *JR East, NTT*. Tokyo: Unpublished.

Yamamoto, Tomejiro. 1935. *Shanai Saabisu Kenkyu*. Tokyo: Denki Koronsha.

Yoshimura, Hiro. 1992. *Toshi no Oto*. Tokyo: Shunjusha.

Part III
Sound Identity and Locality

6 Acoustic Communities Represented

Sound Preferences in the Scottish Village of Dollar

Heikki Uimonen

1. Introduction

Ubiquitous but often unnoticed sounds make the research on everyday sonic environments challenging for anthropologists, ethnomusicologists or anyone studying soundscapes in urban and rural contexts. While conducting fieldwork on environmental sounds, especially meanings related to them, it is crucial not only to focus on acoustical parameters of a given place but also to consult the people who are living within the soundscape being researched. There is no such thing as a universal approach to listening; every individual, every group and every culture listens in its own way (Augoyard and Torgue 2008: 4). Drawing on this, it is evident that applying qualitative methods such as interviews to fieldwork are not only highly recommended but they should be integrated into any research aiming to construct a comprehensive picture on any given soundscape.

Furthermore, it needs to be taken into consideration that soundscapes are not only constructed and interpreted in real-life situations by the people living within a sonic environment, but also represented in various ways such as in face-to-face discussions, in printed texts and in electronic media. This poses a challenge for the researcher interested in community attitudes towards soundscape: in which ways acoustic communities are being produced symbolically and represented and how they reflect the construction of soundscape in study. One way to overcome this obstacle is to apply different fieldwork methods developed among scholars of acoustic communication and soundscape studies. These methods include Sound Preference Test and Recorded Listening Walk.

Sound Preference Test was invented by the multidisciplinary *World Soundscape Project* at Simon Fraser University in 1975. The method was applied in *Five Village Soundscapes* project and further developed by *Acoustic Environments in Change* and the *Soundscapes and Cultural Sustainability* projects (Järviluoma *et al.* 2009, SoCS 2011). The two research projects are intertwined. *Five Village Soundscapes* was the first comprehensive and comparative research studying various and diverse acoustic environments in Europe in 1975. The continuation research *Acoustic Environments in Change* was carried out twenty-five years later, to be followed by *Soundscapes and Cultural Sustainability* project in 2009 (see chapter three).

Sound Preference Tests were carried out during the fieldwork in all villages, including the Scottish village of Dollar, thus enabling a long-term comparison on the pleasant and unpleasant sounds among different generations (see Järviluoma *et al.* 2009, SoCS 2013). A more recent Recorded Listening Walk Method (Uimonen 2011) was first carried out as a pilot study at the University of Tampere, Finland, in 2010. The Dollar field trip presented in this article was planned after this pilot study with the goal of documenting the environmental sounds of the village and to analyse them in collaboration with the members of the community. Another goal for the Dollar research was to further develop the methodology of soundscape studies and to include pedagogical methods in the fieldwork to make the everyday sounds more audible for anyone interested.

Theoretically, the article draws on the concept of acoustic community (Truax 2001) defined as "any soundscape in which acoustic information plays a pervasive role in the lives of the inhabitants". The article elaborates on how the acoustic community of Dollar has transformed sonically over the last quarter of a century and more specifically concentrates on the how the members of the micro community of the local Strathdevon Primary School listen to and construct their sonic environments. The empirical part of the paper introduces the Sound Preference Test carried out in 2011 among school children, paying special attention to how their acoustic communities are represented. The outcome is then presented with the results of the previous test, enabling a comparison of liked and disliked sounds across three different generations.

Before presenting the results of the field work, a theoretical background and key concepts are defined including acoustic communication, acoustic community and the anthropological concept of dirt as "matter out of place" coined by Mary Douglas (Douglas 2000, Truax 2001). The theoretical definition is then combined with the results from previous Sound Preference Test carried out in Dollar in 1975 and 2000 (more detailed information can be found on Järviluoma *et al.* 2009).

2.　Acoustic Communities

Study of *acoustic communication* is concentrating on the exchange of sonic information including the cognitive processes that enable this information to be understood. The approach is clarified by the triangular relationship between sound, listener and environment. Hence, *acoustic community* stands for "any soundscape in which acoustic information plays a pervasive role in the lives of the inhabitants (no matter how the commonality of such people is understood)" (Truax 2001: 11–2). Those living within an acoustic community are not only interpreting sonic information but also constructing their soundscapes through their activities. The model for

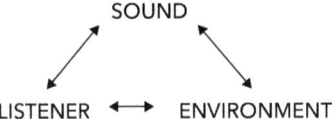

Figure 6.1 Model for acoustic communication.
Source: (Truax 2001: 12).

acoustic communication shows how sound, listener and environment are interactive and intertwined.

The concept of the acoustic community is further elaborated by the fact that sharing of acoustic information within an acoustic space can be quite variable, and it does not always involve simultaneity of any given aural experience. A given signal can be heard at regular times by some members of the community, and at other times by other members, but they share a similar experience and identify and interpret the particular sounds. These communities may be very localized, such as a home, workplace, school, etc. (Truax 2001).[1]

Soundscape competence is defined as "tacit knowledge that people have about the structure of environmental sounds, knowledge that manifests itself in behaviour that interprets such sound and acts upon it." Soundscape competence allows us to understand environmental sounds as meaningful. It can be further divided between *general soundscape competence,* referring to general knowledge of a given area, and *specific* soundscape competence, referring to special knowledge and to the meanings of certain sounds (Smith 1993: 401–2, Truax 2001: 57–8, Uimonen 2011: 257).

Construction of acoustic community and soundscape competences can be further elaborated by introducing communication scholar James W. Carey's (1994) *transfer* and the *ritual models* of communication. According to him, communication not only shapes the relationship between the environment and the members of the community, but also creates a social commonality (Ridell 1993: 10). This is what aforementioned *acoustic community* is by definition: any soundscape in which acoustic communication plays a pervasive role in the lives of the members of community. The notion is parallel to Raymond Williams's ritual view of communication. In this context communication is linked to terms such as "sharing", "participation", "association", "commonness" and "communion". More than towards the extension of messages in space, the ritual view of communication is directed towards maintenance of society in time and the representation of shared belief (Carey 1989).

Knowledge concerning sounds of acoustic community and the meanings connected to them can be further theorized with the help of terms of *communication, culture* and *meaning* by saying that culture *is* communication.

Communication consists of symbolic forms and meanings. Human communication presupposes shared cultural meanings, so culture cannot exist without communication. The only difference between communication and culture lies in how they are evaluated: "culture" stresses the structures of symbols and actions whereas "communication" stresses the processes of interaction—the function of symbols (Fornäs 1998: 171–2).

The communicational and cultural criteria are met when these notions are evaluated from the perspective of acoustic communication research. The interactive and symbolic meanings are very much present in ordinary environmental sounds, but also when something extraordinary takes place within the community. This can be elucidated by an example from the Scottish village of Dollar. The acoustic communication in the village was altered interactively and symbolically in year 1990 when village life was connected sonically to global geopolitical issues. Before the Gulf War, the jets and propeller-driven planes from the Royal Air Force station located 65 kilometres east of Dollar in the small town of Leuchars were practicing low-flying along the valley and close to the village changing the soundscape radically with the sounds of their engines (Uimonen 2009: 205).

3.   Douglasian Dirt and Semantic Differential

Research on acoustic communities includes individual, social and cultural values connected to environmental sounds, such as the liked and the disliked, or any other sound heard within community. They can be approached theoretically and methodologically by applying anthropological concept of dirt to research and by using semantic differential in evaluating the environmental sounds.

Anthropologist Mary Douglas defines dirt as a matter out of place or something we find inappropriate in a given context. This leads to a conclusion that communally disliked sounds are sounds in a wrong place. Also the dimension of time needs to be added to definition, since the same sounds can have different meanings depending on the time of the day when they are being heard. Furthermore, whenever dirt exists, there exists some kind of cultural or communal order. Cultures have their conceptions of dirt and about the overall cultural structure, which should be maintained by different means (Douglas 2000: 85–86, 236, see also Bailey 1996, Uimonen 2005).

In addition to the members of the community, who are pro order/equilibrium, there are also those who are breaking or disturbing the sonic order of the acoustic community. The noise making of the rule breakers is usually normalized to the order defined by the majority of the community. At one point the villagers of Dollar were disturbed by the noise of the youngsters made at night in the centre of the village. They were causing anxiety about damage to property or that villagers in the nearby houses would not enjoy a proper sleep. However, the nuisance was temporary since little by little the "youngsters became a bit more responsible", as one informant put it. In this case there was no need to take official action, since according to local authorities no noise complaints were put on the record (Uimonen 2009: 199).

Drawing on this, defining pleasant, unpleasant and even bearable sounds is not just about the individual preferences but also about community values and the predominant power relations: who has the right to define the pleasant and the unpleasant and to make these preferences audible by passing laws and to oversee that these laws are being obeyed (see also Corbin 1998).

When soundscape changes, the definitions of pleasant or unpleasant sounds are also prone to change. This leads to constant redefinition and rearticulation of Douglasian dirt. Conventionally, these disturbing sounds are approached quantitatively by noise measurements. With the help of decibel meter scale, the subjective and undesirably dirty sounds can be disinfected to objectively measurable noise. Thus the problems of undesired sounds—if there are such—are handed over to organizations of specialists typical to modern society. However, it is not only the specialists who are controlling the sound making of the members of the acoustic community or rearticulating the concept of noise. The individuals are enculturated to the society and to its rules and norms and are thus spontaneously, willingly or unwillingly, controlling their own sound making.

Light was shed on the rearticulating of disturbing sounds of Dollar during a preliminary study of the Acoustic Environments in Change project. The elderly couple interviewed in 1999 pointed out that voices and shouts of the intoxicated young women at night-time would have been considered inappropriate a quarter of a century ago. This was underlined by the fact that at those times women were allowed to enter to bars or pubs and to consume alcohol only when accompanied by their husbands (Uimonen 2009: 199). Not only does the change of soundscape reflect the values of the community, but more specifically, it also brings forth the question on what kind of behaviour is considered to be appropriate for different genders.

Douglasian dirt can help in questioning the concepts of something or someone being "liked" or "disliked" and to culturally contextualise the spatiotemporal character of the sonic phenomena of a given community. However, it should be remembered that concepts of liking and disliking are multifaceted and ranging from appreciation to loving or from dislike to disgust or hate.

One way to solve the conceptual problem on a methodological level would be to utilize the semantic differential method applied in assessing the built environment. The semantic differential can be used in eliciting the connotations and meanings attached to the sounds by a given acoustic community. Also, sound preferences can be approached systematically with the polar oppositions instead of the personal likes and dislikes, which may differ considerably from each other.

Semantic differential method has been carried out by asking the informants to evaluate pictures of landscapes with the help of the adjective list of opposing adjectives such as beautiful-ugly, active-passive, etc. The adjectives are arranged across a numerical range of seven points (1 to 7) with the purpose of finding out how well the adjectives can be used in describing the landscapes portrayed. In soundscape studies, this method has been applied by recording the local environmental sounds, by playing them to informants and asking them to give their opinion on these sound events and soundscapes (Uimonen 2005: 109).

The semantic differential should not be considered as a substitute or a separate method, especially when sounds and their meanings are being scrutinized. Semantic differential can raise connotations which would otherwise be difficult to recall from memory and thus hard to verbalize. Polar oppositions can also serve as a catalyst capable of evoking emotions and memories when connected to the sounds of the environment. Furthermore the semantic differential can also be applied to a sound preference test when a large number of people are being surveyed (Uimonen 2005: 110, Kang and Zhang 2009).

4.   European Villages and Recorded Listening Walks

In 1975 Canadian World Soundscape Project research group carried out the first large-scale soundscape research in Europe called *Five Village Soundscapes*. Twenty-five years later, the Finnish *Acoustic Environments in Change*

Figure 6.2 Six villages studied.

Source: (Järviluoma et al. 2009: 17).

research team visited the villages of Skruv, Bissingen, Cembra, Lesconil and Dollar in Sweden, Germany, Italy, France and Scotland, respectively. In 2000 a Finnish village of Nauvo was added as sixth village to research.

Both research teams were applying quantitative and qualitative methods in fieldwork while researching sonic environments. The methods included listening walks and aforementioned sound preference tests (Schafer 1977, Järviluoma *et al.* 2009).

In general, the recurring qualitative phenomena can be coded to statistical representations. After this, the results of the quantitative analysis can be used as leads. However, it should be remembered that the essence of the qualitative research is the interpreting of the meanings (Alasuutari 2011: 53).

This was applied in the methodology of Acoustic Environments in Change study. The acoustic rhythms and densities of the villages were studied by collecting numerical data on traffic, signals and other acoustic events in all different areas of the villages. Also, the listening walks were applied during which the analytical listening and systematic classification of environmental sounds were carried out by dividing the heard sounds into ten categories. The categories were motor traffic, human traffic (e.g., footsteps, bikes), voices, indoor human activity, outdoor human activity, domestic animals, electroacoustic sounds, signals (non-regular), other transportation sounds (brakes, doors, ignition, etc.), and planes (Uimonen 2011: 258). It goes without saying that this quantitative information on acoustic phenomena was often brought up and discussed in personal and group interviews and thus integrated with qualitative research.

This utilising of qualitative and quantitative data was also pointed out in the Acoustic Environments in Change publication, when the Sound Preference Test was evaluated. It was clear that when reading the percentage from the tables, one needs to bear in mind that they are not meant for statistical analysis but to arrange information for more profound qualitative analysis (Järviluoma *et al.* 2009: 226).

Another methodological goal for the *Soundscapes and Cultural Sustainability* project stated in the research plan was to organise courses and "Ear Cleaning" listening exercises at local schools. The exercises were combining pedagogical actions, field research and participatory methods: the children were observing and documenting their own sonic environments with most of the classes held outside the school building (SoCS 2013). Furthermore, the reflective methods such as the Sound Preference Tests and listening walks were applied.

Recorded Listening Walk is a method for studying the meanings of environmental sound with the help of recording equipment, documenting the verbal descriptions of the recording event and by filling out the questionnaires. It was first carried out at University of Tampere, Finland, in order to find out how individual recordists experienced their soundscapes, whether they wanted to change their sonic environments and how recording events changed their modes of listening. Some of the comments on recording events compared to everyday listening were as follows: "You tend to listen in a more analytical way." "You seldom listen in everyday situations." "The mode of listening is more analytical than everyday listening," "After this kind of task, you walk in your everyday surroundings with your ears open" (Uimonen 2011: 260).

As a result, better sound insulation and acoustics were suggested as desirable changes in school premises. In general, the recordists wanted to get rid of the hums and buzzes and retain the sounds of human interaction. The pilot research also shows that interpretation of soundscape is affected not only by these factors, but also how individuals have been educated or how they have educated themselves to listen to and interpret sounds—musical or other—and how they apply this competence to environmental sounds (Uimonen 2011: 260).

In Dollar, Recorded Listening Walks were applied in different ways: at home and in the schoolyard. First, sixteen pupils of Strathdevon Primary School took part in morning listening exercise. The participants aged seven and eight were listening to their everyday sounds and also making sounds in the schoolyard in groups of fours. The pupils were asked to describe verbally sound-making to someone who is not present to witness what is actually happening during the recording event. These few-minute soundwalks were recorded and edited to sound samples. As a result a diverse compilation of rhythms and timbres of the sounds that usually go unnoticed were documented: soft polystyrene foam, crisp packets, empty plastic bottles, railings, different surfaces under the feet, sounds of the swing and so on (SoCSblog 2011).

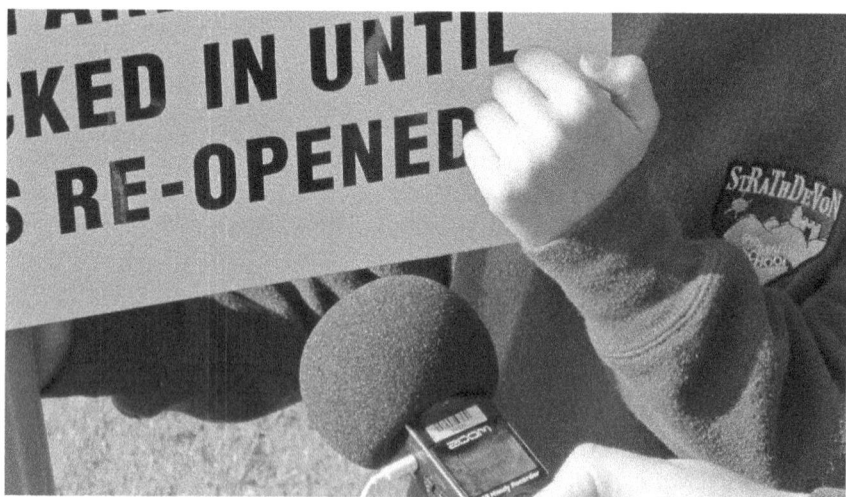

Figure 6.3 Recording everyday sounds.
Photo: Heikki Uimonen.

- **Document 1:** Soundwalks with Strathdevon School Pupils on 28th April 2011. Recorded by Heikki Uimonen & Viika Sankila.

Second, three 10-year-old students of Strathdevon Primary School took portable digital recorders and earphones home. They were advised to document their soundscapes by searching for the sounds they like and dislike. In order to make the documents identifiable, they were asked to tell their names and what they were documenting to the recording. The next day the outcome was introduced to the rest of the class, who participated by telling their opinions and commenting on the sounds. The recordist described where in the Dollar area the recording homework was carried out how they thought they succeeded in their jobs (SoCSblog 2011). The liked sounds were the ones of laughter, running water and crunching leaves. The disliked were a revving car, high heels on the pavement and voice of a little brother.

- **Document 2:** Three Homework Recordings by Strathdevon Primary School Pupils Finlay, Megan & Leah on Wednesday 27 April 2011.

Besides the recording event, a new and somewhat exciting sound-related experience for the recordists was to hear one's voice recorded for the first time. This was actually somewhat surprising in this day and age of smartphones and computers with voice-recording options. The detailed description of the Recorded Listening Walks and Homework Recordings including the sound samples and pictures can be found on the Dollar Soundscape Blog (SoCSblog 2011).

5. Sound Preference Tests at Strathdevon Primary School

As noted, the listeners' relation to sonic environments is affected by several individual factors, such as how they are encultured to their acoustic communities, how they have been educated or have educated themselves to listen to music or environmental sounds. This enculturation lays a foundation

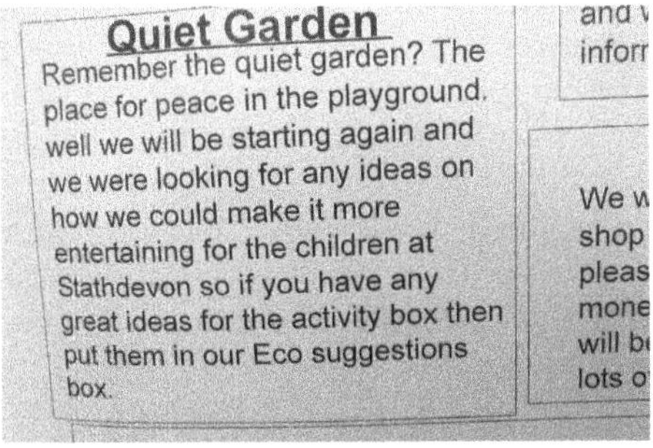

Figure 6.4 Quiet garden announcement.
Photo: Heikki Uimonen.

for how the values of a given acoustic community are reflected in sound preferences. Although music education is integrated to contemporary curriculums at schools, education on environmental sounds seems to play a minor if not a practically nonexistent part (Kankkunen 2013).[2] It should be noted, though, that the issues of sounds had already been taken into discussion at Strathdevon Primary School. A place called Quiet Garden located in the school area was characterised as "the place for peace in the playground" (SoCSblog 2011).

While conducting the Sound Preference Test, the children were advised to write down the sounds they found pleasant and unpleasant. Pupils of Strathdevon Primary School participated in the test on Thursday 28 April 2011. The informants were requested to write down five sounds they liked and five sounds they disliked and where in Dollar these sounds could be heard (Schafer 1977, SoCSblog 2011).

The most *pleasant* sounds according to the 10- to 11-year-olds (31 pupils) were the sounds of the Dollar Burn and the birds. Dollar Burn is a small river that streams in the middle of the village. Its sounds can be heard distinctively in the yard of Strathdevon Primary School. According to the answers, the singing of birds can be heard in Dollar almost everywhere. Other favourite sounds mentioned were the rustling of the leaves of the trees.

The results are equal for the answers of 1975 and 2000, when the aforementioned sounds were selected to be the most pleasant, too. An explanation for this might be simply the fact that the sounds of the birds are practically omnipresent in Dollar. This was also as stated in the answers. Again, the popularity of the Dollar Burn could be explained by the omnipresence of its sound: it is clearly audible in the schoolyard of Strathdevon Primary school. Sounds of nature were preferred also in other five villages, probably due to the same reason: they were very much present in these acoustic communities, such as sounds of the sea and seagulls in Lesconil, France, or birds in Skruv, Sweden. (For more comparison, see Järviluoma *et al.* 2009.)

The most pleasant sounds are presented in the table and compared to information collected from *Five Village Soundscapes* and *Acoustic Environments in Change* projects in 1975 and 2000.

Category for *other sounds* provided some interesting preferences, not to mention that the percentage of these sounds was remarkably high. In 2000 over sixty and in 2011 over 40 percent of the pleasant sounds were classified in this category.

First music. As stated in a study from 2000, it is difficult to believe that children in 1975 were not listening to any kind of music. The explanation for this lies in the fact that possibly musical sounds were not considered to be included in sound preferences (Järviluoma *et al.* 2009, Uimonen 2012). Furthermore, the answers are in strong contrast with the dissemination of the new music technology of the 1970s. Compact cassettes introduced in 1963 were revolutionising personal and collective music listening, home taping and sharing of music being practically everywhere in the world during

Table 6.1 Most pleasant sounds.

	1975	2000	2011	1975	2000	2011
Birds	19	11	25	26 %	14 %	18 %
Dollar Burn	13	6	31	18 %	8 %	22 %
rustling leaves	13	6	18	18 %	8 %	13 %
Water	10	1	0	14 %	1 %	0 %
clinking coins	8	0	0	11 %	0 %	0 %
Rain	5	0	1	7 %	0 %	0 %
Wind	5	6	4	7 %	8 %	3 %
Other sounds		49	63		62 %	44 %
Signals		6	6		8 %	4 %
Voices		9	7		11 %	5 %
Music		5	13		6 %	9 %
Nature		5	–		6 %	0
objects, action		7	15		9 %	10 %
technology		13	5		16 %	3 %
Animals		4	17		5 %	12 %
Total	73	79	142	100 %	100 %	100 %

the 1970s. It would be hard to imagine that these innovations would have left Dollar untouched. Drawing on that, it does not come as a surprise that twenty-five years later radio and music were mentioned on the list of pleasant sounds.

Also in 2011 music and mobile listening equipment were mentioned in many answers. The favourite artists (Cyrus, Fred) were considered pleasant; also different listening devices and ways of disseminating music, such as radios, iPods and internet music services, were mentioned, including YouTube. It goes without saying that new technology becoming popular among the children has changed not only acoustic communities but also music sharing. According to recent studies, American teenagers listen nowadays to most of their music from YouTube, surpassing radio and CDs (Guardian 2012).

Additional pleasant sounds included sounds of animals and voices and from the category *objects/action*. Apart from a single wild animal ("fox"), the animals were mainly domestic ones, such as cats, dogs, sheep on a local golf course and one gecko. Human sounds such as laughter, chatting and whistling were considered pleasant as well. A minor acoustic community of Strathdevon Primary School was represented by sounds of ripping paper and scissors. Also a novel sound event presumably spread to different parts of the world is plastic bubble wrap, because of the entertaining popping sound it makes when the bubbles are being deliberately deflated.

The most *unpleasant* sounds according to the 10- to 11-year-old children, were traffic, including loud engines. The percentage was even higher in 2011 when compared to previous answers. In 2000, 54 percent of the unpleasant sounds were human voices. Twenty-five years earlier it was only screaming that was disliked among the human sounds. In 2000, disliked human sounds included neighbours, mother's voice and a shouting teacher, among others. Furthermore some sounds of their own families were annoying to the respondents. The human voices and sounds were disliked by the children in other villages as well. For instance in Finnish Nauvo, the boys of the age of 14–15, who had their ongoing love/hate relationship with girls and their voices (for more comparison, see Järviluoma *et al.* 2009).

In 2011 the percentage of unpleasant human sounds had dropped to 25 percent of all answers. The category "voices" included people shouting, screaming, swearing and crying babies. Alongside with physical response to loud sounds, the answers are telling about upbringing: what you are supposed to say and what not, such as profanities or swearing. Another explanation for disliking human sounds can be the fact that that school children spend most of their days in environment where acoustic community is shared with other sound-making people: teachers, schoolmates, siblings and the rest of the villagers. As with sounds of nature, the references for the liked and disliked sounds are repeatedly selected from soundscape you live within.

The most unpleasant sounds are presented in the table and compared to information collected from *Five Village Soundscapes* and *Acoustic Environments in Change* projects in 1975 and 2000.

High percentage of disliked sound in category *objects/action* included building sites, domestic and again, sound of schools such as knives on plates, paper ripping, pencils on desk, sharpeners scraping on tables, nails on chalkboard and the paper cutter (called "guillotine" at school).

"Rain all the time" was not liked. Also, upbringing is notable here: splashing in muddy puddles is supposedly something that pupils are not allowed to do and thus considered a disliked sound. Another disliked sound is "TV that no-one is watching", which can be explained by parents telling their children to switch off the television. Signals such as ambulance sounds, alarm clocks and car alarms were not liked either. Other sounds considered unpleasant were the sandpaper and rolling baskets in the local grocery store. Also, barking dogs and birds in the trees (sounds that were actually liked very much, too).

The international music industry and the musical tastes of the children were present in the answers. Loud and noisy music was disliked in general, pop star Justin Bieber in particular (SocSBlog 2011). Disliking Bieber can be explained by the change of the youths' media use, which includes forming of various fan groups or followers of certain artists. Popular music is used in constructing one's identity and belonging to a certain group. The meanings attached to a certain piece of music or artists might cause the informants to give their answers in more emotional way than what they would do when

Table 6.2 Most unpleasant sounds.

	1975	2000	2011	1975	2000	2011
Traffic	5	6	31	14 %	8 %	23 %
chair scraping floor	5	2	0	14 %	3 %	
screeching brakes	4	0	0	11 %	0 %	
chalk on blackboard	4	1	7	11 %	1 %	5 %
door slam	3	1	0	8 %	1 %	
desk banging	3	0	0	8 %	0 %	
Rain	3	2	0	8 %	3 %	
screaming	3	0	0	8 %	0 %	
squeaking	3	0	0	8 %	0 %	
styrofoam	3	0	0	8 %	0 %	
Other sounds		59	96		83 %	71 %
Nature		3	0		5 %	
objects/action		9	36		16 %	26 %
technology motor traffic		6	0		11 %	
Animals		3	14		5 %	10 %
Signals		7	13		12 %	10 %
Voices		31	33		54 %	25 %
Total	36	71	134	100 %	100 %	100 %

evaluating the non-musical environmental sounds. Also, music is what you select deliberately to listen to, unlike environmental sounds, thus making it a special acoustic sound phenomenon compared to other sounds.

For comparison, the Sound Preference Test was carried out with the 7-year-old children, too. In their age group (27 pupils), the most *liked* sounds were the sounds of the birds "in trees", "in garden" and "everywhere". Other sounds mentioned were quite diverse, including rain, sounds of cars, rustling of the leaves and "barking in my house" (pet dog, presumably). Music was liked both indoors and outdoors, i.e., "in the car" and "Dollar Academy Band", the latter referring to the Dollar Academy Pipe Band, which is a local bagpipe orchestra rehearsing outdoors during the summer semester.

The most *disliked* sounds according to the 7-year-olds were, again, voices and human sounds: people shouting and screaming at school and home (teacher, parents). Whispering in the house was not liked either, not to mention the siblings ("Sally asking me to play when I'm reading"). Disliked sounds included cars, trucks and engines. Also, wind on the window, turning pages at school, kettles boiling and cracking of glass were mentioned. The older ones pay more attention to the traffic sounds not present most of the time whereas the little ones are more sensitive to shouts, screams and cries around them. In the school environment, the high-pitched sound of the blackboard was equally disliked. Music was evaluated both qualitatively ("bad music") and quantitatively ("really loud music in my sister's room").

6.   Conclusion

The outcome of the *Soundscapes and Cultural Sustainability* project was elucidated as follows: to develop theory and methods of participatory cultural ethnography and have practical final outcomes. As a result the degree of soundscape awareness in the regions studied will be at a higher level than before. Special attention was paid to young people and children. With this in mind, the research and fieldwork was carried out at Strathdevon Primary School: to make the everyday sounds more audible and to underline that soundscape consists of diverse sound that construct the everyday life of the children.

In this article this was approached theoretically with the model of acoustic communication. Methodologically this goal was partly achieved by introducing the listening walks combined with soundscape recordings and the Sound Preference Tests. The latter was utilised to find out how the changes in acoustic environment are reflected in sound preferences. As the model of acoustic communication shows, the individuals are not only interpreting but also constructing their acoustic environment: how children have been acculturated in making sounds and evaluating sounds as members of their communities.

The sound preferences of the acoustic communities are representations of the soundscape of a given place. They are not notions of the pleasant and unpleasant sounds to be generalised. Dollar Burn was considered a pleasant sound by the respondents. Objectively it is debatable whether that is a typical Dollar sound, since any river may have these same sonic qualities. However, for an insider living within a given acoustic community it certainly is, and in research should be treated as such. When examining the relationship between sounds and spaces, it should be noticed that alongside with spatial and temporal conditions of physical signal propagation, sound is shaped subjectively by the auditory capacity, attitude, psychology and culture of the listener. As previously stated every individual, every group and every culture listens in its own way (Augoyard and Torgue 2008: 4). These qualitative data can then be combined with the quantitative ones such as measuring sound propagation or acoustic properties of a given space.

The sound preferences of the Strathdevon Primary School pupils are reflecting the enculturation and upbringing and thus making the Douglasian dirt visible in the answers. On the other hand, from time to time children are not "politically correct" in evaluating the sounds they like and dislike. Disliking a sound of eating with your mouth open is clearly something that the children are advised not to do; disliking the sound of a little brother is clearly a personal preference. Interestingly, when the recording of the little brother's voice was played as a disliked sound, the whole classroom found it highly amusing. In general it is not appropriate to dislike your sibling, so what the classroom heard was *actually* and personally a very unpleasant sound, although at the same time somewhat hilarious.

The increase of individual and collective music consumption was visible when compared to the year 2000. Unfortunately we did not have information from the year 1975 at our disposal. However, there is a potential pitfall when one asks the pupils to talks about music as a sound preference, since instead of evaluation of environmental sounds you might get the list of favourite bands or singers the pupils like—or the ones they do not like. However, in this way you might get quite realistic picture on what a soundscape of today's teenagers actually is.

This also raises a question on what the commonly shared soundscape is if we evaluate it in terms of acoustic and electroacoustic communities. With the iPods, cellular phones and other electroacoustic devices becoming popular, the acoustic and electroacoustic communities are definitely overlapping, and communities have become fragmented not only individually but also socially. The questions of defining the borders of private and public soundscapes and acoustic communities in the future are thus highly relevant, too.

Also, we should be aware that the ideals of preferable sonic environment are in some cases presented by the adults to children. Sometimes pupils tend to give the "right" answers, which is somewhat evident in place like classroom, where you are *supposed* to give right answers when your skills and education are being tested. In one of the European village schools the teacher had just talked about noise and tinnitus, so not surprisingly the most disturbing noise was considered to be tinnitus. The answer was not stated in other European schools studied (Järviluoma *et al.* 2009: 228). However, this proves that the school children are actually listening to what their teachers are telling them, which of course provides a prominent channel for future sound education.

Sound Preference Tests were not accomplished in laboratory settings, which means that some of the results reflect the environment where the test was carried out. It was biased towards sounds heard at school, but on the other hand, this provides an opportunity for acoustic design in getting rid of the unpleasant sounds. This is parallel to the principle for the soundscape studies in the first place: to research sonic environment in situ with the informants in order to provide tools for perceiving, analysing and taking the necessary steps in improving their soundscapes if the informants find that preferable.

Also pedagogical aspects should be taken into consideration and developed further. This could be used in collaboration as part of music education in pointing out the elements of music that can be found in everyday surroundings. Another way of improving the knowledge of soundscape—if such a need exists—would be to integrate so-called "ear-cleaning"/listening exercises to curriculum.

Notes

1 Barry Truax, *Thanks—30 second "elevator pitch" contributions*. Email at acoustic-ecology@sfu.ca, June 12, 2012.
2 At least the Finnish education system does not recognise the teaching on environmental sounds.

References

Alasuutari, Pertti. 2011. *Laadullinen tutkimus 2.0* [Qualitative Research 2.0]. Tampere: Vastapaino.
Augoyard, Jean-Francois and Henry Torgue, eds. 2008. *Sonic Experience: A Guide to Everyday Sounds*. Translated by Andra McCartney and David Paquette. Montreal: McGill-Queen's University Press.
Bailey, Peter. 1996. "Breaking the Sound Barrier: A Historian Listens to Noise." *Body & Society* 2 (2): 49–66.
Carey, James. 1989. *Communication as Culture: Essays on Media and Society*. http://www3.niu.edu/acad/gunkel/coms465/carey.html.
———. 1994. "Viestintä kulttuurisesta näkökulmasta" [Communication as Culture]. *Tiedotustutkimus* 2 (94): 81–97.
Corbin, Alain. 1998. *Village Bells: Sound and Meaning in the Nineteenth Century French Countryside*. Translated by Martin Thom. New York: Columbia University Press.
Douglas, Mary. 2000. *Puhtaus ja vaara: Ritualistisen rajanvedon analyysi* [Purity and Danger: An Analysis of Concepts of Pollution and Taboo]. Translated by Virpi Blom and Kaarina Hazard. Tampere: Vastapaino.
Fornäs, Johan. 1998. *Kulttuuriteoria. Myöhäismodernin ulottuvuuksia* [Cultural Theory: The Dimension of Late Modern]. Translated by Mikko Lehtonen, Kaarina Hazard, Virpi Blom, and Juha Herkman. Tampere: Vastapaino.
Järviluoma, Helmi, Meri Kytö, Barry Truax, Heikki Uimonen, and Noora Vikman. 2009. *Acoustic Environments in Change and Five Village Soundscapes*. Series A, Research papers 13. Tampere: TAMK University of Applied Sciences and Studies in Literature and Culture 14. Faculty of Humanities, University of Joensuu, Faculty of Humanities.
Kang, Jiang and Mei Zhang. 2009. *Semantic Differential Analysis on the Soundscape of Urban Open Public Spaces*. www.informedesign.org/Rs_detail.aspx?rsId=3515.
Kankkunen, Olli-Taavetti. 2013. Suomalaisen perusopetuksen kuuntelukasvatus [Listening Education in Finnish Basic Education], manuscript for doctoral dissertation, University of the Arts Helsinki, Helsinki.
Michaels, Sean. 2012. "YouTube Is Teens' First Choice for Music." *The Guardian*, August 16, 2012. www.guardian.co.uk/music/2012/aug/16/youtube-teens-first-choice-music.
Ridell, Seija. 1993. "Kommunikaation ihmeelliset seikkailut: Viestinnän käsite kertovan fiktion tutkimuksessa—ja vähän tiedotusopissakin" [The Amazing Adventures of Communication: The Concept of Communication in Fiction and Communications Theory]. *Tiedotustutkimus* 1 (93): 9–21.
Schafer, R. Murray. 1977. *Five Village Soundscapes*. The Music of the Environment Series. Vancouver: A.R.C. Publications.
Smith, Christopher. 1993. *The Acoustic Experience of Place: An Exploration of the Soundscapes of Three Vancouver Area Residential Neighbourhoods*. Simon Fraser University. http://summit.sfu.ca/item/5580.

SoCS. 2013. *Soundscape and Cultural Sustainability Project Description.* http://
socsproject.blogspot.fi/p/about.html.

SoCSblog. 2011. *Dollar Soundscapes.* http://socsproject.blogspot.fi/.

Truax, Barry. 2001. *Acoustic Communication.* Westport: Ablex.

Uimonen, Heikki. 2005. *Ääntä kohti: Ääniympäristön kuuntelu, muutos ja merki-
tys* [Towards the Sound: Listening, Change and Meaning in the Sonic Environ-
ment]. http://tampub.uta.fi/bitstream/handle/10024/67535/951–44–6442–7.
pdf?sequence=1.

———. 2009. "Stories of Sounds: The Narrated Past of Scottish Village." In *Acoustic Environments in Change*, edited by Helmi Järviluoma, Meri Kytö, Barry Truax,
Heikki Uimonen, and Noora Vikman, 194–208. Tampere and Joensuu: TAMK
and University of Joensuu.

———. 2011. "Everyday Sounds Revealed: Acoustic Communication and Environmental Recordings." *Organised Sound: An International Journal of Music and
Technology* 16 (3): 256–263.

———. 2012. "My First Compact Cass: Home Taping and Music Consumption in
1970s Finland." In *IASPM 2011 Proceedings*, edited by Ed Montano and Carlo
Nardi, 253–258. Grahamstown: International Association for the Study of Popular Music.

7 Mics in the Ears

How to Ask People in Cairo to Talk About Their Sound Universes

Vincent Battesti[1]

Figure 7.1 Traffic hum in Wast al-Balad, Downtown Cairo, April 21, 2011, 07:10 p.m. Photo: Vincent Battesti.

Introduction

I was amazed to hear the vibrant and bustling sound ambiance of the Egyptian capital, and it seemed to me a surprisingly overlooked aspect of Cairo urban life.

- **Document 1:** Recorded ambiance in front of the Azbakiyya Park, by al-26 yūlyū, Downtown Cairo, April 14, 2011 at 3:25 p.m. (recorded by Vincent Battesti).

An ethnography of local sound ambiances received and produced in Cairo is possible (Battesti 2009, 2013), and sound studies taught us the necessity for close observations of these neglected dimensions of our relationship—which is first of all sensorial—to the ecological and social environment. To understand local ways of dealing with sound matter in the everyday life requires first being methodical, by setting up an ethnological analytic grid, and then by improving ethnological survey tools, as the main resistance to the study is to gather relevant verbalizations.

How to tackle the idea of an "acoustic community" (Truax 1984), if one makes sense in Cairo? As a social anthropologist, my interest focused on the everyday experience of the Cairene people with the sound environment of their city. To explore these experiences, I tried out a set of tools. Observations and interviews met the pitfalls of studies of the senses—the difficulty for the informants to verbalize this part of their life. When we get more specific about sounds or ambiances of the city—this word "ambiance" is relevant, *gaw* in Egyptian Arabic, as it is a key notion for understanding the local practices and mobility of its inhabitants (Battesti and Puig 2011)—the judgments tend to be summed up in mere polarized hedonistic terms. A more efficient way was the "aural postcard experiment", kind of "reactivated listening" (Augoyard 2001). I used sound ambiances I recorded in different neighborhoods, and informants, while listening with headphones, had to comment on them. It was interesting, not because they were able to localize precisely the recording—most of the time they could not—but because they informed me of their own categories of the sound-city: for example what a *šaɛabī* (popular) neighborhood should sound like, or what the sound key-elements of a place are. But still, this aural postcard remains steeped in the researcher's culture (it is a montage), and the difficulty of capturing the intimate experience of a sound city persists: it has to be seized *in situ*. The commented-walk method (Thibaud 2001)—a walk recorded by the investigator with an informant describing (while walking) the sound and his impressions—could offer some results, but because it was too artificial, would miss the very everyday interactions of the informant with his socioecological environment. It is the reason Nicolas Puig and I set up the idea of "mics in the ears": a mix of the two former methods. Binaural mics in informants' ears record the most possible intimate exposure to sound ambiance during a routine alone trip. This chapter will first present the grid I offered to use in order to document the social nature of the sound ambiance—it will help also to give an insight into the peculiar Cairo ambiances—and then a short presentation and some early results of the "mics in the ears" protocol and its contribution to our knowledge of the various social experiences of Cairo sound ambiances.

Hypothesis

Let's recall that considering a unique sensorial dimension seems a bit mistaken: the sensorial experience—from a physiological, social, and perceptual standpoint—is ruled by the combinative nature of the senses (see Candau 2010). This sacrifice is nonetheless necessary in order to isolate some potential sociological features of hearing. Listening or hearing is anything but "natural": it is not sufficient to possess functioning ears. It is about organizing and understanding, consciously or not, the various signals from a wavelength phenomenon from our environment that meets the ear, and from there, the brain. We do not hear the sound waves; we receive them and "hear" a brain-processed signal. Our hearing equipment is "distorted" in the way all our sensorial equipment results from an education: we learn to perceive by limiting or increasing the possibilities of our sensoriality. This is part of our personal history, our education and learning, and our social conformation: because learning to "feel" the environment is first done with others, with our own different social groups. This organization of senses is therefore social (Corbin 1990) and evolves with social changes.

Every social group defines the arrangement of sensory filters, or to be more precise, the presence or absence of perception, the balance among senses, the qualification of perceptions (value, good taste/distaste, discomfort, pleasure, etc.).

My position is that sound ambiance is not only ambient sound. This study on Cairo starts from the premise that the sound ambiance of a place is indeed the result of the activities taking place there (passive definition), a side effect, but also a collective—and more or less voluntary—construction by producers of sound phenomena (active definition). Then, this study assumes that people of Cairo do live in different sensorial universes. Consequently, the main hypothesis is the existence of a social sound structure. Sound ambiances (produced and received) of the urban fabric and the qualities they inherited are organized according to the "strong and sound" social structure of urban Egyptian society.

In order to demonstrate this, and to ascertain that sound ambiances are social productions and do not appear by mere coincidence, I used an analytical grid elsewhere (Battesti 2009), which proves the possibility of an anthropological hold over this intangible dimension of day-to-day urban life. This chapter presents only a summary of this four-rubric analytical grid, which is partially inspired by an ethnomusicologist's work (Feld 1984: who used six partly different rubrics).

An Analytical Grid

This patchy and improvable grid is simply a tool to test the social readability of sound ambiances, through the competence, the form, the production, and the views expressed about the sound environment.

The Competence

I differentiate between the competence to listen to and the competence to produce sound ambiance.

There are two ways to listen to urban sound environment, although they often coexist and work simultaneously: a competence of natural listening and a competence of discriminative listening. Both are "ordinary listening", according to Schaeffer (Chion 1983), who contrasts it with the "reduced listening."[2] In natural or discriminative listening, the sound is a vehicle allowing us to reach other objects, while, in "reduced listening", our intention targets the sound object for its own sake and not the values it carries or suggests. At any rate, immersed in Cairo urban life, with no real option to escape from its sound dimension ("earlids" do not exist in the way eyelids do), people give meanings to the sound objects or phenomena they hear: are they the sound expression of a street wedding of a popular neighborhood or a political demonstration downtown, both electro-amplified? "Natural listening" allows a comprehensive listening, and the competence is that capacity to recognize sound indices and signs as a meaningful whole. The reality of sound signatures of the diverse territories of this socially hierarchical city is obvious for any urban dweller. However, the competence is acquired. This signature is analyzable; it is possible to discriminate among the dozens or hundreds of different sounds, identified or not, composing this sound ambiance. Yet, the meaning here is given by comprehensive listening, and not by each one of its sound components (as also asserted by *Gestaltpsychologie*). With the "aural postcard experiment" (a kind of acousmatic experiment), Cairenes can determine not always by name, but at least the type of neighborhood that I previously recorded, and which they are listening to in their headphones. In doing so, they offer an *ex-post* typology of Cairo neighborhoods. The comprehensive listening allows them to identify a set of sounds with a place, but when they have to objectivize their answers, pressed by me to justify them, the experimental subjects put some chosen sounds or sound effects forward.

Listening to a busy evening in downtown Cairo, it will be for instance the density of car horns or the hawkers' cries and especially the newspapers sellers (*"al-Ahrām, al-Akhbār, al-Gumhūriyya!"*—the three major Egyptian titles).

- **Document 2:** Walk between Talaat Harb square and Sherif Basha street, Downtown Cairo, November 4, 2009, 7:45 p.m. (Recorded by Vincent Battesti).

Listening to a differently busy shopping street of the old Fatimid neighborhood of Darb al-Aḥmar, the relevant sound effects noticed were the *šibšib* (flip-flops) dragged through the dust, the familiar or offhand manners people address each other, the usual greetings used among acquaintances (which signals territories of acquaintanceship, unlike anonymous strolling territories of downtown).

- **Document 3:** Same day, about one hour later, walk between al-Bibani square and ḥara al-Meɛamār, Darb al-Aḥmar, Old Islamic Cairo, November 4, 2009, 9:05 p.m. (Recorded by Vincent Battesti).

Some sounds can signal quite certainly an urban area type: the *roba vek-kiyya!* (from the Italian *roba vecchia*, old things) cry of the ragman/junk gatherer that reverberates between the high apartment buildings to reach the last floors (to inform he's picking up any junk) is only possible in a bourgeois neighborhood.

- **Document 4:** "*Roba vekkiyya!*" cry of the ragman/junk gatherer in the street, recorded from the seventh floor of a Haussmannian-like building, in a pedestrian area, Downtown Cairo, November 6, 2009, 8:57 a.m. (Recorded by Vincent Battesti).

Obviously, a competence for discrimination is used alongside the competence for natural listening. Without ignoring the overall context, it allows one to extract from a whole sound environment one or a couple of sounds that make sense in a peculiar situation. This competence is noteworthy as sounds surround us, are not frontal, and come from everywhere: to establish the source is not always an easy task. The psychoacoustic studies explain this ability to segregate sound in the brain in various "auditory streams" (like in the "cocktail party effect", see Bregman 1990). This ability may be necessary and salutary in urban life: the pedestrian must hear in the ambient noise of engines, horns, and shouts, the acute little music of the continuous bell of the often-brakeless-bicycle of the Cairo bread carrier: weaving in and out of traffic and people, one of his hand holding the *ɛaīš baladī* (common flat bread) arranged on a large palm rack balanced on the head, the other holding the handlebars. Drivers and strollers alike must extract and identify the shrill warning: all have to yield to this bike.

- **Document 5:** In the outstanding traffic ambiance of the Ramsīs square, the cries of the microbus touts can still be heard by the potential fares, in Cairo, November 2, 2003, 11:24 p.m. (Recorded by Vincent Battesti).

The competence to produce sound ambiance allows participation in the sound environment of the city. For instance, to know how to whistle in the street, where, when, and at what age is indeed a competence. In the same way, to know how to act like this "jaded woman filling the world with her cries at dawn, as a relative of the brother of the husband of her aunt Um Ahmad is dead!"[3] is a competence on the proper use of lament and permissible encroachment in the acoustic space of the neighborhood. Similar are the women's ululations of joy, or the ability to "overplay" the cries of dispute between cafe patrons during a football match on television. This production competence is socially stratified: it depends on gender, age, social class, etc. The attention modes, the perception's thresholds, the meaning given to the sounds, the respective position of the tolerable and the intolerable—all this is experienced differently by everyone but with certain sociological patterns.

The acquisition of this competence and this knowledge is sometimes socially problematized or acknowledged: socially, such as your authority to call the waiter, also professionally such as the cries of the microbus touts, or the street peddlers who can pitch their voice (often nasal) to carry in their sound environment, or the fluency of the *nabatšī* (see Puig 2010), the MC of popular street weddings.

- **Document 6:** A street greengrocer's cry in the residential Doqqi neighborhood, Cairo, December 5, 2009, 1:21 p.m. (Recorded by Vincent Battesti). Her cry is very modulated and difficult to perform but highly recognizable by the potential customers.

Moreover, these competences are learned, and evolve over time: they have a history. With the Egyptian Revolution of 25 January (2011), new competences spread: the appreciation and participation in demonstrations' ambiances are, from a social perspective, a new thing for many Cairenes. Arguably, for the last decades in Cairo, the first training in demonstration dates back to late 2002 with the mobilizations against the war launched by the U.S. in Iraq, and then in 2005 with the demonstrations related to "Kifāya!" movement ("Enough!", al-Ahnaf 2011), and this culminated of course with the last, ongoing, revolution.

- **Document 7:** Street demonstration against an American invasion of Iraq, a few left-wing intellectuals met and enjoyed coming back to the street (unthinkable for a long time), on the sidewalk in front of Sayeda Zeynab mosque, Cairo, February 15, 2003, 1:21 p.m. (Recorded by Vincent Battesti).

Hitherto, demonstrations involved mostly few urban actors close to intellectual, artistic, and left-wing political circles, but new social groups, lower middle class and urban proletariat, have since experienced and learned to take part in the festive or electric ambiances, learning for instance patterns become fairly universal (enjoying and singing political slogans like "*al-šaɛab yurīd isqāt al-niẓām*"—the people demand the fall of the regime).

- **Document 8:** Street demonstration for the January 25 Revolution, and against the military, by protesters of different social classes on Talaat Harb street and Tahrīr square, Downtown, Cairo, October 31, 2011, 10:38 p.m. (Recorded by Vincent Battesti).

The Form and Its Means

The form of sound ambiances depends on both the means of production combined with the invested intentions and local possibilities of arrangement of these productions. These means are both the presence and use of audio production tools, and the availability of a material and social context of production.

Silence is hardly ever total. The silence of a mosque or a Coptic church, apart from the ritual celebrations, has the tinge given by the architecture, the marble or the carpets, the murmuring of the city. The social and material contexts could be the royal Poinciana (*Delonix regia* Raf.) in Doqqi (a middle-class residential area) where certain species of whistling birds nest, or the unevenness of a narrow street of beaten earth near the butcher's in the old Islamic Cairo good for penning in bleating sheep, or these more or less green open spaces or building roofs where children play soccer or fly a kite, loudly, or that balcony building whose owner did not dare refuse allowing the self-proclaimed muezzin of the neighborhood to install a loudspeaker and so on.

- **Document 9:** At dusk, birds that populate a huge villa's garden, in the chic residential part of Mansuriyya, country suburb of Cairo, February 25, 2007, 7:00 p.m. (Recorded by Vincent Battesti). No doubt those who can afford to enjoy such a sound ambiance in Cairo are a very happy few (this bourgeois villa belongs to a businessman and former minister).

They are both tools and settings: a setting of Haussmann-like buildings in downtown Cairo does not offer the same sound opportunities as do the alleys of Fatimid Cairo or this deep and narrow lane between high red brick buildings of the *εašwā'iyyāt*, the said "informal" suburban districts (built without official authorization). Here and there, the asphalt is rare, the reverberations and absorption play differently, and automobile and pedestrian traffic vary. The density of human bodies ranks among the relevant variables, especially regarding the ambiances: despite the undergoing homogenization (800 to 1,500 inhabitants per hectare in Cairo), the megalopolis remains one of the densest global cities, with high disparities (7 inhabitants per hectare in Maadi, a chic suburb, for instance). Whether these spaces are structured by the vegetal (parks) or mineral (neighborhoods), the "soul" (*rūḥ*) of the place matters for their Cairene users, whose first manifestation is the co-presence of other human beings, sonic transmitters and receptors (Battesti 2006). Strollers come to enjoy the ambiance and take part in the show the city generates by looking at or listening to itself.

More regular means of sound production exist, whether or not it was their first design: the megaphone of the preacher collecting for a hypothetical new mosque, the roar of a truck, the clinking of glasses, the gurgling of narghilé, the scraping of PVC chairs dragged on the pavement, the hum of thousands of *takīf* (air conditioners) and so on.

- **Document 10:** Same day, two and a half hours later, ambiance in a local café of Suleymān Gawhar (Doqqi), with patrons playing *tawla* (backgammon) and dominoes, smoking *šīša* (narghilé), February 25, 2007, 9:30 p.m. (Recorded by Vincent Battesti).

We cannot neglect the world of audiocassettes, widely amplifying popular music from Vespas and microbuses in the public space (Puig 2011) or Muslim sermons that accompany everyday life (Hirschkind 2006). Obviously, means are inequitably shared out in the Cairo urban society: producing sound with a combustion engine requires owning a car, an unaffordable luxury for most people; preaching an Islamic sermon requires know-how (and first off, being a Muslim), etc.

The form of the sound environment is therefore reliant on the arrangement of these means of sound production. This leads to a consideration first of layout and patterns, and second of aesthetics.

Concerning layout, all means of production are not implemented all together, of course, but selectively. No one imagines firecrackers at the mosque, but in the street during religious festivals, nor megaphones in a cafe, but loud radio or television, with Egyptian light music or American wrestling, as sound background is well conceived. With "aural postcard experiments", it was clear that some patterns make sense to Cairo people, for instance: cars and newsboys or *šibšib* and "people greeting each other".

The notion of esthetics is therefore obvious since there are voluntary productions and assessments. When the urban working classes claim "the atmosphere is great" (*al-gaw ḥalū*) in a park at a given time, it means they are experiencing something likely to qualify this time and this place, it means they attach a great importance to their feelings, even if hard to express, and finally it means they come here to partake in this ambiance (see the Giza Zoo in Cairo, Battesti 2006). Difficult to formulate, assessment criteria would vary at least between good and bad, good taste and bad taste. The dividing line between them is shifting, notably according to social categories. To define in a word the popular aesthetics (that make sense for most) of a "great (sound) ambiance", I would pick "saturation". It could be the electrical saturation (amplifier effect), but more generally the saturation of the sound space. Excellent examples are the popular wedding street parties (the *faraḥ baladī*) or the *mawālid* (plural of *mūlid*, simultaneously saint festival and patronal fair). There, amplified music with electro-saturation effects—which would be avoided (almost) anywhere in the world—fills all the public space and dominates it.

- **Document 11:** Saturated sound space in the popular neighborhood of Sayeda Zeynab during her *mawlīd*, the annual saint's festival (for a week), Cairo, October 1, 2002, 11:26 p.m. (Recorded by Vincent Battesti).

The muezzin as well tends to push the effects (echo and reverb) of his prayer hall loudspeaker. Even more than esthetics, in Cairo we come close perhaps to the notion of *ṭarab*: the absolute and positive assessment, a state of ecstasy while listening to music and lyrics. Some ambiances do indeed induce trance (especially during *mawālid*), but do Cairenes pursue this *ṭarab* through more mundane urban ambiances?

Figure 7.2 In a packed street, a newsstand on the immediate edge of Tahrir Square, Wast al-Balad, Cairo, April 11, 2011, 8:28 p.m.
Photo: Vincent Battesti.

The Production

This rubric will deal with the sound production issue in urban ambiances through spaces and times of production, coproductions, and ends of production. Unlike a "deterritorialized" electronic music listenable on any medium, a sound ambiance has to be experienced in its space-time of production.

- **Document 12:** Religious sounds (prayer from a small mosque nearby) heard in a composed ambiance with other incidental and accidental sounds during a walk inside an informal overcrowded market in Azbakiyya, downtown border, Cairo, February 19, 2007 (Recorded by Vincent Battesti).

In other words, ambiances are necessarily part of precise spatialities and temporalities. They also have producers, often multiple, who may or may not share a common purpose.

- **Document 13:** Religious sounds (Friday's sermon from the local mosque) heard in a composed ambiance with other incidental and accidental sounds, from an apartment in the neighborhood of Suleymān Gawhar, Doqqi, Cairo, February 16, 2007 (Recorded by Vincent Battesti).

Urban spaces are not only a physical potential of sound effects: their qualifications by people of Cairo—what they say about them, how they

use them—turn spaces into places (Depaule 1991). The old town is qualified differently from downtown, or a middle-class neighborhood, or a gated
community of recent nearby desert towns. Some practices are possible here
and not there. Urban users are limited by formal and informal regulations
(Battesti 2006) to such-and-such sound productions. The mesh can be even
thinner: open spaces differ from enclosed spaces; what can be done on an
avenue is not what can be done in these downtown passages: the ambiance is
different because its users and "producers" read or hear that the atmosphere
is more intimate there and feel they should comply with it.

What applies to the space of production applies to the time of production. The sound event can be unique (a demonstration, a street altercation,
a crowd pursuing a thief) while having to happen in a peculiar place. The
sound event can occur at given hours and punctuates the course of the day
(a typical example is the structuring contribution of calls to prayer). A sound
environment or any part of it (a sound event) may recur daily like pupils
coming out the school or the closing of stores' metal shutters, or may vary
in intensity with the course of day (more or fewer cafe or street restaurant
patrons, more or fewer hawkers)—and needless to say with night and day
(for some neighborhoods, this does not contrast silence with noise but different ambiances)—with the course of the seasons—temperatures change
the sound, and the incessant hum of *takīf* (air conditioners) stops in the fall.

Sound environments are inherent to space-time, as are soundscapes. Tim
Ingold rightly criticized the neologism "soundscape" (2007). The definition
here of "soundscape" (*paysage sonore*) is my own (Battesti 2013) as I distinguish "soundscapes" from "sound environments" by the regularity or the
reproducibility of the sensory event, of the set of sound effects that gives it its
iconic nature and allows identifying it as the sound signature of an (urban)
territory. A bell sound is a bell sound; it is a sound event. A bell sound mixed
with other incidental sounds, composite or composed, still do not together
make a clear identifiable signature (the situation can be recognized but not
identified yet as a space/time signature, as an iconic sign): it is a "sound
environment". The "sound landscape" (or soundscape) is therefore a combination of sound events that signs a place and a time, an identifiable "sound
environment" (it remains to be seen who can read the signature).

The various examples of ambiance productions given above demonstrate
that they often depend upon more than a single producer. We should therefore think of them as "co-productions", since an accumulation of producers
and productions often happens. Although sound productions are restricted
in place and time, "ambiance producers" most often seem chaotically to
join in a whole that makes sense as ambiance only at that holistic level (the
principle of emergent phenomena). However, since there are layouts and
patterns, this "sound individualism" is never complete. Even actual cases
of deliberate coproductions can be given. Music performances are obvious
examples of coordinated people shaping an ambiance, but the usual "horn
concerts" in the heavy Cairo traffic clearly are also: an acknowledged fact is

that the police officer directing the traffic at an intersection changes the direction only under the pressure of the vehicles expressing their impatience by sounding their horn, and there is an actual rhythmic cooperation of motorists to break the official down. Different grades of productive cooperation could be distinguished, from "one to one" (I coordinate with one other, and it can spread eventually to more people) to "one to all" (I agree with the dominant ambiance to "add" my own production to it).

• **Document 14:** Cries close to screams of young peddlers selling T-shirts at night on Talaat Harb street, Downtown Cairo, April 14, 2011, 8:20 p.m. (Recorded by Vincent Battesti). With the revolution, people took up the street again, especially vendors. In strong competition, they cry or scream to draw customers, but nonetheless they sometimes cooperate to create a specific street ambiance.

Finally, what about the intentionality of this production? Let us say that any action-producing sound is grounded on intentionality: it cannot be said, however, that all the produced sounds were intentional. They could be incidental to the main purpose of the action. Cairenes have to move around in the urban fabric, the carpenter has to work the wood, the butcher the meat, etc. Nonetheless, sounds accompany the action; they can be enjoyed or expected. The sound production can also be manifest and deliberate. The intentions can be to back an idea of party, celebration, leisure-activity, urbanity, aesthetic, protest, wellness, or to draw customers or believers, to announce the urban culture you belong to, etc. The purpose of a sound production can be nil or to overthrow a regime.

Views Expressed

The last rubric of this analytical grid concerns the language used and the views expressed about the sound of urban Cairo life. Some sound ambiances may offer the opportunity for discourse; not all are a discursive object.

Broadly speaking, all sensorial feedback loops between perception and sensation—fast-flowing (almost synchronous) and self-fulfilling—are often unconscious, probably avoiding cognitive overload. Does the unconscious nature of the mechanism explain why they are so poorly "expressible"? Anyway, only a few words are in use in Cairo to verbalize this sound dimension, even though ambiance is a central dimension of urban life.

This phenomenon is actually recurrent in sensorial studies and deprives the ethnologist of his main material. To have urban actors of public spaces say more than "I like" (*baḥibb*) or "I don't like" (*mabaḥibbš*), possibly "it's noisy" (*dawša*), is rare and difficult and the verbalization restricted to hedonic or intensity terms is a real challenge. "The atmosphere is great" (*al-gaw ḥalū*). That's it.

Two types of discourses differ in this case, those of Cairenes in/on the public space, and those of a smaller population of intellectuals, politicians, and media people in the public sphere. The latter have over the past few years gone through a wide public debate—in which the notion of "noise pollution" occurs—about the governmental decision to replace the thousands of amplified muezzins by an automatic, synchronous, and centralized broadcasting of recorded *azān*, call to prayer (Battesti 2013 and in detail Farag 2009). Indeed, the language used and the views expressed on the sound component of the city vary according to the social class of the speaker and of the addressees, with obvious intentions of distinction, in the sense Bourdieu (1979) means it. People from any Cairo neighborhood do not talk of their own ambiances in the same way they would talk about the ambiances of the others: Cairo is a juxtaposition of urban micro-cultures (about urban "over-differentiation", see Battesti and Puig 2011), which are all different sensorial and perceptual universes. To be a little simplistic (but to take up the classical local bipolarity), silence is adorned with virtues in the discourse of the upper classes (*al-būrgwasiyya*), which are now freed from urban sounds through residential segregation (in private neighborhoods, gardens, or cities, they say they value the muffled ambiance in cozy lounges, a withdrawal from the hub-bub, see also Said 2013), and on the contrary, popular classes (*šaɛabiyya*), always associated by the former with the noisy (*dawša*) and dense (*zaḥma*) crowd, express their satisfaction at the warmth of pleasant (and festive) company, of the reassuring "sound coating" of the neighborhood environment. The latter see the silence of the former as possibly desirable—far beyond the issue of loudness—because associated with a comfortable life, with the signature of a *rāqī* (luxury) neighborhood. Popular classes, however, also quickly associate this silence with loneliness and isolation, whereas the primary wealth of popular universes is the interlacing of social networks, the density of the fabric of everyday encounters necessary for survival in an informal economy. Upper classes celebrate *zaḥma* and *dawša* ambiance only as a form of nostalgia for the popular, without any desire to experience it: for them, *zaḥma* and *dawša*, much like poverty, dirt, and rustic ignorance, are popular. A "muted" fear keeps them away from getting a foothold in these neighborhoods (see Battesti and Puig 2011).

This last rubric most lacks the resources to run its program. Tools for analyzing a verbalization of the intimate relation to the sound environment have to be improved upon or invented.

Getting Cairenes to Verbalize

Keeping my distance from the linguistic determinism (the Sapir-Whorf hypothesis) which assumes that "we conceive a universe that the language has already patterned" (Benveniste 1966: 6), the fact remains that I have to consider semantic distinctions and inbuilt ontologies within the language: obviously, language affects the ways we conceptualize our world, our *world view*, or *world hearing*, as it may be. Furthermore, as we use language as a medium to share our perception of the world, a better understanding of the words used to express the everyday life experience remains the requisite for social researchers.

I already brought up two different procedures employed in the Cairo fieldwork: the "aural postcard experiment" and the "mics in the ears" experimental setup. The first procedure was used to get interesting, but insufficient, data. With this technique, some words already came out, especially to describe the general ambiance, and fortunately also some local—*emic*—categorizations of Cairo neighborhoods according to the sound status evaluated by Cairenes (noisy, quiet, or jammed, crowded, etc.), and according to some sound-key features: footsteps, peddlers' screams, greetings, tone and accent of the voice, presence of Vespas, etc. It would be possible to establish a cartography of preferences, of liked and disliked sounds ambiances of Cairo, suited to each social groups, but we would have learned nothing about the way people live or experience this sound dimension.

To be closer to the intimate and daily experience, we had to find access to another stage of verbalization. First to get a set of local descriptors, a terminological survey seems unavoidable. It was the first purpose of this procedure, the "mics in the ears", Nicolas Puig and I set up: an innovative experimental procedure, still under development. A dozen in-depth interviews reassured us about its efficiency (a later paper will present detailed results).

A Procedure: In the Street

The technique uses stereo binaural microphones/earphones (Roland), small enough to fit inside the ears (like intra-aural headphones), along with a digital recorder and a GPS device. We asked people to have a daily walk route in their neighborhood—or from home to work, to go shopping in local stores, etc.—for twenty to thirty minutes alone with this non-intrusive equipment.

It is not the recording of a "soundscape". This technique results in a unique and personal experiment and gives unique and personal results, specific to an informant and a space-time. But still, only sounds reaching informant's ears are recorded, not what this informant is listening to. I haven't yet stressed this dimension in this text, but we will simply quote Barry Truax (1978: vi–vii) who wrote thirty-five years ago:

> In any of these measuring systems, no matter how sophisticated, one sound is treated similarly to any other sound; there is no way to distinguish what meaning the sound has for those making or hearing it, [. . .] whether it is perceived as background or foreground, wanted or unwanted. In other words, any such device or system treats sound as a signal to be processed, instead of information to be understood.

I am not looking for an objective or unbiased recording, quite the opposite: even the shape of the informant's head plays a role (the shape of the nose and ears, of the use of a veil or not, etc.), and also, of course, how this informant behaves in the street, bends his/her head, greets people, and turns his/her head to talk, or to react to sound, smell, contact, and visual *stimuli*— especially because while walking, his/her environment is changing (the use of a "dummy head" would not render that). His/her body is immersed in the city ambiance. These recordings are the most accurate reproduction of the reality experienced by the informant. However, microphones are recording everything: background and sound events, regardless of their personal or social qualities.

A Procedure: After the Walk

A second step has to take place: the "reactivated listening". The idea of *écoute réactivée* dates back from twenty years ago (Amphoux 1993: 22–30), but this technique, perfected by Augoyard (2001), relies on listening to a montage of recorded sound ambiance. The approach here differs in the way our informants have to listen to their own and very personal twenty-thirty-minute recording (during which recording they did not practice expert listening), not our montage. Therein this listening is, for us, "reactivated" (the psychoacoustic effect of binaural recordings are noticeable) or we should say, "re-immersed": informants are brought back into their own actions, movements, and displacements in their neighborhood. They are reliving their routine trip in the city, and here we record their comments: "Please, tell us what do you hear?" We expect to produce reaction, to induce reflexiveness, beyond the simple dichotomy of hedonic or intensity terms. We are interested in the very words (in Egyptian/Cairo Arabic) used by our informants as descriptors. The form adopted to express this hearing reactivation interests us also: for instance, slow speech flow, gestures of concentration, and use of "I" (people speak in the first person) express the recollection of this precise daily walk.

The GPS device helps us to check the route the informant took, and accompanying the comments, it helps to spot the threshold effects, when "entering" a *hāra* (sub-neighborhood, alley), entering a shopping street, home, a new ambiance, etc. After the listening, we always have a brief further talk with the informant to deepen some topics.

Some First Results

To relive one's own walk is not an easy task. Informants can at first be confused by the experience: to hear through headphones is obviously an acquired skill. And maybe especially for this kind of recording: they are Hi-Fi stereo binaural recordings, creating a 3-D stereo sound thanks to psycho-physiological properties of human hearing for localization of sounds: unlike light—ear space is not eye space—sounds can come from everywhere, other rooms, other streets, other spaces, and be heard. It is the ubiquity effect (on this, read Augoyard and Torgue 2006). The listener will get the sensation of actually being in the very same situation as the informant recording his/her walk (and all the more since the listener is the informant).

Aside from this small confusion, the personalities of our informants are an important factor to consider. It is always a challenge for a social anthropologist to link up the particular and the collective, psychological, and social dimensions. We first tested this procedure with inhabitants of Cairo among our acquaintances or usual informants. Nicolas Puig and I have both known most of them for a long time and so assumed interpreting the results would be easier. To present samples of the results here, I will refer to two people from the same family: Wā'el, living in historic Islamic Cairo, and Malak, one of his daughters, married and living at the far end of city, Baštīl, part of ɛašwā'iyyāt "informal" districts. All are popular neighborhood dwellers and poor.

Malak went to buy some electrical wires with her three-year-old son. During her walk in her neighborhood, head covered by her veil (she is a Muslim), she was in constant interaction with her child. During the reactivated listening, she gave us a minute and detailed description of every element she heard. She started to describe her actions and to repeat every conversation she had or simply heard in the street, but she was most focused on herself, on her own movement, and seemed constantly on the go. But movements are dual-actions or dual-systems of reference: her movement and the movement of the world. For instance, she commented: "I go downstairs . . . this is the sound/noise of the wedding [in streets of the neighborhood], it is loud, the wedding, Ibrahim [her son], a car coming along the [narrow] street, the wedding, it's noisy, the wedding gets further and further away".

With Wā'el, it was different. The father is also a working-class musician. The sound dimension of the experiment interests him but the performing dimension of the experiment, much less. This walk seemed to him useless and especially since he could not take his mobile phone (I feared possible interferences with the mics). He took a few cigarettes at least but left with the feeling of a *fāḍī* (useless) walk, even if his wife found the opportunity to ask him to get something from the store. Contrary to his wife, nonetheless, he is, in the street, playing the customary affable man, observing the *bienséances* (proprieties), cheering a lot of people. He knows his male lines in the (popular) Cairo human comedy. Concomitantly, Wā'el was very forthcoming when time came to give his comments, but it was actually less localizing his route in the neighborhood than giving a lot of theories about his own society. He started like the others ("Here is the sound/noise of the street . . ."), but he slipped quickly into interpretation:

> man has been created to live in society, and in the sounds here we hear, in the relationships here we hear, there's a lot of humanity, because we're walking in the street, a narrow street, and the sound of motorcycles is annoying, and I endure that, and at the same time, I let him get away with it, because he finds it worth his while, because life's going on, and

all of us have to bear each other, and perhaps I've a motorcycle too that bothers my neighbor and my neighbor tolerates it, and that's an aspect of love, that's love. But, from another point of view, we can regard it as noise pollution.

Although unequal or uneven, none of our experiments has "failed". Much is meaningful: words used to describe this part of the sound environment, and silence to pass over this other one. These verbalizations make audible the sound experience of a life in Cairo.

With careful generalization, it would be possible to move on issues for which Schaeffer's theories and semiology (1966) will be useful. For instance the distinction made between "natural listening" and "discriminative listening" on the one hand and "reduced listening", as the latter is not actually used: informants refer to sound events only as signified, vehicles of exchanges or social situation ("a child cries", "the call to prayer begins"), no one describes the quality of the sound itself, the signifier, or qualifies the music heard; they just notice the "wedding event" (ordinary listening). To take this study further, we should investigate the notion of intentionality, as sound seems to be heard at least as indices (in the semiotics sense), as something that can be interpreted as having an unintentional meaning ("[I hear] The butcher's boy is pounding the meat with a mallet", so I'm near the butcher), and which is nonetheless able therefore to communicate information to the listener ("[I hear] this guy tooting his horn because he's in a hurry"). This semiotic

Figure 7.3 Coffee patrons on the sidewalk, looking at the television, in the loud ambiance of the popular neighborhood of Darb al-Aḥmar, old Islamic Cairo, March 31, 2011, 9:53 p.m.

Photo: Vincent Battesti.

perspective seems fruitful, as it is possible to distinguish between index and sign—the sign is with the clear intent of passing on a message ("A woman has an argument with a child", "The call to payer just started").

Conclusion

To conclude, I must repeat that the analytical grid has no pretention of being definitive but of offering an anthropological hold on the sound dimension of a city, received and produced by Cairo's inhabitants. Our "mics in the ear" experiment is still a work in progress. This study we conduct in Cairo has a double perspective: to document the local perception of sound environment, and also to think about a sound ecology of Cairo.

Our experiments underway engage our informants in a kind of introspective work: urging people to verbalize, to put their everyday relationships into words or speech, as listeners and producers of the sound dimension of their city. They perform a selection of relevant sound phenomena, but still we are not sure they all choose to "voice" the same "classes" of those sound phenomena, which are audible or inaudible to them. So far, our Cairo informants have more pointed to sound as vehicle than described the sonorities: maybe the average Cairo citizen is much more a semiologist than an acoustician.

We may have to dig up issues raised by Edward T. Hall; he contrasted "Arabs and Americans" to underline "how the senses are used by different peoples" (1966: 3). Beyond cultural approaches and stereotypes about "Arabs", interesting considerations concerning proxemics and the abilities to screen out sound remain. In Wā'el's comments, the notion of the self-regulations of proprieties regarding the daily sound dimension already came up (Goffman 1956 would be useful). The idea that in urban—especially popular—situations, people have to cope with others, because their lives encroach upon one another, seems contrary to the right to quietness and tranquility demanded by members of other social classes. The study has to be continued.

- **Document 15:** Saturated sound space during the popular annual saint Festival of Sayeda Zeynab, during the *layla kabīra* (the last and greatest night of the *mawlīd*), Cairo, September 24, 2003, 0:37 a.m. (Recorded by Vincent Battesti).

Notes

1 This chapter uses and summarizes in part work published in French (Battesti 2013), with the permission of its editors J. Candau and M.-B. Le Gonidec.
2 "*Écoute réduite*", named in this way in reference to the notion of phenomenological reduction (*epoche*).
3 Passage taken from the lyrics of Bayram Ettounsi's song, c.1920, "*Hatgann*" ("I go crazy").

References

al-Ahnaf, Mustapha. 2011. "Débats intellectuels et intellectuels en débat." In *L'Égypte au présent: Inventaire d'une société avant révolution*, edited by Vincent Battesti and François Ireton, 1105–1151. Paris: Actes Sud/Sindbad.

Amphoux, Pascal. 1993. *L'identité sonore des villes européennes*. Vol. 1, *Techniques d'enquêtes*. Grenoble: CRESSON.

Augoyard, Jean-François. 2001. "Entretien sur écoute réactivée." In *L'espace urbain en méthodes*, edited by Michèle Grosjean and Jean-Paul Thibaud, 127–152. Marseille: Éditions Parenthèses.

Augoyard, Jean-François and Henry Torgue. 2006. *Sonic Experience: A Guide to Everyday Sounds*. Montreal: McGill-Queen's University Press.

Battesti, Vincent. 2006. "The Giza Zoo: Re-Appropriating Public Spaces, Re-Imagining Urban Beauty." In *Cairo Cosmopolitan: Politics, Culture, and Urban Space in the New Globalized Middle East*, edited by Diane Singerman and Paul Amar, 489–511. Cairo: The American University in Cairo Press.

———. 2009. "Ambiances sonores du Caire: Proposer une anthropologie des environnements sonores." *Les Cahiers du GERHICO* 13: 35–49.

———. 2013. "'L'ambiance est bonne' ou l'évanescent rapport aux paysages sonores au Caire: Invitation à une écoute participante et proposition d'une grille d'analyse." In *Paysages sensoriels: Essai d'anthropologie de la construction et de la perception de l'environnement sonore*, edited by Joël Candau and Marie-Barbara Le Gonidec, 70–95. Paris: Éditions du Comité des travaux historiques et scientifiques (CTHS).

Battesti, Vincent and Nicolas Puig. 2011. "Comment peut-on être urbain? Villes et vies urbaines." In *L'Égypte au présent: Inventaire d'une société avant révolution*, edited by Vincent Battesti and François Ireton, 145–182. Paris: Actes Sud/Sindbad.

Benveniste, Émile. 1966. *Problèmes de linguistique générale*. Vol. 1. Paris: Gallimard.

Bourdieu, Pierre. 1979. *La distinction: Critique sociale du jugement*. Paris: Édition de Minuit.

Bregman, Albert S. 1990. *Auditory Scene Analysis: The Perceptual Organization of Sound*. Cambridge: MIT Press.

Candau, Joël. 2010. "Intersensorialité humaine et cognition sociale." *Communications* 1 (86): 25–36.

Chion, Michel. 1983. *Guide des objets sonores: Pierre Schaeffer et la recherche musicale*. Paris: Buchet/Chastel and Institut national de la communication audiovisuelle.

Corbin, Alain. 1990. "Histoire et anthropologie sensorielle." *Anthropologie et sociétés* 14 (2): 13–24.

Depaule, Jean-Charles. 1991. "Des espaces qualifiés: Présentation." *Égypte/Monde arabe* 5: 7–12.

Farag, Iman. 2009. "Querelle de minarets en Égypte: Le débat public sur l'appel à la prière." *Revue des mondes musulmans et de la Méditerranée* 125: 47–66.

Feld, Steven. 1984. "Sound Structure as Social Structure." *Ethnomusicology* 28 (3): 383–409.

Goffman, Erving. 1956. *The Presentation of Self in Everyday Life*. Edinburgh: University of Edinburgh.

Hall, Edward Twitchell. 1966. *The Hidden Dimension*. Garden City: Doubleday & Company.

Hirschkind, Charles. 2006. *The Ethical Soundscape: Cassette Sermons and Islamic Counterpublics*. New York: Columbia University Press.

Ingold, Tim. 2007. "Against Soundscape." In *Autumn Leaves: Sound and the Environment in Artistic Practice*, edited by Angus Carlyle, 10–13. Paris: Double entendre/CRiSAP.

Puig, Nicolas. 2010. *Farah, Musiciens de noces et scènes urbaines au Caire*. Paris: Actes Sud/Sindbad.

———. 2011. "Musiques et usages sociaux de la culture." In *L'Égypte au présent: Inventaire d'une société avant révolution*, edited by Vincent Battesti and François Ireton, 1035–1063. Paris: Actes Sud/Sindbad.

Said, Nora Gamal. 2013. "Cairo behind the Gates: Studying the Sensory Configuration of Al-Rehab City." *Ambiances*. http://ambiances.revues.org/252.

Schaeffer, Pierre. 1966. *Traité des objets musicaux: Essai interdisciplines*. Paris: Éditions du Seuil.

Thibaud, Jean-Paul. 2001. "La méthode des parcours commentés." In *L'espace urbain en méthodes*, edited by Michèle Grosjean and Jean-Paul Thibaud, 79–99. Marseille: Éditions Parenthèses.

Truax, Barry. 1978. "Introduction." In *Handbook for Acoustic Ecology*, edited by Barry Truax, v–ix. Vancouver: Simon Fraser University and ARC Publications.

———. 1984. *Acoustic communication*. Norwood, N.J.: Ablex Pub. Corp.

8 Mapping Out the Sounds of Urban Transformation

The Renewal of Lisbon's Mouraria Quarter[1]

Iñigo Sánchez

The Mouraria is a densely populated inner-city neighborhood of winding streets, rundown buildings and a long history of marginalization. Despite its privileged central location, close to Lisbon's downtown and at the foot of one of the city's main tourist attractions, the Castelo de São Jorge, the Mouraria has been conceived of as a territory on the margins of the city ever since its emergence as a Moorish quarter in the twelfth century. First built as a segregated space for the defeated Moors, it then came to be seen as a poor and disadvantaged neighborhood, then as a dangerous and unhealthy place, and finally as a multi-ethnic quarter subject to urban renewal (Menezes 2004: 23–70). The area is home to a heterogeneous population of longtime residents, settled migrants, new immigrants and a recent wave of new residents. Often associated with images of exoticism and multiculturalism, the neighborhood still retains the atmosphere of an "urban village," a repository of history, popular traditions and memories associated with a vernacular popular culture. At the same time, the Mouraria has the aura of being a sordid, dangerous and gritty place, lacking the charm of other historic quarters of the city. These multiple images coexist in the shared public imaginary of the neighborhood (see Menezes 2004).

- **Document 1:** Two neighbors talking from their apartment windows. Travessa do Terreirinho, 27/6/2012. Recorded by Iñigo Sánchez Fuarros.

After decades of neglect and sporadic efforts to address social and physical conditions, the Mouraria was back in the urban spotlight in 2009 when the mayor of Lisbon announced a €12 million plan to revitalize the area.[2] In 2011 the Mouraria embarked on an ambitious two-year urban renewal program called the QREN-Mouraria Action Plan.[3] Following the logic of contemporary urban renewal schemes, the program strives to "open the neighborhood to the city [. . .] and create the conditions to attract private investment, new residents and tourists."[4]

Two years after the arrival of cranes and bulldozers, the physical transformation of certain parts of the neighborhood—streets, buildings and public open spaces—is complete. A new touristic trail crosscuts the neighborhood, motor-vehicle traffic was reduced, new infrastructures have been created and some squares and public spaces have been renovated. Simultaneously, a community development plan involving a consortium of local agencies, grassroots community associations and third-sector organizations was launched to improve residents' quality of life, combat poverty and social exclusion, boost the local economy and attract new residents and most of all, visitors.[5]

This chapter explores the impact of this urban renewal scheme on the Mouraria's sensory environment. By charting some of the new acoustic territories and the changing sonorities of a neighborhood in transformation, the present chapter embraces sound as a means of "exploring the more ephemeral and shifting elements of urbanism" (Atkinson 2007: 1905), namely those qualities of the environment—like ambient sound—that give urban places their unique and distinctive character (Degen 2008, Thibaud 2011). In this sense, the physical makeover and cultural reinvention that the Mouraria is undergoing has wider implications for the sensory qualities of the urban environment. The refashioning of its urban spaces has reshaped the sound environment in significant ways. Moreover, sound and music have been actively used as catalysts for this transformation. New sounds have been introduced into the everyday soundscapes, whereas other distinctive soundmarks have changed or disappeared as a result of the revitalization process. Some of these changes in the sound environment are common to other urban renewal efforts (such as the mitigation of traffic noise due to the pedestrianization of certain areas, or the perennial stream of construction noise filling the air), but other sound interventions are time—and site—specific. This is the case in the three brief ethnographic vignettes around which the chapter is built. Each vignette takes a closer listen to the changes in the sound environment of three iconic urban spaces of the Mouraria: the *Largo da Severa*, the Praça do Martim Moniz and the Largo do Intendente. Together, these three examples offer different points for listening to the new acoustic territorialization of a neighborhood in transformation.

The first case study examines one of the many initiatives embracing *fado*, a popular genre of urban song that developed in Lisbon in the second quarter of the nineteenth century, as a valuable asset for the transformation of the neighborhood from the renewal program's very outset. After decades of absence, the mournful melodies of the Portuguese national musical style resound again in the small streets of what it is considered the "cradle" of this genre, reshaping the sensory experience and perception of the place. The second example describes the transformation of the blurred and hazy sound environment of an open public square, the Praça do Martim Moniz, into a controlled acoustic enclave in which the sounds of carefully selected pre-recorded music structure and regulate the uses of this public space. Finally I examine the role that noise abatement policies play in upscaling a zone known for prostitution and the illegal drug trade. I discuss the controversy surrounding a group of resilient local bars located in the Largo do Intendente

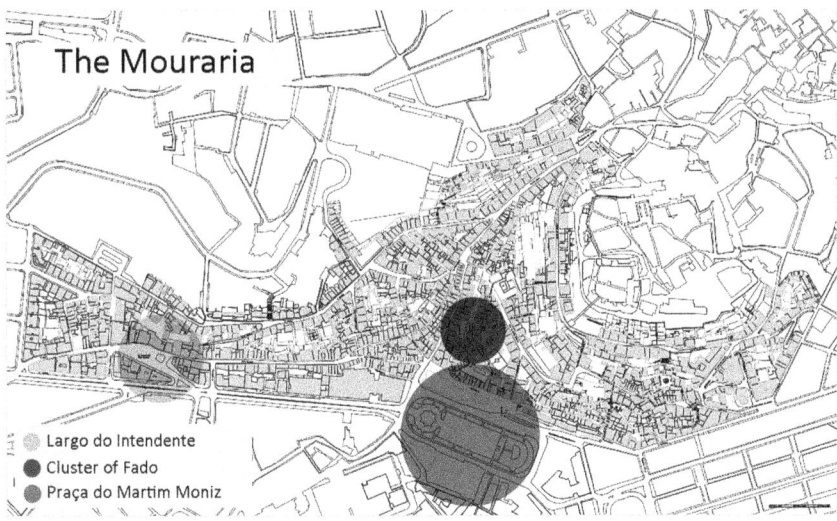

Figure 8.1 Map of the Mouraria.

that are in the municipality's sights for their association with "noisy," "unde-sirable" and "marginal" activities.

This chapter is based on field research conducted in the Mouraria since the Autumn 2011, mostly in the form of observations, informal conversations and participation in the everyday life of the neighborhood. In addition, I conducted participant observation in official meetings and other institutional events. The research also included consultation of blogs, social media and newspapers.

Returning Fado to the Mouraria's Public Space

On a pleasant summer evening, a dense crowd crawls along the gloomy Rua do Capelão, a small, narrow side street that penetrates deep into the maze of tortuous streets that characterize this area of the Mouraria. A local guide with a megaphone explains the place's significance in the history of *fado* to the visitors.[6] The story is that there, in the labyrinth of streets and dark alleyways, in the old bars and brothels, among prostitutes, aristocrats and ruffians, *fado* was born in the mid-nineteenth century.[7] Although rich in history and memories of its legendary past as a *fadista* quarter, today there are barely any remaining material or sonic traces of that period other than a few nameplates or the amplified sound of *Rádio Amália* playing in a small bar where a handful of visitors and local patrons enjoy a *ginjinha*, Lisbon's most typical liqueur.[8] Outside the bar, the metallic voice produced by the bullhorn—an unusual sound signal that manifests the Mouraria's recent incorporation into the city's touristic routes—cuts across the constant murmur of the audience, which is more focused on photographing every detail of its surroundings than attentively listening to the enthusiastic guide. Amplified by the spatial configuration of the place, the continuous drone of indistinct sounds disrupts the usual tranquility of the street where the legendary *fado* singer Maria Severa lived. A neighbor disturbed by the commotion leans out of her window to see what it is happening below; another beats his way through the crowd blocking the narrow side street. Never before has the presence of visitors been so visible and audible in the Mouraria's urban space.

Meanwhile, a group of local residents gathers around the benches of the Largo da Severa, a charming square located at the end of the Rua do Capelão. As neighbors arrive, they exchange sonorous greetings with their acquaintances. On days like these, the square becomes a hub of intense local social activity. A regular group of inhabitants attends the outdoor *fado* performances organized by the Museu do Fado (*Fado* Museum) in collaboration with a local grassroots association since the summer of 2012.[9] These musical acts are part of the *Visitas cantadas na Mouraria,* a series of free singing tours designed to attract visitors and tourists by combining a walking tour of the neighborhood with outdoor *fado* performances.[10] While participants from outside the neighborhood see these tours as an opportunity to "discover" this overlooked part of the city and listen to *fado* in its "natural" environment, these outdoor *fado* performances have opened new spaces of "music sociality" for local residents (Holt and Wergin 2013) in which interactions between "guests" and "hosts" are negotiated.

The sun is going down over the buildings and two *fadistas* (*fado* singers) chat away and share a cigarette while they wait for their performance. One of the guitarists warms up by playing some scales beside them. The wait is punctuated by jokes and banal conversation. The neighbor's voices' inflection, modulation and rhythmic pattern are important sonic markers that differentiate those born and raised in the neighborhood from outsiders. These voices' vocal materiality and melodic contour invest the place with a distinctive character. As the sound of the rowdy horde approaches, one of the neighbors exclaims, "Here come the tourists!" and moments later the Largo da Severa is flooded by a wave of people, mostly Lisbonites visiting the Mouraria for the first time, but also tourists and *fado* aficionados.

- **Document 2:** *Visitas cantadas* participants arrive at Largo da Severa and the fado performance starts. Largo da Severa, 22/9/2012. Recorded by Iñigo Sánchez Fuarros.

At this point, the *fadistas* and musicians take up their place. The staging is sober, only a few folding chairs and a round plastic table covered with a red polka-dot tablecloth. A piece of black fabric disguises the metallic fence protecting a building under construction, the future *Casa da Severa,*

Figure 8.2 Pedro Galveias and Conceição Ribeiro perform for visitors and local residents in the Largo da *Severa*.

Photo: Iñigo Sánchez Fuarros.

the first *fado* house to be opened in the Mouraria in decades. The crowd quickly forms a semicircle around the musicians. Some inhabitants follow the action from their apartment windows. As soon as the *fadista* starts singing, a bitter quarrel arises between one of the neighbors seated on a bench and a newcomer blocking her view of the musicians, the former admonishing the latter out loud with a "Shhhhh!" People ask for quiet, and the hubbub slowly fades away under the sorrowful tone of a fado song singing to the crumbling Mouraria.

The music is not amplified. The square is enclosed by three- to five-story buildings. Its reduced dimensions and confinement act as a natural resonating box. The pedestrian streets, the absence of automobile traffic and the "authentic" aura emanating from the aging buildings of this part of the neighborhood reinforce a feeling of time standing still. The absence of sound amplification enhances the perception of immediacy and the naturalness of the music. The performance is dominated by the customary silence that normally accompanies *fado* singing. However, the audience is strongly involved and interacts with the *fadistas* in various ways. During the most emotive moments exclamations such as "Ah, *fadista*!" can be heard; some people hum the song refrains in a low tone. When the *fadista* makes a reference to the Mouraria the neighbors explode with joy, enacting a resounding sense of belonging and community by calling out exclamations such as "*Ié, ié, ié. Mouraria é que é!*" ("Hey, hey, hey, there's no place like Mouraria") or "*A Mouraria é linda!*" ("Mouraria is the loveliest!").

- **Document 3:** Interaction between the *fado* singers and participants in the Visitas cantadas. Largo da Severa, 22/09/2012. Recorded by Iñigo Sánchez Fuarros.

But this ritual silence is also frequently broken by mundane sounds coming from the open windows of nearby apartments, birds singing or the outbursts of a well-known local boozer. In fact, the ordinary noises and rhythms of daily life do not stop while *fado* is being sung: a woman hangs clothes on her apartment's line to dry; a couple of drug addicts cross the square on their regular route to buy their daily dose; some men are playing cards on the veranda of a local bar; a domestic dispute erupts inside a house; etc. Music is ingrained in the daily sonic texture of the place as much as the everyday sounds of the Mouraria become an integral part of the music.

The status of *fado* as "an unquestionable identifying marker" of the Mouraria has placed this sonority at the forefront of the regeneration process.[11] The recent inauguration of a *fado* house and a permanent exhibition of *fado* portraits on the walls of the streets speak eloquently to efforts to create a new, easily recognizable, exportable and consumable urban image of the Mouraria as a *fadista* quarter. In this sense, *fado* has become the dominant soundmark of the renewed Mouraria. The sensory/sonic transformation of the Mouraria into a living *fadista* quarter has not only transformed the perception and experience of the place for outsiders but for its inhabitants as well, who have embraced this new sensory environment as a source of pride and empowerment.

The multiplication of sounds, images and symbols that attempt to set the *fadista* character of the neighborhood may turn the Mouraria into a(nother) theme park for tourism consumption, as was the case a few decades earlier in Alfama, Lisbon's *fado* quarter *par excellence*. This will be demonstrated in the next section. A possible side effect of the tourism-led renaissance of the Mouraria, thematizing the sound environment has been at the core of the renovation of the neighborhood's main open public space, the Praça do Martim Moniz, the example I will discuss next.

Tuning In to the Multicultural: The Praça do Martim Moniz

The Praça do Martim Moniz is a 1.5 hectare sun-bleached piazza built on the void left by the demolition of the lower Mouraria (see Colvin 2008). Named after a Christian knight who died trying to keep the city gates open during the crusade against the Moors, the space is dominated by the overwhelming presence of the Hotel Mundial and two massive shopping centers.[12] Opposite the tiny sixteenth-century Church of Nossa Senhora da Saúde, the only remnant of the old Mouraria that disappeared under the Estado Novo's "civilizing" urban crusade, stands a row of unfinished apartment blocks for sale under the promotional slogan *tenha uma casa com vistas para o fado* ("own a house with a *fado* view").[13] The promised view could not be more picturesque: old Mouraria's jumbled and aging architecture spreading across the northern slope of Sao Jorge castle.

The Praça do Martim Moniz is a transitional space that connects the Mouraria to the city center (Menezes 2009). Created in the fall of 1997, the plaza added new open space to a dense neighborhood that lacked in open public spaces. The square is surrounded by wide roads with fast-moving traffic. The relentless sound of cars is accentuated by the occasional sound of the tram horn, frequent ambulance sirens on their way to a nearby hospital and the constant circulation of trucks delivering goods to the area's prosperous wholesalers. The sparse concrete square outlined with green areas is accessible via several pedestrian crossings that are distributed all around its perimeter. Water is a central design element, with interactive fountains running its length and a big star-shaped fountain crowning the northern end. Entering the plaza from the south and approaching a replica of the medieval city gate in homage to the legendary Martim Moniz, the sound of rushing water creates an enveloping effect in the midst of the area's typical agitation. The sound of running water, along with the occasional sound of South-Asian children playing cricket and background traffic noise, are some of the mundane sounds that shape the square's muddled sound environment. However, a new sound event, which is both cause and effect of the place's new urban dynamics, has been recently incorporated to the plaza's everyday soundtrack: a continuous stream of amplified recorded music that comes from a PA system installed on the northern side.

- **Document 4:** The muddled sound environment in the vicinity of the Praça do Martim Moniz, 1/9/2012. Recorded by Iñigo Sánchez Fuarros.

In the shadows of the Mouraria's revitalization, the central area of the square has been transformed into a slick outdoor multicultural food court and weekend market.[14] Inaugurated in June 2012, the Mercado de Fusão has altered the square's morphology. Ten pre-existing kiosks have been adapted to house new food stalls that serve prepared food from different parts of the world: Japanese sushi and macrobiotic food, Peruvian *ceviche*, Cape Verdian *cachupa*, Italian pizza. Two rows of solid white tents have been set up to create a central esplanade with a seating capacity for 300 people. The tents also provide shelter for a weekend market and other activities. Colorful flags, bamboo pots, mobile structures for commissioned graffiti, exhibitions of exotic travel photography and timely public art interventions are also part of the design. There are a few informal lounge areas and hammocks scattered

Figure 8.3 The Mercado de Fusão. Note the DJ booth overlooking the square.
Photo: Iñigo Sánchez Fuarros.

over the space. A permanent DJ booth oversees the whole area, and several CCTV cameras monitor the market perimeter.

Beyond the visual and the material realm, the Mercado de Fusão has redefined the plaza's sonic environment as well. During operating hours there is a continuous stream of music accompanying the market's daily rhythms.[15] The music flows from a couple of loudspeakers installed on each side of the DJ booth. The soothing music stream brings together an array of exotic sounds from diverse locations: Lusophone music, *fado*, electronic music, reggae, "world beats," Latin music, tango. This programmed music is not meant for contemplative listening; rather, it functions as background music for other activities such as eating, drinking or relaxing. The resulting sound, which could be easily described by the marketing category of "world music," creates a soundscape that is at once seemingly foreign and yet close to the socio-cultural milieu in which the square is inserted. In fact, the area is home to various ethnic groups that settled there since the 1970s (Malheiro *et al.* 2012).[16] These groups have gradually appropriated the plaza and the urban spaces around in their own terms by inscribing their culture and uses into the territory they inhabit (Gésero 2012). The Mercado de Fusão draws on this pre-existing ethnic and cultural diversity to craft a multicultural discourse that celebrates and appropriates that diversity, aiming to attract not those immigrant groups, but a young, upwardly mobile, urban cosmo-politan clientele avid for new urban leisure consumption experiences. The continuous flow of globalized sounds composing the Mercado's soundtrack thus functions as a form of "aural tourism" (Cosgrove in Connell and Gibson 2003: 155) that, in consonance with the visual and gustatory elements, and instead of incorporating the preexisting surrounding sonic diversity, conveys a particular sonic experience of consuming the "exotic other," the space occupied by so-called "world music" being a "ubiquitous nowhere" (Erlmann 1996: 475).

In this way, the acoustic design and use of sound in the Praça do Martim Moniz construct the plaza as a commercial space. Jonathan Sterne (1997) has called attention to the centrality of programmed music as an environmental factor in commercial spaces and its role in organizing and producing space. In the shopping mall, Sterne notes, "the sound becomes the presence, and as that presence it becomes an essential part of the building's infrastructure" (Sterne 1997: 23). Meanwhile, recorded and electronic sounds effectively contour the Mercado de Fusão's shape and acoustic horizon. The central position of the speaker system ensures that the background music is audible in the food stalls and the eating areas but fades out when moving away from the center of the square. On the other hand, the pervasive continuous program of "world music"-style tunes contributes to the market's branding by recasting its image from one associated with the harsh reality of immigration to that of a haven for cosmopolitan urbanites.

Changes in the plaza's sound environment can also be read as an attempt to restore civility to this public space, along the lines of the "privatization" of the square suggested by Guterres (2012). A traditional gathering place for immigrant communities and scene of informal and illicit activities (Reginensi and Menezes 2011), prior to the Mercado de Fusão's opening the square, activity revolved around three ethnic food kiosks that served casual food and drinks, respectively run by people of Chinese, Cape Verdian and Eastern European origin. Each had its own clientele and particular dynamics and a distinctive sonority build of the various languages spoken and the different musical styles played on rudimentary sound systems. The refurbishment of the *praça* meant the closure of these establishments. The square's private management not only took possession of the kiosks, but it also minimized the plaza's possible dissonances by masking the nuances of the plaza's original sound environment through controlled musical programming. By offering pleasant surroundings, reducing the risk of "disturbing" encounters, and re-creating multi-ethnic interactions as civilized ideals, the Mercado de Fusão emerged as an acoustic enclave; in other words, as an artificial island of calm inserted in an area marked by systemic inequalities and social exclusion.

While the new imposed sonority of the Praça do Martim provided effective isolation from unpleasant- surrounding sounds, the regular presence of guest DJs and musical groups connected the area to other parts of the city through an intricate network of sound and the Mercado de Fusão and the renewed

Mouraria burst onto Lisbon's urban nightlife circuit. As a result, one of the common problems associated with nocturnal leisure activities, excessive noise, became a matter of concern for new residents and local authorities. The following section examines the redefinition of which noise levels are and are not acceptable in the renewed Mouraria by looking at a controversy over a group of resilient bars located in the area of the Largo do Intendente.

Policing Noise: The Largo do Intendente

In June 2012 a group of residents issued a complaint to the city council about excessive noise levels in the Largo do Intendente and vicinity, a rundown area infamous for prostitution, crime and drugs located on the northern end of the Mouraria. The residents urged local authorities "to take the necessary measures to limit the noise and disruptions in the Rua dos Anjos," indicating several bars as the source of their woes and exhorting the council to take action against them. On July 18, the owners of eight bars in the area received official notification of restrictions on their opening hours, declaring that the bars would have to close earlier on both on weekdays and weekends, or face severe fines. To justify the measure, the order justified itself in terms of the "psychological disturbances" and "pathologies" that the "excessive noise" inflicted on the local population's "quality of life" and "the terrible effects" that this disturbance could have for "the revitalization efforts that have been made in this part of the city." Based on the alleged noise nuisance, the document crafted a persuasive argument establishing a clear link between the degradation of the area and the activities developed around these bars, some of which have been open for over 30 years.

The crusade against the "noisy" bars took place at the same time as the grand opening of the renovated Largo do Intendente, the hallmark of the Mouraria's urban renewal.[17] Over that summer, hundreds of people flooded the square to attend the many outdoor concerts and activities organized to celebrate the "rebirth" of an area commonly thought of as a "bad area." The redevelopment of this open space included new stone paving, benches, trees, lighting and public art installations, transforming a derelict place beyond recognition. Vehicular traffic was limited. Where once there was a parking lot for moving vans, there is now a public square with several slick bars with outdoor seating. A former *azulejo* tile factory building was renovated to host the mayor's office. A new hostel with an art residency program occupies a former boarding house, and on the opposite end, the driver of Largo do Intendente's gentrified nightlife—a collectively run space serving as café, nightclub, concert venue and cultural space—opened on the first floor of a carefully restored nineteenth-century mansion. Since the renewal began, new shops have opened and a large dormitory for foreign college students was under construction while this text was in preparation.

Those involved in the debate shared a feeling that the concurrence of these three episodes—the resident's complaint, the renovated square's inauguration and enforced reduction of bars' opening hours—was not a mere coincidence, and that the noise complaint was just a pretext to strangle the languishing bars. In a tense meeting with a city council representative, the bar owners expressed their suspicion of the complaint's legitimacy ("who were those residents, anyway?") and insisted that the disturbance came from the presence of people in the street late at night, not the noise coming from inside the bars.[18] Moreover, some argued that they had made significant investments in soundproofing their establishments to adapt to the new regulations. At the end of the meeting, the bar owners decided to join forces to make a legal appeal against the city council's unilateral decision, but the city council representative informed them that the chances of winning the lawsuit were slim, and encouraged them to "jump on the bandwagon of change."

That meeting revealed that the inevitable ebb and flow of the old-timers' sense of origins and the new-comers' feelings of new beginnings (Zukin 2010) that is inherent to these revitalization processes and which is manifest here in the domain of the sound environment. In this sense, the city council's project of creating "a calm, safe, daytime atmosphere" that could attract new investment, visitors and residents alike somehow collided with the "rowdy" notoriety of the area, the Largo do Intendente and the adjacent streets of Rua do Benformoso and Rua dos Anjos having long been associated with marginal activities such as prostitution, the illegal drug trade and petty delinquency. A hot spot for street-based prostitution since the beginning of the twentieth century (Gomes Afonso 1984), the area absorbed the drug addicts and dealers displaced after the demolition of Lisbon's shantytown Casal Ventoso in the 1990s. In addition, gradual population loss, the closing of traditional businesses, and the degradation of public spaces led to widespread perceptions of decline and insecurity. Throughout all this, the group of persisting bars have remained key actors in the complex urban ecosystem of the place, adapting themselves to the changes the area has experienced over the last 30 years while catering to the variety of marginalized populations present there, including prostitutes, street hustlers and local residents.[19] The widespread association between the bars and these marginal activities made them into a scapegoat in the larger municipal strategy to upscale this part of the neighborhood.

The concern with noise underlying the dispute between the bars and the municipality reflects broader anxieties about the control of the uses of urban spaces in the Mouraria's revitalization. Since the process of urban upscaling in the area of the Largo do Intendente began, certain previously tolerated uses and appropriations of the public space have been deemed disagreeable and "noisy." This war against excessive noise raises questions about how sound is valued and devalued in strategies of urban rehabilitation. Which sounds are considered to be "noise" and which ones are not? Is the noise of a band of affluent young revelers who patronize a trendy club in the Largo do Intendente judged in the same way as the noise produced by the frequent fights between the drug addicts who occupy the same streets? Who has the legitimacy to ultimately decide what is a "good" or a "bad" sound environment—local authorities, the new residents or the long-time residents?

Largo do Intendente's revitalization illustrates how, despite improvement of the physical environment, the transformation of this part of the neighborhood from an infamous red-light district to a safe place of "riskless riskiness" could not be completed until the municipality intervened in the sound environment. By extending urban policies into the domain of sound, local authorities tried to remove the vestiges and spatial practices of socially undesirable inhabitants whose presence was viewed as an impediment to the area's redevelopment.

Conclusion

The ephemeral quality of sound makes the urban auditory environment particularly sensitive to processes of urban change. In urban renovation schemes like the one I just presented, the changes observed at the level of the sound environment can be considered as both cause and effect of larger processes of urban transformation. As the case of the Mouraria illustrates, an intervention on the sonic environment can instigate profound changes in the meanings, functions and experiences of urban space. Likewise, the rehabilitation of the built environment of areas under renovation or the development of new urban policies will inevitably result in changes on the sound environment.

Reshaping the milieu of sound can be a powerful tool in transforming the urban dynamics of a given place. The analysis of the revival of *fado* is a good example of how an intervention on the domain of sound can catalyze the revitalization of a neighborhood. The restitution of the sonority of *fado* to the Mouraria's public and semi-public spaces has both re-enacted and re-created a local sonic memory connecting past mental images of the neighborhood to the present. It has also become the main attraction of this renewed Mouraria, now exposed to the unrestrained presence of visitors and tourists. The sensory/sonic transformation of the Mouraria into a living *fadista* quarter has not only transformed the perception and experience of the place for outsiders but also for its inhabitants, who have embraced this new sensory environment as a source of pride and empowerment.

Intervening in the sound environment can be an effective means to regulate and structure the experience of public spaces. The example of the Praça do Martim Moniz exemplifies how the installation of a PA system and the programming of a continuous stream of "piped music" can effectively transform the sensorial environment of a community. The case study analyzed here shows the transformation of an open public square into a commercial space. The music flow creates an acoustic enclave that functions as a sonic envelope, masking various sounds from the environment now deemed unpleasant. Intervention on the sonic environment is also actively used to rebrand the public space, recasting its associated image from the rough-and-tumble reality of immigration to a haven for cosmopolitan city-dwellers. Evaluating the appropriation of pre-existing sonic markers of the area's extant cultural diversity and their dissolution in a celebratory multicultural sonic discourse that embraces "world music" as its soundtrack problematizes the production of this sanitized "ethnic soundscape."

This text is also attentive to how processes of urban transformation contribute to producing new sonic/aural sensitivities. It is interesting to note that in the Mouraria's renewal process, local sounds that were previously tolerated came to be perceived as irritating noises and ultimately ended up becoming criminal offenses. From this perspective, noise control emerges as an effective tool for controlling anti-social behavior and regulating the use of urban space by socially undesirable inhabitants. The controversy surrounding the bars in the Largo do Intendente shows how auditory perception of the sound environment is not unconditioned, but in fact context-dependent; in other words, it changes as the process of urban revitalization progresses. As a new sonic sensitivity descended on the vestiges of the spatial practices of the poor and marginal that characterized this part of the city, the "noises" associated with them and their activities became decontextualized and had to be erased. Thus, municipal efforts to fight the "excessive noise" need to be understood as part of a larger strategy to cleanse the area of its previous associations with prostitution, illegal drug trade and petty delinquency.

Analysis of the three spaces discussed here strongly suggests that the renewed Moraria is undergoing a process of acoustic thematization or put another way, an equalizing process that aims to smooth out the area's original rowdiness and dissonance.

Notes

1 I am grateful to Christine Guillebaud for the faith and patience that allowed this article to take shape, as well as for her comments and critical insights on early versions of this chapter. I could not have successfully completed the first and second drafts of this article without the generous and reassuring support of Fernando Salmón. Finally, I owe thanks to Andy Dyo for his help editing the photographs for all the plates. Field research was supported by a post-doctoral fellowship from the *Fundação para a Ciência e a Tecnologia* (SFRH/BDP/70411/2010).

2 Lisbon's municipality turned the Mouraria into a priority of public investment between 2011 and 2013. Besides the €7.5 million from the QREN program, the city council allocated another €4 million from PIPARU, a local program that supports urban rehabilitation actions. In addition, €1 million from the *orçamento participativo* (participatory contribution) was invested in the neighborhood. Moreover, several projects were funded under the BIP/ZIP program, a municipal program created in 2010 to support a variety of grassroots urban interventions in neighborhoods with social, economic, urban and environmental deficits.

3 Detailed information on this plan's various actions is available on the renewal program's website: www.aimouraria.cm-lisboa.pt, accessed October 2, 2013.

4 From a speech by Antonio Costa, mayor of Lisbon, at the public presentation of the QREN-Mouraria Action Plan. *Largo do Intendente*, September 30, 2011.

5 The so-called *Plano de Desenvolvimento Comunitario da Mouraria* (PDCM) was built around four axes of intervention: economic development, active aging,

populations at risk and the promotion of *fado* music as an identifying marker of the Mouraria.

6 Richard Elliott (2010) has explored *fado's* relationship to the city of Lisbon, with a particular emphasis on its presence in the song texts. For a more detailed study of the relationship between the Mouraria and the history of *fado*, see Colvin (2008).

7 As with any musical genre, tracing the origins of *fado* is a controversial undertaking. For a comprehensive history and description of the genre see Vieira Nery (2010).

8 *Rádio Amália* is a local radio station specializing in *fado* music.

9 The first edition of the *Visitas Cantadas* took place every Friday through Sunday in the summer of 2012. Due to the positive response, the singing tours were expanded from the Mouraria to Alfama, Lisbon' *fadista* quarter *par excellence,* in 2013.

10 "Discover the Mouraria quarter through the voice of its artists" ("*Descubra o bairro da Mouraria pela voz dos seus artistas*") was the catchy phrase that appeared on posters and leaflets promoting the initiative.

11 In the QREN-Mouraria Action Plan guidelines, *fado* is presented as "an unquestionable identifying marker" of the neighborhood that should be "assessed," "disseminated" and "dignified." The PDCM also views the *fado* as "a key dimension of the Mouraria's identity and memory" and "an excellent lever to stimulate the local economy and the cultural life of the neighborhood" due to "its capacity to attract new publics, particularly tourists." Source: www.aimouraria.cm-lisboa. pt/valoracao-das-artes-e-dos-oficios/sitio-do-fado-na-casa-da-severa/descricao. html. *Programa de acçao*, accessed October 10, 2013.

12 As part of the area's revitalization, two shopping centers, one on each side of the Praça do Martim Moniz, were built in the 1980s: The *Centro Comercial Mouraria* and the *Centro Comercial Martim Moniz.*

13 The *Estado Novo* (the New State) was an authoritarian regime ushered in by António Salazar in 1933. The Carnation Revolution would lead to the fall of the *Estado Novo* in 1974, changing the authoritarian regime from a dictatorship to a democracy.

14 The city government awarded the concession to operate ten stainless steel kiosks and install a weekend market to NCS, a private corporation linked to the successful revitalization of other areas of the city such as Cais do Sodré and the LxFactory in Alcantara. The *Mercado de Fusão* was inaugurated in June 2012, with the media playing an important role promoting the area's new image.

15 The food market operates daily from 11:00 a.m. to 10:00 p.m. At the weekend, it closes at midnight.

16 According to the latest census (2011) the population of immigrant origin represents one-third of the total population of the neighborhood.

17 For an informative study of recent changes in this area from a visual anthropology perspective, see Veiga Gomes (2011).

18 The meeting took place in the *Sport Clube Intendente* on July 23, 2012. This analysis is based on my field notes from that day.

19 Although some of the women involved in prostitution and some of their clients patronize several of these establishments, prostitution does not happen on the premises. The bars also offer shelter to these women while they are waiting or in the case of bad weather.

References

Atkinson, Rowland. 2007. "Ecology of Sound: The Sonic Order of Urban Space." *Urban Studies* 44 (10): 1905–1917.

Colvin, Michael. 2008. *The Reconstruction of Lisbon: Severa's Legacy and the Fado's Rewriting of Urban History*. Lewisburg: Bucknell University Press.

Connell, John and Chris Gibson. 2003. *Soundtracks: Popular Music, Identity and Place*. London: Routledge.

Degen, Monica. 2008. *Sensing Cities: Regenerating Public Life in Barcelona and Manchester*. London: Routledge.

Elliott, Richard. 2010. *Fado and the Place of Longing: Loss, Memory and the City*. Aldershot: Ashgate Publishing.

Erlmann, Veit. 1996. "The Aesthetics of the Global Imagination: Reflections on World Music in the 1990s." *Public Culture* 8: 467–487.

Gésero, Paula. 2012. "O espaço é o lugar: O Martim Moniz na migrantscape de Lisboa." *Sociologia: Numero temático* 1: 159–180.

Gomes Afonso, Maria G. 1984. *Estudos de casos: Prostituição e espaço social; O caso do Intendente*. Lisbon: UNL-Facultade de Ciencias Sociais e Humanas.

Guterres, Antonio B. 2012. "Interações reflexivas sobre o novo plano Martim Moniz." *Buala*. www.buala.org/pt/cidade/interacoes-relexivas-sobre-o-novo-plano-martim-moniz.

Holt, Fabian and Carsten Wergin, eds. 2013. *Musical Performance and the Changing City: Post-Industrial Contexts in Europe and the United States*. New York: Routledge.

Malheiro, Jorge, Rui Carvalho, and Luis Mendes. 2012. "Etnicização residencial e nobilitação urbana marginal: Processo de ajustamento ou prática emancipatória num bairro do centro histórico de Lisboa?" *Sociologia: Numero temático* 1: 93–124.

Menezes, Marluzi. 2004. *Mouraria, Retalhos de um imaginário: Significados urbanos de um bairro de Lisboa*. Oeiras: Celta.

———. 2009. "Praça do Martim Moniz: Etnografando lógicas socioculturais de inscrição da praça no mapa social de Lisboa." *Horizontes Antropológicos* 15: 301–328.

Reginensi, Caterine Odile and Marluci Menezes. 2011. *Pratiques: Entre formel et informel dans les espaces urbains; Lisbonne—Portugal et Rio de Janeiro—Brésil*. http://hal.archives-ouvertes.fr/hal-00605013.

Sterne, Jonathan. 1997. "Sounds Like the Mall of America: Programmed Music and the Architectonics of Commercial Space." *Ethnomusicology* 41 (1): 22–50.

Thibaud, Jean Paul. 2011. "A Sonic Paradigm for Urban Studies." *Journal of Sonic Studies* 1 (1). http://journal.sonicstudies.org/vol01/nr01/a02.

Veiga Gomes, Hèléne. 2011. "Le visuel dans la ville: Croisements et perspectives à partir du Largo do Intendente." Proceedings of the Second International Conference of Young Urban Researchers. http://conferencias.cies.iscte.pt/index.php/icyurb/sicyurb/paper/viewFile/219/133.

Vieira Nery, Rui. 2010. *Para una história do fado*. Lisboa: Público.

Zukin, Sharon. 2010. *Naked City: The Death and Life of Authentic Urban Places*. Oxford: Oxford University Press.

9   Listening to the City
The Sonorities of Urban Growth in Barcelona

Claire Guiu

The city sounds and resonates. In Barcelona, the rhythms of traffic and passers-by, of passages and construction sites, of conversations being chanted, all allow us to hear movement, dynamics and change. Under the beats of pneumatic drills, the concrete makes it clear for spectacular monuments to appear. Trucks pour sand to widen the beach. New pavements flatten the bumps and edges to let bicings[1] whisk by. At a syncopated pace, bathers rush toward a public space devoted to leisure: the seaside. In the urban islets of the fisherman's neighborhood of Barceloneta songs of household canaries, the shouts and exaltations of the inhabitants and their televisions mix with exhalations of the sea breeze, sun cream and churros. The advertising of cleaning carts, the loud clanking of the recycling services, the multilingual echoes of the loudspeakers on the beach announce the transformation of an industrial, Mediterranean Barcelona into a global, festive city.

- **Document 1:** Rambla Santa Monica. 2007. Recorded by Ciudad Sonora.

The multidisciplinary team Ciudad Sonora (2010) chose to listen to small and large urban mutations by focusing on the insignificant, the pluralities and the fragments of everyday life in movement (Augoyard 1979).[2] Between 2006 and 2009, three anthropologists, an ethnomusicologist, a psycho-sociologist and a geographer chased down sound fragments and events that continuously redefine the city. They investigated the sonorities of urban growth in Barcelona through an audio-ethnography of the waterfront.[3]

The fieldwork was chosen according to its "value as a social indicator" (Augoyard 1979), as both the theater and the driver of urban and social actions. Indeed, from the 1990s, large urban renewal projects were developed between the Zona Franca and the Plaza del Forum, along the coast. The 1992 Olympic Games initiated the development of urban renewal. The Poblenou industrial zone, integrated to the first Metropolitan Strategic Plan, has been transformed into a cluster development area based on the knowledge economy.[4] If the industrial city was once correlated with noise (Schafer 1977), we wonder how the post-industrial city resonates. With the spread of urban landmarks, such as flagship projects, art installations and territorial marketing, can we also witness the development of "soundmarks" (Schafer 1977: 274)? Can we analyze a "sonic legibility of the cityscape" as Lynch (1960) suggested for images? In a contemporary city characterized by socio-spatial segmentation, do the multiplication of otherness, aesthetic experience and tension surrounding the sensory dimensions of spaces reveal the rise of new actors and new forms of identification?[5]

After presenting the methodological framework of our research, we characterize sounds in coastal zones that have experienced recent development (new urban area, urban district renewal). Afterward, we suggest how sound, as well as related discourses and images, participate in the process of the appropriation, qualification, spatial organization and transformation of place.

1. Methodologies

> Saturday morning. The Ramblas seem saturated with people and traffic rumors. Wheeled suitcases resonate on the undulated pavement. A bus brakes. Screech of tires. Flight of pigeons. An ambulance siren bursts loudly, covering for a short moment the peep of sparrows and budgies. I am sitting down in front of the Santa Monica Art Center. Garbage men turn on the water pipes and start watering the ground. The water splashes and pours, shaking left over cans. Gasp of trucks. A man comes by. "What are you doing? Are you recording?"
>
> (Sound register, July 2007, Rambla Santa Monica)

The space is fluid, changing. This is a space of circulation, interactions and events. The tones, volumes, heights and rhythms of sounds are constantly moving, creating new "colors" or "sound signatures" (Augoyard and Torgue 1995).

This research is inspired by the works of artists, as well as by social science research mainly from the 1980s, that invite us to listen to and explore the dimension of sound in the city, going beyond an approach based on "noise" or "music".[6] We use some of the sound analysis tools developed by CRESSON research team such as the "sound effects" (1995) or the analytical methods of the "urban sound identity" (Amphoux 1981).

During the fieldwork, we conducted an audio-ethnography of the waterfront, based on "sound postcards",[7] exploratory free recordings, first systematic, and then directed toward specific events. A database was created with 20 hours of recordings associated to maps, photographs and descriptive notes. The survey consisted of four phases of listening and recording.

First, the waterfront was explored through sound *dérive* ("drifting") and floating listening. *Dérive*, defined by Debord as a "technique of rapid passage through various ambiances", involves "a playful behavior that differs in every aspect to the classical notions of journey or stroll" (1956). It evokes the "floating observation" developed by Pétonnet (1982)[8] and invites the discovery of unexpected places.

Second, urban sound spaces were approached with the goal of being representative and systematic. Listening from a fixed point for long intervals, or in "dérive", allowed us to grasp spatial and temporal discontinuities and to identify spatial unities. In four areas (Zona Franca, Passeig Colom, Mare-magnum, Barceloneta, Olympic Port, Playa-Forum), we chose eight fixed and continuous recording points.[9] Every week, between 10:00 a.m. and 8:00 p.m., one or two researchers went out to record sounds for 3 to 3.30 minutes. These recordings allowed us to approach the rhythms and temporalities of daily routine and everyday sounds: the exuberance sound of the restaurants on the port at lunchtime, the "awakening" of Barceloneta Square, the tourists on the Maremagnum walk during summer afternoons, etc.

During the third phase of fieldwork, we focused on four areas that are representative of current urban changes in order to more precisely understand their organization and their dynamics.

The last phase of research focused on soundsmarks in public events and ephemeral gatherings (festivals, sporting events, and demonstrations).[10] The aim was the analysis of public situations, sketches of everyday life, "remarkable atmospheres", defined by their sensory, collective, temporal and imaginary characteristics (Torgue 2004). In the "festive city", performances are more and more frequent. Benefitting from heavy media exposure, they become the stage for shaping urban identity and contribute to the auto-visibility of the city.

During the three years of research, the listening was interrogative. "To listen is to be straining toward a possible meaning, and consequently one that is not immediately accessible" (Nancy 2002: 19). We listened to the urban space not as an acoustic phenomenon, but as a "resonant meaning, a meaning whose sense is supposed to be found in resonance, and only in it" (Nancy 2002: 21). Listening, then, engages our whole body in a reso-nant orchestration with the city (Bandt *et al.* 2009). As the rythmanalyst defined by Lefebvre,[11] we take "the pulse of the city" (Torgue 2005). The collective dimension of research here is essential: it is through the compari-son between resonances, the sharing of disciplinary listening and the recur-rences between the multiple interpretations that writing the sound of the city becomes possible.

2.   Listening to Spaces

The first way to consider the sonorities of urban transformation is to listen to places newly created or in transformation. In Barcelona, since the end of the nineteenth century, the organization of international events has driven the transformation of the city (1888 International Exhibition, 1992 Olympic Games and 2004 Universal Forum of Cultures). Along with the rise of Cata-lan nationalism, these events have helped put into play a "Catalan identity", and developed the "capitality" of the city opposite Madrid (Monclús 2000). However, since the 1990s, the scale and conception of development proj-ects, as well as the actors involved, have all changed. Large urban strategies have prevailed over city planning (Barcelona 2000 strategic plan) and have allowed for an integrated tourism plan. The city is perceived as a whole and forms now a "collective actor" (Degen and García 2012: 1027). In parallel, the importance given to urban design has favored the development of small-scale interventions dedicated to rethinking public spaces and framework of identification of the city. The 1992 Olympic Games led to new constructions, and to the reinvention of cultural practices and politics. The initiatives conducted transformed Barcelona into a "lab city" and an exemplary site. The city's regeneration was considered as the development of the "strategic urbanism" and the revelation of a "Barcelona model".[12]

Transformations started along the waterfront, in a particularly rapid and radical way, along several kilometers of coastline. Already, since the 1960s, it had been envisioned "to re-open the city towards the sea, to which it had turned its back." This ambition was defined from the 1980s as a strategic axis. The construction of an American model of 'Waterfront' was accompanied by a rhetoric of reconquest. Boardwalks and beaches won territory over the sea. The entire coast was marked by these rapid transformations, at the level of urban development (urbanization of new spaces, increase of mobility and new practices), commerce (creation of large shopping centers) and demography (tourism, immigration).

Three dimensions were chosen for our research: the spatial dimension, social practices and the imaginary (Amphoux 1981). The *Répertoire des effets sonores* (1998) proposes a framework to analyze and qualify spaces. The sound postcards, the multiplicity of collected anecdotes and micro-events, the floating recordings, systematic or punctual, allow us to search for recurrences and formulate characterizations. However, our aim is not to confine the evanescence of sound in rigid cartographies. Spaces are considered as singular forms and moments. Nonetheless, there is a sort of "stickiness" of sound in place (Atkinson 2007), produced by the activities, functions and history of these urban spaces. "The spatial and temporal ordering of the urban soundscape, its ebb and flow, is often programmed, regularized or ordered in ways that can rarely be defined as random" (Atkinson 2007: 1906).

In the following, we describe a route through different places on the waterfront, from the Moll de la Fusta to the Forum of Cultures. For each sector, we associate a sound register, in some cases photographs and a characterization of the city area. The sound registers were mostly written in the first person singular and evoke only the situation observed. The characterizations provide information on the history of the built environment and the general types of sonorities heard; photographs are chosen as emblematic images of the area studied. These three elements coexist as different discursive regimes. They do not demonstrate; they expose; they give to see and hear.

On the Moll de la Fusta: Small Footsteps and Panoramic Views

I walk to the end of the Moll de la Fusta and settle in front of the port, a microphone directed towards the *golondrinas* (tourism boats). The space is open, facing the sea and Montjuïc. The engines of the *golondrinas* blend with the staccato?[13] rhythms of a helicopter, the continuous echo of a plane and the call of seagulls. The funicular crossing the harbor is far away, but I have the feeling that I hear its continual vibrations. Behind me, the ongoing hammering and sliding of the footsteps on the wooden deck. Fireworks blow up, far away. It is St John's Day. Two meters away, by my side, a young man sells small mechanical dogs that walk with the music. Another one sells magnets that vibrate and bump into each other when he throws them in the air. Whistling. Beside them, two older men watch out for the police.

The transformation of the old port, abandoned since the transfer of port activities to the southeast of the city, has considerably changed the water-front with the construction in the 1990s of the Moll de la Fusta, a festival marketplace on the sea containing an aquarium, a shopping center, an Imax cinema, restaurants and bars. A wooden deck, called "Rambla del Mar", connects this leisure area, managed by the Autonomous Port, to Las Ramblas of Barcelona. The space is marked by the rumble of the traffic and the plurality of the sounds, music and languages (mostly French, English and Mediterranean languages). The recurrence of users' flow and the continuity of the leisure activities create a specific sonic identity.

Figure 9.1 View of the Moll de la Fusta, Port Vell, 2007.
Photo: Ciudad Sonora.

When Barceloneta Square "Awakens"

It is still early. There are few people in the square. Two shopkeepers open the metal blinds of their stores, the bar keeper removes the chains tying the chairs together and takes out the tables on the terrace. I start recording, sitting on the bench by the bar. Four people sit in front of me on the other benches, including two street musicians that have placed their guitars and accordion on the ground. Two people pass with their bags and greet. Some pigeons fly away. A dog barks in an apartment in a side street. In the parallel street, an ambulance passes. Its siren interrupts the peacefulness of the square, yet without disturbing it.

(Sound register, 17 May 2007, Barceloneta square)

Physically separated from the rest of the old town, Barceloneta, built during the eighteenth century and hosting fishermen's families, is a working-class neighborhood characterized by a dense and linear urban fabric, made of long and narrow blocks, heritage of the 1754 Barceloneta Plan. The Special Plan for Interior Reform adopted in 1986 included different projects to build new equipment and renovate public spaces. The aim of the plan was to open the city to the coast, the development of the waterfront avenue and the renovation of the eastern part of the neighborhood (Ter Minassian 2013). Since the mid-2000s, the increase in the cost of real estate, the housing transactions and the rise of tourist apartments have made it difficult for some local inhabitants to maintain their residencies. The neighborhood has recently been transformed again with the reconstruction by Josep Trias of the old market, originally built in 1884.

In this area, Barceloneta square is a space characterized by rhythms of sociability. It can be considered as a morphogenic space (i.e., a place in which the transformation of its global composition by singular, random events is always possible). It is a sound environment that has a signature where micro-social sounds clearly appear. The "sound texture" of traffic flows is largely absent. The observations made in the square show that it is used as a relaxing space at some time of the day, as a meeting place and for festivals, events and performances. The square allows for multiple uses and forms a unified space.

The Passeig Maritim: Connection and Sound Bubbles

We sit on the side of the Passeig, looking at the beach. Behind us, pedestrians' footsteps and bicycles. We can hear the traffic on the Ronda, especially the ambulances' sirens. From an uncertain place, surely a restaurant, we hear the air conditioning rumbling. We settle on the footbridge, facing the marina and above the restaurant La Fonda situated below us. We are surprised to note the low level of the restaurant echoes at lunch time. [...] We move then in front of the restaurant. Sounds from inside clearly resonate. Plates, cutlery and glasses slamming, waiters' calls, laughs, clients' conversations cover the sounds of the sea and the traffic. Only few ambulances' sirens can be heard. [. . .] We sit then in front of one of the quays. The grating of ropes and the jingling of the moorings under the quiet movement of the sea mix with the sounds of the passers-by and the intense traffic in the port area. The siren of an ambulance, again; the horn of a car; a helicopter far away and the barking of a dog.

(Sound register, July 2007, Olympic port)

The Passeig Maritim crosses the Olympic Village built in the 1990s, identified by the Mapfre tower (shopping center and luxury hotel), and connects a marina, a wharf, restaurants and beaches. This passage leads to the Bogatell beach. It is made of different lines parallel to the sea with different functions: in front of the marina, at the bottom, are the pathway, the road and a row of restaurants. Above, we can see a row of lights and trees and some terraces and restaurants that hide the passage of la Ronda de Littoral. In the urban plans of the end of the 1980s, passages were supposed to offer a barrier protecting the beach from the city and to become essential urban elements, places for contemplating the sea, symbols of the city and axes of cohesion in the urban fabric (Nóvoa 1998). The recordings show here the importance of sounds due to traffic and flows (helicopters, roads on each side, bicycles, suitcases rolling on the pavement and multilingual conversations). The density of the "sound magma" both connects and hides the micro-social life happening in the different places. The music from the shops, for example, can be perceived only from the terraces. We have here an "apocryphal" space, where the micro-social sound signatures are hardly distinguishable. The global appropriation of the space by the sound is made difficult by its physical shape. However, one characteristic of this area is the diversity of its acoustic horizons. Everything is mixed together: the helicopters' hammerings that resonate both in the whole area and at a smaller scale, "sound bubbles" created by the ambiance of the cafés, the marina and so on.

The Residencies in Diagonal Mar, Listening to a Seashell

Diagonal Park, scattered with few luxury residences in construction, close to a shopping center. Some advertising signs promote second homes. Few resonances here. We attempt to record emptiness. There is no one in the park, except for a mother and her daughter. Bangs and vibrations of building works sound. Few activities outside the passage of trucks, cars and motorbikes, two tourist buses and some bicycles. The planes resonate with the tree leaves of the park.

(Sound register, July 2007, Diagonal Mar)

The northern area, called Diagonal Mar, underwent different development projects during the 2000s, including the urbanization of the avenue,

Figure 9.2 View of Diagonal Mar residential area, 2007.
Photo: Ciudad Sonora.

the construction of transport facilities and a shopping center. These interventions aimed to connect one of the central axes of the city (the diagonal) to the sea and to build luxury residences and office buildings. The residential part of the area, along the Passeig Garcia i Faria, on the old industrial Macosa site, can be described as a staccato space, where each sound is well delimited, but also as an anonymous one. The sounds made by the construction works resonate. There are no soundmarks of sociability. This empty space is yet invested with rhetoric on sound, brought to the urban landscape by images or protest signs. In this luxury residential area, the location is valued through the prism of amenities. The sea is promoted as a panoramic view. Advertising uses images of island and shell as metaphors for the place. The social and residential island promises silence, or a chosen and privileged listening, among a specific social group. Diagonal Mar is a space in which the "collective desire for the coast", as narrated by A. Corbin (1988), is subsumed into images for the promotion of real-estate. The shore is a horizon, giving a "sense of infinite" (Sansot 1983: 75). However, the inhabitants here protest with signs that the visual horizon is threatened by the densification of construction along the waterfront.

A Forum of Cultures Without Resonances?

End of the afternoon on the Forum. Few people. The sewage treatment plant makes a continuous bass sound. Very clearly, we hear the voices of some children far away, roller-blading or running on the immense cemented square. In the background, traffic sound from the Ronda de Littoral.

(Sound register, 28 October 2007, Forum of Cultures)

In the Diagonal Mar area, on the edge of Besós and above the sewage treatment plant, the square of the Forum of Cultures building, conceived by Herzog and De Meuron and now named Museu Blau, hosted the Universal Forum of Cultures in 2004, an important cultural event that lasted for four months and was supported by UNESCO. These constructions, defined for their function, participated in the rise of the Poblenou area as a cultural neighborhood. The place, the largest square in the city, now hosts various cultural events and performances, but remains empty the rest of the time. Its concrete square offers a practice area for roller skaters, joggers or cyclists. A bagpipe player sometimes practices there to avoid being heard. Nonetheless, the sounds alternate between crowds and shows on the one hand, and to non-use on the other. The Forum is an open, staccato place, where sounds seem to vanish because of a lack of resonance.

Figure 9.3 View of the Forum of Cultures, 2007.
Photo: Ciudad Sonora.

Preliminary Conclusions

This overview of sounds reveals different types of spaces, according to the scale of resonance available there, to the possibilities of 'sound appropriation' given to the inhabitants, to the diversity and richness of the tonal colours, of the volumes and the timbres possible. It invites us to forge a link between the sensory dimension of places and the urban project that created them.

Indeed, the areas of Diagonal Mar and the Forum are spaces in construction, characterized by emptiness and uninhabited temporalities. "Works still in progress of their realization", said Hartog on generic cities (2012: 18), these spaces only find their rhythm in the staccato of an event. Different scales can be heard (helicopters, planes, road traffic), but the sonic characterization of such spaces by its users is not easy. The absence of resonances and the poorness of the score composed there can be considered as convergent elements, the same diagnosis being made by many specialists. Indeed, "for many [. . .], the Forum and Diagonal-Mar are indicators of the demise of the 'Barcelona model' in the face of pressure from a neoliberal global context necessitating increasingly aggressive entrepreneurial urban regeneration, but also in part the consequence of the success of the prior modernization strategy which located the city on an international map" (Degen and García 2012: 1031). With their low densities, fragmentation, poor quality of public space and hollow sonorities, these spaces appear to be the antithesis of the concepts promoted by the "Barcelona model". Built earlier, the Passeig Maritim and the Moll de la Fusta are composite spaces cadenced by leisurely temporalities and characterized by a wide listening horizon. In general, a notable aspect of the areas created since the 1990s is the breadth of their acoustic horizon, given by the simultaneous presence of discontinuous events. In the sounds of helicopters, planes, conversations and footsteps, shouts and whispers, micro and macro sound and resonate together. "The opening of Barcelona to the sea" translates not only into the multiplication of panoramic landscapes, but also into the widening of the acoustic field.

Beyond these distinctive spaces, four elements appear transversally in the recordings: the sounds of helicopters, sirens and footsteps, words in different languages and comments on the city.

The passage of helicopters is frequent on the waterfront, expressing both the strength of the control over the city and also the importance of new practices offered to tourists. Indeed, a visit of the coast by helicopter is proposed by different companies. "Está pasando un helicóptero. No te oigo. Hablamos luego" ("There is a helicopter flying by. I can't hear you. Let's talk later") shouts a woman in her cellphone. Alert signals and control sounds in the city certainly provoke a collapsing of scale. Such panoptic soundscapes interfere with the intimate, the micro-social and the mundane.

Walking sticks and canes, wheelchairs and footsteps are part of the recurring elements in the sound registers. "Interlacing footsteps shape spaces.

They weave places together" (de Certeau 1990). Walking sounds depend on the type of pavement, the buildings' acoustics, on practices, behaviors and ways of life. The rumbling of suitcases is heard numerous times along Rambla Santa Monica and Passeig Maritim. Above all, the grating of the sand under flip-flops is perceptible in Barceloneta square, along all the beaches, in the Forum or the Moll de la Fusta leading toward the Maremagnum.

> I take a seat on the seawall. The percussion of people slapping shoes on the concrete, eliminating the remaining sand. I listen to the footsteps, with or without shoes on, lazy shuffling and the trotting of sweating athletes. The wheels of single or tandem bicycles, unicycles, and baby-strollers, as they slide on or pat the ground.
>
> (Sound register, July 2007, Barceloneta beach)

The diversity and variety of languages and intonations also constitute one of the recurring elements of observation. English, French, Portuguese, Italian, but also Russian, Chinese, Hindi and Arabic, produce a murmur that is prominent in several recordings and reveal a moving topophony of linguistic practices. It is possible to determine some periods in which the Catalan language is predominant, as in some recordings from Barceloneta or in Bogatell beach.

An ethnography of the senses focuses on the ordinary, the little nothings that make the city. Listening and recording allow access to conversations and anecdotes without the interference of the researcher. Some recordings evoke the echoes of cultural activities taking place in the city. Other conversation snippets comment on the city in the making: "*mira, allà faran el nou hotel*", "*què bonic*", etc. A group of friends sit down on the grass. They speak of Woody Allen's imminent visit. In effect, the recording was done while the movie *Vicky Cristina Barcelona* was being filmed. All these fragments reveal the expansion of a cultural city, commented, represented, even personified.

3.   "Soundposts" and Regulations: "*Barcelona, Posa't Guapa*" . . . "*Barcelona, Posa't Silenciosa?*"[14]

If the urban space is fluid and dynamic, it is also made of signposts regulations. Sonic territories are shaped by norms and imaginaries. These framing processes can be addressed at different levels. The sounds considered as "noise" are regulated at different scales, from the EU directives to the municipal by-laws. But sound can also be used as techniques to bypass, appropriate and subvert spaces. They contribute to these "microbial practices", to the "often minuscule ruses of discipline" that "draw their efficacy from a relationship between procedures and the space they compose to make an 'operator' out of it" (De Certeau 1990: 144). Finally, they participate in the development of new forms of expression and imaginaries of place.

Putting the City Into Order

With the development of the "Barcelona Brand" since the 2000s, there is a multiplication of city icons and symbols, defining it as a whole. The urban image is at stake. The increasing number of views from the top of iconic buildings, the funiculars on different hills (Montjuïc, Tibidabo), the cruise boats or the helicopters, all construct the unity of the city from a variety of visual panoramas. At a smaller scale, the city council has led a campaign to protect and improve the urban landscape by funding the renovation and embellishment of the facades and public spaces, advertised by the slogan: "*Barcelona, posa't guapa*".

With the arrival of massive numbers of tourists and the multiplication of leisure activities, the regulation of practices and sounds consists of, first, creating leisure zones in non-residential or peripheral areas (Maremagnum, Montjuïc, Fórum de las Culturas) and then, controlling the festive and sonic activity in residential zones. The civil order of the 24 of January 2006 lists some measures to "promote and guarantee urban coexistence in Barcelona public spaces" (interdiction to spit, to play or to organize spontaneous sport competitions, to drink alcohol outside designated areas, etc.) Urban design leads to new behavioral norms and impacts on spatial and social practices. The city council adopted a pedagogical policy based on messages and speeches on the city, which it defined as "an action based on complicity and everyday life" that "also evokes, calls for and offers to do it with the B style of Barcelona" ("Fem-ho B"). The urban landscape is arrayed with texts (recommendations, advice, interdictions, suggestions) that aim to induce civic behavior through an identification to the city. Public space becomes the medium and the center of the discourse on citizenship and "living together".

This is especially the case along the beach. At the edge of the sand, many signs recall municipal bylaws: it is forbidden to sleep, but also to use percussions, loudspeakers or megaphones. In addition, since 2005, the city council has led a campaign named "La platja et parla".[15] In the sand, large comic strips show characters such as "Supernoinet" ("Super clean boy") or "La Protectora de la Sorra" ("The Beach Protector"). Speech balloons, hammered in the sand, give a human voice to the beach: "I am a beach, not a huge ashtray, okay?" "Walking in the sand is good for your health. Keep in shape. Walk to the trash cans". Finally, twenty-four loudspeakers, spread along the beach, broadcast a masculine voice in four languages (Catalan, Castillan, French and English) that informs beachgoers on the state of the sea, the presence of jellyfish, etc. Sometimes, the tone changes to become informal.

"Your attention please, to all bathers, the beach is talking to you", a serious masculine voice says.

"Dear friends, this is the beach, the beach itself", goes on a feminine one. "First of all, I would like to greet the new comers. Then I would like to ask you all . . . all of youuuu!! Please, use the bins. There are plenty of them, so don't be lazy, heh!"

"Your attention please, to all bathers, the beach is talking to you."

"Listen, I have heard many people complaining because I burn. Of course I burn!! Would you be happy if someone put out a cigarette on your navel every two minutes? Then, don't use me as an ashtray, okay?"

The messages depend on the events. During St John's Day's celebrations, the beaches are marked by a repetitive recommendation: "Thank you for using the bins and collaborating with the cleaning service of Barcelona City Council. Don't forget, at 6 A.M., you must leave the beach in order to let the cleaning services circulate" (2007). As underlined by Juan Cantavella and Sánchez Fuarros (2010), the beach sounds like a swimming pool.

•   **Document 2:** Loudspeaker in the beach, 21/06/2007. Recorded by Ciudad Sonora.

These messages constitute a new form of coastal soundmark mixing shouts, laughs, flows and the sound of the waves and the wind. They express "the power of sensuous ideologies in framing cities" (Degen 2008).

Our approach to sound also allows us to analyze the disjunctions between the sanitary and aesthetic intentions of the city and the effective actions of urban policies. For example, the passage of cleaning carts in Barceloneta neighborhood makes a loud noise in the middle of the night, and the residents complain about it (Martí 1997).

The Global Sound of the City

In parallel with urban policies and regulations, several actors participate in the construction of a global image and "sound of the city". For example, the *chiringuitos* (small bars), located all along the beach, have been reorganized with the opening of the seafront. They now sell cocktails and fruit juices and broadcast salsa, house and chill-out music. Next to the Olympic Port, some of them mark the sonic space with a low-frequency beat. The music seems to be the vector of a rhythmic unification of the waterfront, the instrument of a collective orchestration. At the Barceloneta beach, however, the *chiringuitos* located less than 100 meters from inhabited areas do not have the right to broadcast music and must respect strictly regulated hours (Municipal bylaw that came into force in 2007). The Association Xiringuitos protested by creating T-shirts worn by the waiters and sold for 10 euros: "Shhh . . . Be quiet! This is Barcelona", "500,000 customers X one neighbor = NO MUSIC!" Through music or the evocation of its interdiction, "noises" and "sounds" are invested with meaning in highly public spaces, and they participate in a polyphonic composition that continually (re)qualifies the city.

Figure 9.4 T-shirts sold by the Barceloneta Chiringuito, 2007.
Photo: Ciudad Sonora.

Sound in general, and music in particular, contribute to shape imaginary spaces that integrate the city within multiple worlds. "Music does not then simply provide a marker in a pre-structured social space, but the means by which this space can be transformed" (Stokes 1994). It can evoke in one place other places, or even create a *lieu de condensation* (Debarbieux 1995). On the Barcelona waterfront, the importance of South-American music groups that play in the Passeig Maritim or in the passage Juan de Bourbon in the Autonomous Port (that benefits from a different legislation concerning the use of the public space), the generalized introduction of the batucadas during traditional celebrations in Barceloneta and the music broadcasted by the *chiringuitos*, all create a "brazilisation of sound" on the waterfront, and more generally, a globalization of musical sounds in the city.

Being Heard in the Interstice

While sound is subject to territorialization, rules and regulation, it also contributes to many practices of circumvention. On the beach, the illegal vendors use sound effects of *créneau*[16] to be heard: "agua, cerveza, beer." Others shake and make their goods sound without showing them. Young people on the beach call out to each other from afar using specific whistles. On St John's Day's celebrations, firecrackers, drunken people singing, laughs and shouts totally cover up the voice of the loudspeakers on the beach which seems out of place. In the Poblenou Park, on the 22nd of July 2007 (before its restructuring by Jean Nouvel in 2008), 7:35 p.m., the same loudspeakers formed the sonic background themselves. On the grass, groups of people play cards. A gypsy family sets up domestic birds in cages on the trunk of four trees that form a rectangular zone. Some images of Cameron, the flamenco singer, are stuck to the bottom of the cages. One of the men takes out his guitar and starts playing. The family marks here its territory through the music and the bird songs that echoes with the loudspeakers.

- **Document 3:** Poblenou Park, Barcelona, 22/07/2007. Recorded by Ciudad Sonora.

Being Heard With Resolve

Finally, sound contributes to the construction of groups. Speeches, projected music and sound signals sounds are vectors for mobilization within urban space. They create unification, the constitution of a community of listening, even an "imagined community" (Benedict Anderson). They show new forms of communities and political expressions. The *casserolades* (banging on pots and pans in protest) organized every Thursday in Barcelona during the war in Iraq resonated throughout the whole city. Similarly, the fireworks of St. John's Day are sparsely lit during the afternoon, but come the evening, they cover all other sounds at the scale of the entire city. On a smaller scale, the social tensions linked to conflicts of use, and problems of noise are present in the public space. This forms a space made of expressions and challenges. The claims concern the evolution of the city, the perceived threat of excessive tourism (mobilization in Barceloneta Square against tourist apartments, posters on balconies above the terraces of the Ribera, etc.).

Conclusion

In 1983, Sansot suggested that "the screams in large capitals had a common aspect; surely because they came from a certain type of economy" (1983: 82). What, then, is the sound of a post-industrial city? Listening to the sounds of the city allows us to draw several tendencies. It shows striking contrasts between different coastal areas and reveals the variability of the modes of practices, governance and priorities which preceded their construction. The functional spaces of Diagonal Mar and the Forum appear, for example, to be areas without echoes, without resonance. The privatization of spaces in Diagonal Mar is characterized by the absence of communities of listening. Numerous sounds allow us to hear the integration of Barcelona in the list of globalized cities: the framing of the sensory experience via bylaws and regulations, showing a new sensory ideology of the city; the broadcasting of "Brazilian" or chill out music along the waterfront; the multiplication of the sound of footsteps, of foreign languages and of vehicles; the opening of acoustic horizons by the multiplication of types and scale of sources of sound. Most tourist sectors of the waterfront witness the emergence of soundmarks. However, they share more stereotypes (the image of the shell, or the Brazilian and chill out music) than sharing of experience. The shared dimension, however, is also composed every day in another way. The multiplicity of ruses and bypasses deployed by users, the new forms of political mobilization and identity spread by sound, the expression of conflicts between different groups concerning the use of public space, all demonstrate the presence of an active citizenry in movement, and of constantly reinvented sonic and spatial practices.

Notes

1 B*icing* is a public bicycle renting service created in 2007 by the City of Barcelona.
2 This research was conducted by Sandra Anítua i Jorge, Miguel Alonso Cambrón, Noel García López, Claire Guiu, Anna Juan et Íñigo Sánchez, members of the collective Ciudad Sonora, dedicated to sound anthropology. It was funded by the Catalan Institute of Anthropology and the Inventari del Patrimoni Etnològic de Catalunya (*IPEC*) (Cultural Department of Catalonia Generalitat) and was developed in collaboration with the "Orquestra del chaos" of the Barcelona Center for Contemporary Culture (CCCB).
3 An "audio-ethnography" (Smith 1994: 233) is a sensory ethnography based on listening and data collection (sound registers, floating listening, sound postcards).
4 In "knowledge economy", knowledge would replace natural resources and physical work as tools for economic development. This theory encouraged cities to invest in high technology, communications and also the creative sectors.
5 For references on other fields, see Colon in Pecqueux (2012) or Guiu *et al.* (2015).
6 For a synthesis on these researches, see Guiu (2006) and Guiu *et al.* (2014).
7 The "sound postcard" is the result of an interview conducted with a person picked randomly who was asked to imagine a postcard—not based on the visual but on the sound—of the place he/she is and he/she would like to send to a loved one.
8 According to Pétonnet (1982: 39), the floating observation "consists of staying in all circumstances available, without fixing the attention on a specific object, but to let it 'float' in order that information comes in with no filter, no a priori, until points of reference and convergences appear and we can discover implicit rules."
9 Monjuïc, port, at the crossing between the Rambla and Passeig Colom, Mercè square, Barceloneta square, Passeig Maritim, at the crossing between Bogatell and Mar Bella, Forum square.
10 Many events were attended: dog shows, Peruvian party, Caramelles, Corpus celebrations, Barceloneta celebrations, sport competition, traditional Catalan cultural events, Music Day, Barça game retransmission, processions, etc.
11 "The rhythmanalyst is all ears. He listens not only to words, however, but to everything happening in the world. He hears things that are usually hardly noticed: noise and sound. He pays attention to the babble of voices, but also to silence [. . .] He is always listening to his body, to whatever it communicates to him" (Meyer 2008).

12 The Barcelona model was defined not by its content but by its governance, by a particular way to think about city planning that looks for citizen consensus and a balance between public and private stakeholders (Monclús 2000). However, this model is criticized by several researchers who condemn its drifting toward the privatisation of urbanism, speculation, and the development of an entrepreneurial urban politics (Capel 2005, Monclús 2003, or Delgado 2007, among others).

13 "We borrowed from the music vocabulary the articulation 'staccato' that insists on the precision of the contour and the distinction of sound objects" (Augoyard 1983: 117).

14 "Barcelona, make yourself pretty" . . . "Barcelona, be quiet."

15 "The beach is talking to you."

16 "A temporary diminution of the ambient sound level which allows the producer of a sound to send a signal to his audience" (Augoyard and Torgue 1995: 46).

References

Amphoux, Pascal, ed. 1981. *Aux écoutes de la ville: La qualité sonore des espaces publics européens; Méthode d'analyse comparative; Enquête sur trois villes suisses.* Grenoble: CRESSON.

Atkinson, Rowland. 2007. "Ecology of Sound: The Sonic Order of Urban Space." *Urban Studies* 44 (10): 1905–1917.

Augoyard, Jean-François. 1979. *Pas à pas: Essai sur le cheminement quotidien en milieu urbain.* Paris: Éditions du Seuil.

———, ed. 1983. *Sonorité, sociabilité, urbanité: Méthode pour l'établissement d'un répertoire des effets sonores en milieu urbain.* Rapport de recherche 4. Grenoble: CRESSON.

Augoyard, Jean-François and Torgue Henry, eds. 1995. *À l'écoute de l'environnement: Répertoire des effets sonores.* Marseille: Éditions Parenthèses.

Bandt, Ros, Michelle Duffy, and Dolly Mackinnon. 2009. *Hearing Place: Sound, Place, Time, Culture.* Cambridge: Cambridge Scholars Publishing.

Capel, Horacio. 2005. *El modelo Barcelona: Un examen crítico.* Barcelona: Edicions del Serbal.

Ciudad Sonora. 2010. *Acústiques del litoral de Barcelona: Una aproximació etnogràfica a l'espai sonore urbà.* Barcelona: IPEC.

Corbin, Alain. 1988. *Le territoire du vide: L'Occident et le désir de rivage (1750–1840).* Paris: Champs-Flammarion.

Debarbieux, Bernard. 1995. "Le lieu, le territoire et trois figures de rhétorique." *Espace géographique* 24 (2): 97–112.

Debord, Guy. 1956. "Théorie de la dérive." *Les lèvres nues* 9.

De Certeau, Michel. [1980] 1990. *L'invention du quotidien.* Vol. 1, *Arts de faire.* Paris: Gallimard.

Degen, Mónica and Marisol García, eds. 2008. *La Metaciudad: Barcelona; Transformación de una metropolis.* Barcelona: Editorial Anthropos.

———. 2012. "The Transformation of the 'Barcelona Model': An Analysis of Culture, Urban Regeneration and Governance." *International Journal of Urban and Regional Research* 36 (5): 1022–1938.

Delgado, Manuel. 2007. *Sociedades movedizas: Pasos para una antropología de las calles.* Barcelona: Anagramma.

Guiu, Claire, ed. 2006. "Géographie et musiques, quelles perspectives?" Special issue, *Géographie et Cultures* 59: 1–144.

Guiu, Claire, Guillaume Faburel, Marie-Madeleine Mervant-Roux, Henry Torgue, and Philippe Woloszyn, eds. 2015. *Soundspace: Espace, expériences et politiques du sonore*. Rennes: Presses Universitaires de Rennes.

Hartog, François. [2003] 2012. *Régimes d'historicité: Présentisme et expériences du temps*. Paris: Éditions du Seuil.

Juan Cantavella, Anna and Iñigo Sanchez Fuarros. 2010. "Escoltant la ciutat: Del paisatge sonor a l'espai sonor." *Revista d'Etnologia de Catalunya* 35: 160–166.

Lynch, David. 1960. *The Image of the City*. Cambridge: MIT Press.

Martí, Josep. 1997. "When Music Becomes Noise: Sound and Music That People in Barcelona Hear But Don't Want to Listen to." *The World of Music* 39 (2): 9–17.

Meyer, Kurt. 2008. "Rhythms, Streets, Cities." In *Space, Difference, Everyday Life: Reading Henri Lefebvre*, edited by K. Goonewardena, S. Kipferm, R. Milbrou, and C. Schmid, 147–160. London: Routledge.

Monclús, Francisco-Javier. 2000. "Barcelona's Planning Strategies: From 'Paris of the South' to the 'Capital of West Mediterranean'." *Geojournal* 59 (1/2): 57–63.

———. 2003. "The Barcelona Model: An Original Formula?" *Planning Perspectives* 18 (4): 399–421.

Nancy, Jean-Luc. 2002. *A l'écoute*. Paris: Galilée.

Nóvoa, Manuel. 1998. "Una reflexión sobre la reciente transformación de Barcelona." *Porto: Revista da Faculdade de Letras: Geografia I* 14: 61–75.

Pecqueux, Anthony, ed. 2012. "Les bruits de la ville." *Communications* 90: 1–227.

Pétonnet, Colette. 1982. "L'observation flottante: L'exemple d'un cimetière parisien." *L'Homme* 22 (4): 37–47.

Sansot, Pierre. 1983. *Variations paysagères*. Paris: Klinsieck.

Schafer, Murray. 1977. *The Soundscape: Our Sonic Environment and the Tuning of the World*. Rochester: Destiny Books.

Smith, Susan J. 1994. "Soundscape." *Area* 26: 232–240.

Stokes, Martin, ed. 1994. *Ethnicity, Identity and Music: The Musical Construction of Place*. Oxford: Berg.

Ter Minassian, Hovig. 2013. *Changer Barcelone: Politiques publiques de gentrification dans le centre ancien (Ciutat Vella)*. Toulouse: Presses Universitaires du Mirail.

Torgue, Henry. 2004. "Figurer: Vers un répertoire d'ambiances remarquables." In *Ambiances en débats*, edited by P. Amphoux, J.-P. Thibaud, and G. Chelkof, 233–279. Grenoble: A la Croisée.

———. 2005. "Immersion et émergence: Qualités et significations des formes sonores urbaines." *Espaces et Sociétés* 4 (122): 157–166.

Part IV

Sound Arts and Anthropology

10 Not Just Tones, Noises too![1]

On Sound Poetry[2]

Jean-Charles Depaule

"Things used to be clear," wrote Emmanuel Hocquard in 1995. "Without getting into the details, in poetry, whatever style the example (regular rhyming verses or free verse), there was always a family resemblance. Those who wrote poetry called themselves poets." But now, he added, "things are no longer so simple. The book ceased to be the exclusive place for poetry. I am thinking of Sound Poetry, which resembles performance in making sound, the body, the voice, intervene directly" (Hocquard 2001: 227). In the latter half of the twentieth century, some poets would indeed decide to free the poem from the page, some of them going so far as to object to the category of poem by seeking intersections with other artistic forms that would accentuate the sound or visual qualities of their work (Baudelaire and his dream of correspondences, for a start . . .) Some aspired to multidisciplinarity, or even a total art. In the 1950s it was difficult to imagine the future their efforts might have, but in time they would develop in several directions, leading to a nebulous collection of trends. Very few people know that the public reading of poems *by their authors* is among the effects of this rebellion, since it has become such a common and institutionalized phenomenon by this early twenty-first century.

Poets who chose to privilege the voice, the body and sound left behind much more than the constraints of the book and the page. As we shall see, they were also driven to test other limits, subverting the concept of the text (written and/or spoken) by playing on and with the structural and phonetic constraints of language, sometimes to the point of dislocation. Some temporarily or permanently abandoned articulated language to explore nonverbal modes of expression and production of meaning. Many became (and remain) interested by the sound environment. Thanks to the technical means at their disposal, they echo this environment or incorporate fragments of it in their work. These practices invite us to revisit seemingly established distinctions and categories, not only in the area of poetry, but beyond—especially the postulated difference between sound and noise.

In this study, it was impossible to explore how contemporary poets work on sound material, especially how they deal with sound milieu, without relating their work to wider perspectives. To do so, I chose a few points of

Figure 10.1 Bernard Heidsieck. "Canal Street, Revue parlée, Centre Georges Pompidou, 1980".

© Françoise Janicot, reproduced by kind permission.

reference. I tried to identify the concentrations and gaps, as well as echoes and constellations, based on a few "cases," even if this meant setting aside others that may be just as significant as those I chose.

Two Difficulties

Study of this poetic domain faces two difficulties. The first is of a taxonomic order: there is a vast range of designations. The second is more genealogical in nature. "An abundant burgeoning of terms flourishes all around sound poetry: '*Lautpoesie,*' 'phonetic poetry,' 'acoustic art,' '*neues Horspiel,*' '*ultralettrisme,*' 'verbal music,' 'spatial poetry,' '*poesia Sonora,*' '*poésie action,*' 'text-sound composition,' 'verbophony'" (Barras 1999: 27). There is no point in complicating matters by expanding on the list. It is possible, though, to sketch out archipelagos, with tangent points, intersections, and nesting components. As far as the distinction between sound poetry and oral or vocal poetry goes, Jean-Michel Espitallier (born 1957), himself a poet and musician, draws a clear division:

> Sound poetry is not oral poetry. [. . .] It is not music, either. The poetry that gives voice to voiceless texts is not sound poetry. Sound poetry remains silent to the non-sound poem. Sound poetry in the book is not written poetry. In short, sound poetry is not the oralization of texts with the possibility of using mechanical devices, but a practice that engages, remunerates, and *treats sound as raw material,* returns the sonic dimension to the word, stripping it of its meaning (which forms a screen) in order to produce other meaning-effects.
>
> (Espitallier 2006: 219–20. Emphasis our own)

Such a distinction appears to be culturally situated, holding true for "France at least. [. . .] The rigid distinctions of the French have not appealed to British artists and performers" (Sheppard 2005: 2). This serves as a reminder that my own study probably also fails to escape such ethnocentrism.

The diversity of label names shows something of the fragmentation of this poetic domain, in which competition and hostilities may sometimes be quite lively (especially in the 1950s–60s, when the lettrists, in their claim to exclusive legitimacy, fought considerably with newcomers who did not place themselves in their lineage). It is also true that periodically, when advocates of strictly textual poetry mount an attack, sound and vocal poets are capable of banding together, if only for a moment.

The other temptation, or difficulty as we termed it, is that of genealogy, to which the same Jean-Michel Espitallier, in his amused-amusing savant manner, invites figures from Aristotle to Kurt Schwitters and his *Ursonate* (1923–1928), to the first recorded journal, *OU*, created in 1964 by Henri Chopin (1922–2008). Beyond running the risk of name-dropping, there is also a risk of arriving at a limited truth prone to revision. Thus, if one is to believe the reading of a succession of diverse sources and studies, concrete poetry (a general category including sound, visual, and spatial dimensions) was born in Sweden, Switzerland, or Brazil, or all three, or in Germany. Accounts are often preoccupied with identifying a beginning, or failing that, inventing one (as some do to give a foundation to their work) by claiming affiliation with an alleged fundamental origin of song and the word (which one willingly imagines as a primal cry), or more modestly in referring back to erudite or vernacular improvised poetry traditions found around the world, or even to the troubadours. I have not especially tried to settle on an anteriority of phenomena that are often concomitant and have compounding influences, nor have I tried to show the numerous and often reticulated connections, as illustrated by the useful essay of historical typology of Jean-Pierre Bobillot (born 1950), critic and self-proclaimed "noisy" poet (Bobillot 2009).

Places, Knots, Circulations

The poet and performer John Giorno (born 1935) tells this story:

> In 1965 Brion [*Gysin*] had talked about *poésie sonore*, sound poetry. How, in the late 1950s, he, Bernard Heidsieck, Henri Chopin and François Dufrêne innovated *poésie sonore* in Paris. Brion had played for me, in room 703 of Hotel Chelsea in New York, the reel-to-reel tapes of the sound poem "I Am That I Am" that he made at BBC in London in 1960, the *OU* LP featuring works by all of them, and other recordings.
> (2010: 147)

Giorno's recollections shape one of the currents—American in this case—of the great narratives built from the testimonies of various participants for over half a century, Bernard Heidsieck's in particular (1928–2014). In this study we will repeatedly encounter this major French figure of the heroic post-war decades who has frequently and methodically spoken of the personal and collective adventure into which he was pulled by his desire to make the poem active.

Sound poetry is clearly an international phenomenon, and sound poets' internationalism is striking. They publish each other across national boundaries, despite some protectionist impulses, as seen in France with the Fluxus movement. Some places stand out in the geography of their gatherings, like the Cabaret Voltaire in Zurich was for Dada: the American Center on the Boulevard Raspail in Paris in the 1960s is the inevitable example. At the December 1962 Fluxus festival, Bernard Heidsieck discovers Brion Gysin (1916–1986) and his famous permutation *I Am That I Am.*

- **Document 1:** Gysin, *I Am That I Am,* YouTube, January 2011.

Organized very early on, festivals small and large trace out these all but mundane focal points: Sweden, with the Text-Sound Festival founded in

1967; Budapest and Provence with the Cogolin, Allauch and Tarascon gatherings of 1985 to 1993 . . . Last, journals (also international, based in Brazil, Japan, France, Italy . . .) provoke, prolong, and restart discussion; they are printed, sometimes accompanied by cassettes, records, or CDs, then become electronic—the latest being *Celebrity Cafe*, which took over from *Son@rt* in France in 2013. Now there are electronic websites, both specialized and of wider breadth.

The desire that overcame the first "sound" poets to give poetry new life was not entirely new. But for a long time the most frequently cited precursors, still in the most visible context of the book, were audacious pagination and typographical invention: Appollinaire's calligrammes, and Mallarmé's text arrangement of *Un coup de dés jamais n'abolira le hasard* (A throw of the dice will never banish chance; 1897), his last poem. But these authors also had active *sound* preoccupations. Fascinated by the invention of the phonograph, Apollinaire recorded *Le Pont Mirabeau* ("Mirabeau Bridge") in 1912. In *Crise de vers* ("Crisis of Verse"; 1886–1896) Mallarmé described the "exquisite [. . .] fundamental crisis" poetry was undergoing in his time, and the tendency of the "faithful supporters of the Alexandrine," the French verse *par excellence*, to break away from the "rigid and puerile mechanism of its beat" (translated in Lloyd 1999: 227–8). In this programmatic text he used the word *souffle* —breath, breathe—twice, a word that would later be found among poets seemingly distant from Mallarmé's legacy. And in his work *Coup de dés*, the literally shattering disposition of words spread out over two facing pages that come to be one, the distribution of blank spaces, the entirely new cuts and spans, cannot be understood independently of their intonational and prosodic dimensions: line breaks and "encroachments" make an inseparably visual and sound-related scansion, where the blanks are silences. As for "the variations between printed characters," Mallarmé specifies in his preface, "they indicate their importance to oral expression" (1945: 455).

To "stand poetry up." Stop humming along, as Brecht had already said. Despite literary shake-ups since the mid-nineteenth century, regardless of the jolts of Dada and futurisms and the surrealist shiver that would take their place, for some the poem seemed to "be diluted in the white page." Bernard Heidsieck declared in 1961: ". . . so for a poem, standing up straight feet on the page / a page: trampoline for its quest for oxygen" (Heidsieck 2001: 208).

Text, Language, and Beyond

I have already mentioned the return to the cry. The sound poets' project was not exempt from a certain linguistic primitivism: "Language, if we petrify it in the academies, runs off to children and crazy poets," said the Dadaist poet Raoul Hausmann in 1955 (2007: 247). And Jean-Pierre Verheggen (born 1942), inexhaustible brewer and kneader of words and member of the journal *TXT*, declared: "I know that to speak the language well [. . .] you have to produce a stupidly intelligent language" (1991: 141). He compiled a little anthology of major non-conformist authors to support this assertion: Maiakovski, Rimbaud, Burroughs, Khlebnikov, and Artaud, who declares himself to be a "gibberish singer." To these leading names could be added others, suggesting at least a proximity with the Austrian poet-performer and poetician Ernst Jandl (1925–2000) who works in "a regressive German, a *fallen language*" and practices onomatopoetry, assembling "in a flash what seemed to have collapsed and making it into new possibilities for speech" (Tunner 1992: 160–3).

- **Document 2:** Jandl, *Devil Trap,* YouTube, April 2011.

We could also cite the Swede Öyyind Fahlström, who in 1953 spoke of "emphasized rhythm as 'the most elementary, directly physically grasping means of effect' because of its 'connection with the pulsation of breathing, blood, ejaculation'" (Cobbing 1982: 385).

There is also an evocation of the idea of preserving the surge of speech, the immediateness of the here and now, the fragility of the object thus produced. The American David Antin (1932–2016) insisted on this, abandoning reading his books in public so he could improvise his "talk":

> it was like reading   somebody elses words   who was talking through me in a way   i didnt really like   and id sort of mouth the words like an   actor reading his own lips in a film that had shot last year   on a noisy location and was now dubbing it in all over again
>
> (Antin 1984: 151)

David Antin also insisted on interaction with the public, of which he said:

> because what I say   to some degree   is determined by what you   think   and my sense of it
>
> (Antin 1984, 151 and 54)

Finally, "with 'sound poetry,' which mixes cries, sound, breath, speech, and voice, a radical innovation intervenes: the body," wrote Jacinto Lageira, citing Tzara: "Thought is made in the mouth" (Lageira 2006: 18–19). This is the same body through which the poet gets completely involved in the performance. Corporeality includes what happens inside the body (we will come back to this).

In sound poetry, the emphasis is thus on the voice, on the surging word freeing itself, in contrast with the (pre-)written text, and a scale of authors can be made according to the degree of anteriority that writing holds for them in the expression of the poem. Bernard Heidsieck called his first works "poem-scores," taking care to specify, however, that "the poem is only complete when it is 'played,' said" (Interview, 4–7–2013). When questioned about what she calls "oral publications," Michèle Métail (born 1950) explains: "so there is a score [. . .], it's the exact equivalent of a musical score; not everything is marked: the voice and the timbre for example." She also maintains that "telling is the ultimate stage of writing" (Métail and Barras 1992: 149, 151). And Charles Olson: "breath allows *all* the speech-force of language back in [. . .] now, through speech, a poem has solidity" (Olson 1950). On the contrary, David Antin improvises his poems by "talking" in front of and

Figure 10.2 "Michèle Métail (Internationale Festival Phonetische Poesie—Vienne, février 1983)".

© Françoise Janicot, reproduced by kind permission.

with an audience, in front of a recording device, before using the recordings of these "talking pieces" to make books.

Their demand may not merely be to leave the page or the pre-written text, but to break away from all text, even virtual, or even language itself, either by retaining only a few minimal elements, like the letter for lettrists, or by orienting toward the infra-linguistic. In the world of sound poetry this division is illustrated on one side (asemantic, nonverbal) by François Dufrêne (1930–1982) and his *Crirythmes* and by Henri Chopin, who explains: "Little by little I abandoned discursive poetry to go toward sound" (cited in Donguy 2007: 15).

- **Document 3:** Chopin, *Chercher,* YouTube, February 2011.

The other side is exemplified by Bernard Heidsieck and his "action poetry," although most of his work was semantic and verbal, drawing comparison to "miniature operas" (Barras 1999: 29). This tendency is carried on by subsequent generations, such as by Anne-James Chaton (born 1971) who uses "impoverished writings" as material—tickets, receipts, bills, reports, various kinds of statements—and calls on live music, most often that of guitarist Andy Moor.

- **Document 4:** Chaton, *Décade*, http://aj.chaton.free.fr/, 2009.

Another example is the German sound poet and musician Michael Lentz (born 1964), author of the text of reference on *Lautepoesie* (Lentz 2000), who works either *a capella*, varying speed and exploiting the effects of repetition, or starts with a recorded text that scrambles his voice, which is subsequently layered on with overprinting and sound saturation, or Larsen effects. In this case, then, it is a game pushing limits.

Playing on this side of or beyond the articulated and/or the semantic, or simply the understandable, and playing *with* limits are the projects Russian futurists undertook in their day, especially Vélimir Khlebnikov with the invention of *zaoum*, a "transmental" language. How does a sound make sense, Julien Blaine (born 1942) wonders today, phonetically illustrating his comments over the course of our interview by grunting, groaning, and sighing, declaring: "once you're into onomatopoeia, the sound of pain, joy, pleasure . . . sound makes meaning in its expression of a moment of the body or someone's life" (Interview, 21–7–2011).

I will initially keep to the verbal side of this divide, in a "space" where poets apply themselves, positively, negatively, or by default, to or against language in a thousand ways, voice alone or accompanied. Music paved the way, with Philip Glass's decomposition into phonemes, syllables, and letters, or *Omaggio a Joyce* (1958), where Luciano Berio musically mixes elements from Chapter 11 of *Ulysses*. In *Visage* in 1961, vocally "created" by Cathy Berberian, Berio combined phonemes, laughter, digestive rumblings, grunts, sobs, cries, yells, and nonhuman noises that are more difficult to identify. I am also thinking of Bruna Maderna, in *Invenzione su una voce* (or *Dimenzione II*—1960), an electro-acoustic piece on phonemes composed by the German poet Hans Günter Helms (1932–2012). Or of Henri Pousseur for his *Phonèmes pour Cathy pour voix seule* (1967)—"Cathy" is still Cathy Berberian, whose voice carried so many experiments.

Dismantling-remounting. Puns, permutations, homophonies . . . Acceleration or slowing of the delivery of the voice, scrambling or confusing phonetic units and phonemes, variations in intonation . . . the comical effect of such operations is clearly perceptible in Jandl. Counterpoint in the form of teasing echoes and ironic commentaries are also present in Heidsieck, as are variations on a single formulation, such as *"autour de Vaduz/ il y a des . . ."* ("around Vaduz, there are . . .") returning insistently in his eponymous 1974 poem.

The Reel-to-Reel Tape Recorder

Paradoxically (?) some poets refer to what poetry might harbor of archaic foundations, the incarnated cry, voice, and rhythm, the body that deploys itself in performance, or even the rediscovery of ritual values, while at the same time increasingly calling on technical equipment under continual refinement. For everything voice- and sound-related, the arrival of the reel-to-reel tape recorder introduced a tremendous shift by opening the path to experimentation. In 1959, on what was still a rudimentary mono device, Bernard Heidsieck discovered the possibilities of intervening on magnetic tape with a pair of scissors and sticky tape. He knows that he is not the only one working with a tape recorder in Paris at the time: there is François Dufrêne from lettrism, Henri Chopin, and Brion Gysin. Much like "phonography," or at least to the extent to which the deferred effects of the 1877 invention of the phonograph were a "radical point of discontinuity" in the history of music, the reel-to-reel tape recorder became a pivotal factor in the history of poetry that, along with sound/vocal poetry, would "take over from the sound document," to cite Pierre-Yves Macé's study of the "sound document" in contemporary music (2011: 15–16). To the contrary, the performer Bartolomé Ferrando (born 1951) explained the handicap represented by the fact that this technology was still difficult to come by when he was a student in Spain, where he was born in 1951.

"Many [*poets*] are afraid of tape recorders and the idea of using any mechanical means for literary purposes seems to them some sort of sacrilege" (Burroughs and Gysin 1978). But once "tamed," poets refer to their equipment calling it by its brand name, the way they did with their old typewriters, inseparable companions—Julien Blaine recalls the "shitty old Philips" of his youth, and his next one, a Uher, "was a little better" (Interview, 21–7–2011).

The tape recorder offers many possibilities, presented here in order of appearance in the field of the sonic poet. It is a "passive" means (of recording), and disturbing when it reveals the author's own voice to him. It is also active, allowing acceleration/slowing and repetition. It is an *assembling* machine. It lends itself to sampling and cut-up, the form of "cut-and-paste" invented by Brion Gysin in 1959 and enhanced by William Burroughs. Initially practiced on printed texts, "cut-ups can be applied to fields other than writing" (Burroughs and Gysin 1978: n.p.). Gysin would use it on magnetic tape. With multi-track recorders the possibilities multiply: superimposition of sounds, polyphony, or phasing, which Steve Reich exploited by accidentally discovering how the rotation of two identical tapes at a slightly different speed leads to a gradual break of unison, like a stutter. Last, the tape recorder allows collecting samples of noises-sounds, which thus acquire the status of "document" testifying to industrial, warring, metro-(mega-)politan modernity, and/or to life at its most ordinary.

In addition to diffusion, radio (or at least its studios) functioned as sound laboratories thanks to their perfected equipment. Their role in poetic experiments varied from country to country. Certainly in Germany, where radio stations benefited from governmental polycentrism, they were favored by the development of *Hörspiel*, literally "ear games." Among the original contributors at the turn of the 1920s to 1930s were Walter Benjamin, Bertolt Brecht, and the composer Paul Hindemith. Later it would be Henri Chopin in Köln, Georges Perec, and others. We know that in early 1960s London, Brion Gysin perfected his poem consisting of a cyclical permutation of the terms of the assertion "I Am That I Am" based on his first "tape experiments." He explains: "The BBC loaned me their experimental studio with all its machines and technicians." Here indeed he could build upon the swirling dynamic of what he called "The Divine Tautology" (Burroughs and Gysin 1978: n.p), by using an entire range of acoustic processes, overprinting, variations in speed, shunting, and especially the possibilities offered by a delay, such as reverberation, feedback, or room effects. In Berkeley in 1969, Clark Coolidge was given a weekly show open to composers and poets. In France, even if Chopin in particular did broadcasts, it seems that music was the domain of preference of the national radio network RTF (French Radio-Television) and its *Service de la Recherche* (Research Service), whose prestige was associated with the work of Pierre Schaeffer and concrete music. It had taken over from *Club d'Essais* (The Experiment Club) in 1959, established at the Liberation by Jean Tardieu, who himself had taken the reins of *Studio d'Essai* (The Experiment Studio) from Schaeffer, who had founded it during the war.

After the generalization of sound effects, especially the echo, reverberation, and various forms of distortion, technical resources continued to multiply and improve, putting the more fascinated users at risk of falling into exhibitionism.

Musicalities

"It is very difficult to determine how the voice that forms speech differs form the voice that forms *Song*," noted Rousseau (1995: 694): think of the

Sprechstimme (a melodramatically spoken recitation, a pitched declamation) Schoenberg used in *Pierrot lunaire* (*Lunar Pierrot*, 1912) that blurs the boundaries between the genres of speech and song, or the adoption by several poets (sound or other, for that matter) of a *recto tono* diction, i.e., sung on one pitch. I have attempted to place some contemporary poets on a "musicality scale," which would give, for example, a range of musicality from prosodic to musical:

> William Carlos Williams (1883–1963)
> > Charles Olson (1910–1970) //
> > > > Jack Kerouac (1922–1969)
> > > Clark Coolidge (1939–)
> > > > Rozalie Hirs (1965–)

One could continue to build along these lines, of course, adding Verlaine and his "music above all" upstream, or Ezra Pound, who asked the poet "to compose in the sequence of the musical phrase, not in sequence of a metronome." And remember the temptation of music and its influence evoked by Mallarmé, who spoke ironically of the "forced counting" of a petrified system of meter. With his "variable foot," William Carlos Williams laid claim to the prosody of the American idiom, while Charles Olson put the accent on breath with "projective verse." A "projective poet," Olson states, "goes down through the workings of his own throat to that place where breath comes from, where breath has its beginnings" (1950). Jack Kerouac, whose references were Bud Powell, Lester Young, and Charlie Parker, recorded his Beat poems with jazz musicians in the 1950s (Kerouac 1959). In *Mexico City Blues*, he wrote: "I want to be considered a jazz poet." I also place the American Clark Coolidge on this scale, trained as a geologist and also a jazz drummer, who explores various forms of writing, including compositions for magnetic tape, allowing superimpositions, nesting, permutations. He considers himself to be a bop prosodist, practicing bop phrasing (Fayard 2009: 131). The sound poet Japp Blonk (born 1953) from the Netherlands also first appeared as a jazz musician, on the saxophone and as a vocal artist. There is also place for his countrywoman Rozalie Hirs (born 1965), who publishes books integrating visual aspects of writing and composes instrumental and electronic music, pieces that are "also composed of words, bringing us to wonder about the boundary between music and poetry" (Lindner 2011: 42, 47). As for Jackson Mac Low (1922–2004), where and how to place him, if, as Jacques Roubaud indicates, he is part musician, part poet, alternating between formal constraints of different natures (1973: 39)?

I will not make a list of poets having maintained active relationships with the music of their time. I will only remind of the extent to which Bernard Heidseick's discovery of contemporary composers (along with the purchase of a tape recorder) was decisive for his work, especially the Paris concerts of Pierre Boulez's "Domaine musical" and listening to Karlheinz Stockhausen's

Gesang der Jünglinge (*Song of the Youths*, 1955–1956), considered to be the first electronic masterpiece. "A music without performers! The sound swirled. Now that's what poetry should do: project itself into space" (Interview, Heidsieck, 4–7–2013). Among the references shared by sound poets worldwide (even more than the "sound objects" of concrete music's inventor Pierre Schaeffer, it seems to me) figures the Viennese Anton Webern, who favored sound color, timbre, and *Klangfarbenmelodie* (sound-color-melody) in his music.

The Noises of Poetry

Convinced that the prosodic poetry of his time must take account of noise, Brecht commented: "our ear is doubtlessly in the process of being subject to a physiological transformation. The acoustic setting has been extraordinarily modified. Think only of the noises of the street in the modern city!" (1970: 29). In fact erudite musicians had begun to take up these noises early in the twentieth century, with an apparent predilection for big-city sirens, foghorns, and vehicular horns, which they introduced into the orchestra (Paul Hindemith in *Kammermusiken* in 1921, Edgar Varèse in *Amériques* the following year, George Gershwin in *An American in Paris* in 1928 . . .). Before them, and well before Pierre Schaeffer's experiments, the futurist Luigi Russolo had, even more radically, perfected an impressive machinery destined to produce a pure music of *suoni-rumori*, sound-noises corresponding to the new era.

Before imitating or reproducing them via recordings, replicating them raw or after treatment, poets had been attentive to the voice, the cries of the city and its noises, by evoking them *in their writing*, mimetic or not. There is Victor Hugo, but also the American Vachel Lindsay, who I learned of during my study. He was 42 in 1921, when Valéry Larbaud introduced him to French readers: with him, "the jazz band, Salvation Army brasses, Black dances and songs, illuminated signs, and toots of Ford automobile horns came into literature." Lindsay wrote "in the American language," basing all his poetry on the voice, and indicated the intonation in the poems' margins. He reads them "accompanied by drum, cymbals, and cries," crossing the United States "like teachers and preachers when Walt Whitman was a young man" (Larbaud 1998: 493).

Sound poetry, poetry of sounds, of noises? If we are to believe Jean-Jacques Rousseau, who does not shrink from the challenge in his *Dictionary of Music*, distinguishing between organized sounds and noises ("in general all emotion of the Air making itself perceptible by the auditory organ") is part of an essentially musical problem; a distinction Russolo wanted to destroy. If, Rousseau wonders, they are of the same physical nature, then "why would Noise not be Sound?" He supposes that "the latter is appreciable only with the support of its Harmonics, and thus does not include *Noise,* because it lacks them." The difference, then, is structural, and also quantitative: "where does this change from an excessive Sound into *Noise* come from? The violence of the vibrations makes the resonance of so many aliquots perceptible that the mix of so many diverse Sounds then makes its effect ordinary, and then it is only a *Noise*"—as when all the keys of a harpsichord are struck at once (Rousseau 1995: 671–2).

We know that the distinction varies over time and space, and not only in common-sense conceptions: a noise is likely to acquire the status of a sound, and for some, any noise-sound may become music on the condition that it is intentional. Moreover, the universe of noises is itself split between those that are undesirable and upsetting and those that reassure, boundaries that generally follow physical, aesthetic, and social or ethnic appreciations all at the same time. Noble sounds ("ours") and crude noises ("theirs")? No position is guaranteed: a "repressed" noise is likely to return (Gonseth et al. 2011). What interests us here is not only the noise-sound dialectic—I use this pair most often, refusing to choose between two terms whose usage is often confused—but the noise-sound-language (and poetry) dialectic.

The noises (sounds) of sound poets? We will distinguish here, at least provisionally, between the artifacts resulting from sound-effect operations and the noise-sounds sampled from the surrounding environment (Heidsieck speaks of "biopsy"), which poets sometimes think of as accompaniment, sometimes as a material to work on as such, to be reworked. We must not forget noise from oneself—starting with tongues (the language we speak or sing, but also that of the muscle mass we have in the mouth); language as noise-sound; and breath. Or the noises we produce ourselves as "language" (for lettrists), for that matter, or those that we capture, as Bernard Heidsieck did for his series *Respirations et brèves rencontres* (Breaths and short encounters, 2000). "Remember Gherasim Luca's stammering," wrote Jean-Michel Espitallier, "on which all the torn-tearing of the tongue chews, inventing an immediately necessary timbre for itself, a strike, a rustling, irritating them to make throat render, agglutinating or disarticulating the word-material" (2006: 143). Let us also remember "the 'parasites' of speech [. . .] produced (and sometimes accentuated) over the course of a performance" (Barras 2013: 258), all the sound resources of the mouth and the phonic mechanism, and the trunk as a sonic cavity as well, Henri Chopin going so far as to use a miniature microphone in his stomach (Donguy 2007: 15).

There are also "given" noises in the environment where a performance takes place, which might interfere. Evoking an old desire that his texts be heard through forest foliage, Julien Blaine explains: "I work a lot with sounds that happen in a place." They are unintentional, like the echoes, running water, awakening of bats in a grotto, or provoked, like those of printing presses, to which he pays homage at the moment they were put on the scrap heap (Interview, Blaine, 21–7–2011). By revealing the contrast, this attitude toward ambient noises and their possible intervention in works underway allows an improved characterization of the work of *sound artists*, such as that of Yvan Etienne, which consists of "putting a place in resonance" by exploiting its potential (Interview, Etienne, 20–7–2011).

Bernard Heidsieck related how noise-sounds came to enter his poetry, before they took a prominent place, as seen in *La semaine* (The week).

• **Document 5:** Heidsieck, *La semaine* (*Passepartout 5*), in Bobillot Jean-Pierre, *Heidsieck, poésie action*, Paris, Jean-Michel Place, 1996.

Another example is his work *Le Carrefour de la Chaussée d'Antin* (The Chaussée d'Antin Crossing), an everyday portrait of a slice of Paris via the subway, captured through its sounds, voices, motors, and various signals (Heidsieck 2002). In 1961, while he was recording a "very flat" text for his *Poem Partition J*, the cries of children arose outside, and he opened the window to catch them and include them in his edit (Interview, Heidsieck, 4–7–2013). His story has something "Cagian" to it: its simplicity, its contingency to the event, the love he shows for noises, and what he "says" of silence, supposedly silent silence, which proves to be "background" silence, as we speak of background noise. Not only does it come close to a suggestion from *Silence*—"The sounds that had accidentally occurred/ while it/ was being played were in/ no sense an interruption"—but it illustrates another remark: "There is no/ such a thing a silence. Something is al-/ ways happening that makes a sound" (Cage 1966: 157–8, 191).

Bartolomé Ferrando practiced "poetic performance" into which he integrated a great variety of noise-sounds that he produced—mimetic, "expressive," trans-linguisitic or of variable intensities—the rustling and movement of objects of varying densities, micro-percussion . . . His theoretical thinking refers mainly to Cage, more explicitly so than any other artist encountered in my study. Also citing the painter and philosopher Gilo Dorfles, he wonders if equal value might be granted to noises and sounds. We try to not hear noise, but it might be richer, contributing to a perceptual asymmetry inviting discovery.

> "Listen, listen to everything," as Cage said (and Fluxus along with him), the sounds, noises so abundant in the city (Russolo already). That is what I try to do, listen to non-organized music. The same goes for art. It's not the same for a musician to coordinate sounds and noises in a composition or to construct his "concert" any place, in taking you for a walk—it's life as creation, the society of permanent creation: you hear [*we are seated at a café terrace*] a voice to the left, metallic noises to the right, the sound of a spoon . . . it all produces a sort of polyphony that organizes . . . without an organizing intention. Noise can open the art to another way of hearing noise, sound (Ferrando).

Bartolomé Ferrando then comes back to this idea: moving toward the self-effacement, but not the discounting, of the art's producer, who is then one element among all sound elements. The idea is of a multiple perception, decentered, according to which the plastic sound vacuum does not exist (Interview, Ferrando, 19–7–2011).

All That . . .

> I could capture what interested me, street noise, all that . . .
>
> (B. Heidsieck, cited in Collet 2010: 11)

Again, John Giorno:

> Brion [Gysin] and I had two portable 5-inch reel-to-reel tape recorders, like small suitcases. [. . .] On a very hot and humid afternoon, Brion and I went into the subway and recorded random sounds: trains starting and stopping, rolling through the tunnels into stations with screaming brakes, from inside and out; the rumble of trains and people talking; the silence of the subway.
>
> (Giorno 2010: 147)

"What's the point in imitating what can be captured in real life?" Bernard Heidsieck wrote to Jean-Pierre Bobillot (Bobillot 1996: 86). It is possible to import a heterogeneous noise-sound, sampled with a recorder, into the poem. I will suggest once again a connection with the musical domain by comparing this procedure with the way contemporary composers incorporate external elements into their work, pre-recorded "sound documents": for example, voices and factory noises in Luigi Nono's *La Fabricca Illuminata* (1964), voice and musical quotations in Luciano Berio's *Sinfonia* (1968), and *Requiem für einen jungen Dichter* by Bernd Alois Zimmermann (1967–69), forming an enormous collage of languages, voice, extracts from political, religious, and philosophical speeches, musical and literary quotes. I am also thinking of Steve Reich, collecting the noises of New York City for *City Life* (1995) . . . This would eventually lead to what Pierre-Yves Macé calls an "effect document." Or the borrowed fragment may be "de-documented": like a cut-up, its original meaning is apt to change as it changes contexts. Or indeed, as is usually Cage's case, it is only an interchangeable element, "any sound." Otherwise, it functions as a ready-made—the ready-made short-circuiting the documentary intention (Macé 2011: 123, 126, 242, 244).

I will quote John Cage one last time, specifically his monumental *Roaratorio: An Irish Circus on Finnegans Wake* (April 1979), broadcast for the first time by the Hörspiel Studio of WDR3 (Köln, Germany) October 22, 1979, for which he had benefitted from the technical equipment—between 60 and 70 sound tracks—of the newly formed IRCAM in Paris. The most significant traits of oral and sound poetry take shape and come undone in this work that never ends, since its author has the possibility of performing it several times, by combining live "reading" with pre-recorded elements. For one thing, although he is not the author of the words he speak-sings, Cage "produced" a new text by rewriting Joyce's *Finnegan's Wake*. The resulting radio play became "Cagian" by the "conversion" of the original in *mesostics*, literally "mid-verse," an exercise he was very fond of consisting of distributing a text in linked lines of prose poetry so that it reads vertically, on the same central column, letters forming one or more words, in this case J A M E S J O Y C E, repeated for the length of the text. At the same time, Cage appropriates it physically as well: he hums, he plays with the texture of his voice and the resources of his mouth—inhaling, chewing, sucking—using every phonic mechanism. In addition, he exploits a body of Irish musics and brief sound samples of "the 2462 places mentioned in *Finnegan's Wake*" (1083, ultimately), captured by himself or his assistants, who were instructed: "You can simply accept the sounds which are in the place you go to when you make the recording" (Cage 1992: book 1).

- **Document 6:** Cage, *Roaratorio*, disk 1, part 4, New York, NY, Mode records (mode 28 / 29), 1992.

The last case we offer is that of the *Sound Documentaries* (1967–1977) Glenn Gould made for the Canadian radio. This work, although it was imprinted on a record, is not well known. In it Gould mixes recorded voices, interviews, conversations, speech, and song, which he superimposes in an exercise he calls "contrapuntal radio" to musical and ambient sound samples ranging from a bell chiming in the country to the "continuous bass" of a train inside of which the listener is transported, with no commentary or text from the author, who seems to stay in the background. A sound poem without a poet?

- **Document 7:** Gould, *Solitude Trilogy, Three Sound Documentaries—3 The Quiet in the Land*, CBC Records, PSCD 2003–3, 2000.

Although the poets who obstinately reject such experiments, refusing the paths they opened, maintain rather strongly hostile so that we will listen to them, we know less of the more discrete attitude of other authors reputed to be rather textual, like David Lespiau (born 1969), which deserve study. Even if he willingly practices reading in front of an audience, he does not write in this perspective, and in private he does not read himself aloud, but he wonders what to do with the sound material that surrounds and accompanies him. He responds to this issue in making short videos using a "material recorded without an objective," by making some condensations, accelerations . . . by wondering about what he wants "to hear 'in addition,'" he says, "like at home in Marseille, when I work: sound, both far *and* near (like on the beach of my childhood) . . . a lot of Arabic words, and urban noises that I like—I asked someone to come make a recording" (Interview, Lespiau, 16–3–2013).

Henri Deluy's (born 1931) position—at the limits, it can be said—seems particularly interesting. For a long time he showed no interest in sound poetry, thinking, with the members of the journal *Action poétique* (Poetic Action) that he edited (210 issues published until it ceased publication in

2012), that poetry was *the poem*, a *written* thing responding to specific formal demands. In 2013 he specifies that although he used to be close to sharing Jacques Roubaud's severe judgment, referring ironically to "*vroum-vroum*" poetry (Roubaud 2010), his thinking has since changed.

> Today I can accept as poems what poets calling themselves 'sound poets' produce. On the other hand they have a faculty for listening to ambient sound that interests me. It is obvious that we—the poets who are not at all in this domain—we record a lot of things. For nearly twenty years in Ivry [southern metropolitan Paris], I used to stop by a bistro every morning for a coffee and I overheard the conversations, I thought to myself "there's the poem right there." There was what people were saying, and the sonorities also, especially because in a bar people tend to speak rather loudly—there's a noise, you've got to raise your voice—and I really like to hear that, even if most of the time I'm unable to make it work in what I write. But it's important for me and there's no doubt, indirectly, it has an effect.
>
> (Interview, Deluy, 17–9–2013)

These two points of view are not exceptional. Without necessarily "turning to the enemy," some authors (even some avant-garde ones) who had been rather resistant to or distant from sound poetry culture and practice eventually came to change their opinions. Between attention and inattention, familiarity and strangeness, their potential relationship with the sound environment as they evoke it, somehow mediated by sound poetry, seems to be underlain by a dialectic that is not that far from what Walter Benjamin called "casual noticing." Remember that according to Benjamin, it characterizes urban residents' usual perception of architectural objects "by way of habit" (Benjamin 2008: 40), and by extension, one might say, objects composing everyday environments. This relationship emerges in the register of the *ordinary moment* (an object of microsociology), that of banal interactions—unfocused, scattered, distracted, like listening to the radio or hearing the murmur of a neighborhood (Féraud 2010)—whose auditory dimension should be considered as much as its visible dimension, often privileged in analyses.

Here we seem to have reached a threshold—or at least we have come close—where social science researchers (especially those trying to construct an anthropology of sound), poets, "uncredentialed" makers of noise, and listeners may find themselves together, along with "sound hunters" of all kinds, trackers of birdsong, political speeches, marching bands, local rock, and factory noises. We are not at the threshold of the universe of noises—we are already immersed in the world of noise-sound—but we are confronted with these approaches, lines of questioning, and potential forms of knowledge and speech, which, though they may not be "shared," are at least audible by everyone.

Notes

1 John Cage, *Silence*, p. 166.
2 Acknowledgments: Thanks to Bernard Heidsieck, Julien Blaine, Bartolomé Ferrando and Yvan Etienne; to Henri Deluy, Jean-Michel Espitallier, Olivier Cadiot, Pierre Alferi, David Lespiau, Vincent Rioux and Olivier Féraud, who agreed to answer my questions, as well as Christine Guillebaud for her sharp reading, and Eric Giraud for his bibliographic advice.

References

Antin, David. 1984. *Tuning*. New York: A New Direction Book.

Barras, Vincent. 1999. "Poésie sonore." In *Poésie française contemporaine (de l'après-guerre à aujourd'hui)*, 27–30 (+ 1 CD). Collection Cent titres 1. Marseilles: cipM.

———. 2013. "Parole performée." *Communications* 92: 253–261.

Benjamin, Walter. [1936] 2008. *The Work of Art in the Age of Mechanical Reproduction and Other Writings on Media*. Cambridge: Harvard University Press.

Bobillot, Jean-Pierre. 1996. *Heidsieck, poésie, action*. Paris: Jean-Michel Place.

———. 2009. *Poésie sonore: Eléments d'une typologie historique*. Reims: Le Clou dans le fer.

Brecht, Bertolt. 1970. "Notes sur le travail littéraire 1935–1941." French text by Bernard Lortholary. In *Les arts et la révolution, précédé de Notes sur le travail littéraire: Articles sur la littérature*, 9–54. Paris: L'Arche.

Burroughs, William S. and Gysin Brion. 1978. *The Third Mind*. New York: A Severe Book/The Viking Press.

Cage, John. 1966. *Silence*. Cambridge: MIT Press.

Chopin, Henri. 1979. *Poésie sonore internationale*. Paris: Jean-Michel Place.

Cobbing, Bob. 1982. "Concrete Sound Poetry 1950–1970." In *The Avant Garde Tradition in Literature*, edited by Richard Kostelanetz, 385–391. Buffalo: Prometheus Books.

Collet, François and Bernard Heidsieck. 2010. "Entretien." *Dossier Bernard Heidsieck*. Special issue of Cahier critique de poésie 19: 5–12.

Donguy, Jacques. 2007. "Henri Chopin, ou la rupture avec l'écrit." *Le cahier du refuge* 162: 15–20.

Espitallier, Jean-Michel. 2006. *Caisse à outils: Un panorama de la poésie française d'aujourd'hui*. Paris: Pocket.

Fayard, Guillaume. 2009. "Postface." In *Dépositions smithsonniennes et sujet à un film*, edited by Clark Coolidge, 112–113. Paris: Les petits matins.

Féraud, Olivier. 2010. *Voix publiques: Environnements sonores, représentations et usages d'habitation dans un quartier populaire de Naples*. PhD Thesis, Ecole des Hautes Etudes en Sciences Sociales, Paris.

Giorno, John. 2010. "New Demon King." In *Brion Gysin Dream Machine*, edited by Laura Hoptman, 146–147. London: Merrell.

Gonseth, Marc-Olivier, Bernard Knodel, Yann Laville, and Grégoire Mayor, ed. 2011. *Bruits: Echos du patrimoine culturel immaterial*. Neuchâtel: Musée d'ethnographie.

Hausmann, Raoul. 2007. *Une anthologie poétique, précédé de RH l'optophoniste*, presented by Isabelle Maunet-Saillet. Marseilles: Al Dante.

Heidsieck, Bernard. 2000. *Respirations et brèves rencontres*. Romainville: Al Dante.

———. 2001. *Notes convergentes*. Romainville: Al Dante.

———. 2002. *Le Carrefour de la Chaussée d'Antin*. Romainville: Al Dante.

Hocquard, Emmanuel. 2001. *Ma haie*. Paris: P.O.L.

Kerouac, Jack. 1959. *Mexico City Blues*. New York: Grove Press.

Lageira, Jacinto, ed. 2006. *Du mot à l'image et du son au mot: Théories, manifestes, documents; Une anthologie de 1897 à 2005*. Marseilles: Le mot et le reste.

Larbaud, Valéry. 1998. *Ce vice impuni, la lecture. Domaine anglais*. Paris: Gallimard.

Lentz, Michael. 2000. *Lautpoesie: Musik nach 1945*. Vienna: Selene.

Lindner, Erik. 2011. Preface to *Poètes néerlandais de la modernité*, edited by Henri Deluy, 15–48. Paris: Le temps des Cerises.

Lloyd, Rosemary. 1999. *Mallarmé: The Poet and His Circle*. Ithaca: Cornell University Press.

Macé, Pierre-Yves. 2011. *Musique et document sonore: Enquête sur la phonographie documentaire dans les pratiques musicales contemporaines*. Dijon: Les presses du réel.

Mallarmé, Stéphane. 1945. *Œuvres complètes*. Paris: Gallimard, Bibliothèque de la Pléiade.

Métail, Michèle and Vincent Barras. 1992. "Entretien." In *Poésies sonores*, edited by Vincent Barras and Nicholas Zurbrugg, 147–156. Geneva: Contrechamps.

Olson, Charles. 1950. "Projective Verse." *Poetry New York* 3. www.poetryfoundation.org/learning/essay/237880.

Roubaud, Jacques. 1973. "Jackson Mac Low." *Action poétique* 56: 39.

———. 2010. "Obstination de la poésie." *Le Monde diplomatique* January: 22–23.

Rousseau, Jean-Jacques. [1764] 1995. *Dictionnaire de musique*, s.v. "voix" and "bruit." In *Œuvres complètes V*, edited by Bernard Gagnebin et al., 671–672. Paris: Gallimard, Bibliothèque de la Pléiade.

Sheppard, Robert. 2005. "Bob Cobbing and Concrete Poetry." *Pages*. http://robert-sheppardblogspot.fr/2005/03robert-sheppard-bo.

Tunner, Erika. 1992. "Ernst Jandl: Cas unique; Idées subites; Écrire sous le signe de Saturne." In *Poésies sonores*, edited by Vincent Barras and Nicholas Zurbrugg, 159–175. Geneva: Contrechamps.

Verheggen, Jean-Pierre. 1991. "De l'inouïversalité." In *Écrivain cherche lecteur: L'écrivain francophone et ses publics*, edited by Lise Gauvin and Jean-Marie Klinkenberg, 141–147. Paris: Créaphis—VLB.

Discography

Cage, John. 1992. *Roaratorio*. 2 disks, 2 books. New York: Mode records—mode 28/29.

11 Tribute to a Footbridge

Dance and Sound Spaces Improvisations in Choisy-le-Roi

Vincent Rioux

Introduction[1]

Choisy-le-Roi, a city in the southeastern suburbs of Paris now approaching 40,000 inhabitants, was rather drastically reconfigured in the late 1950s. To facilitate smooth and efficient traffic flow through the city and ensure positive social/urban interactions, main traffic thoroughfares were widened and a large concrete slab was built above ground level for pedestrians. A footbridge was later built in order to join the historical part of the city to the shopping center built on the slab. Fifty years later, urban planners completely changed paradigms in favor of a multimodal transport system, necessitating the complete destruction of the footbridge, among other things. The Communist-led city council assumed the public relations work preparing residents for the disappearance of such a charged place, and in the process decided that a collective of young dancers should perform a rather unusual "ceremony" celebrating the life and death of an organic part of the city.[2] Consequently, the Comipok' collective asked me to join them as sound artist, and we prepared and held two performances on the Choisy-le-Roi footbridge on December 15, 2009, at 7:00–11:00 am and 3:00–6:00 pm.

This paper will show how these improvised sessions were technically and artistically conceived and realized, explaining our choice to combine post-contact improvised dance (Louppe 2004) and computer-based live compositions in this situation. After having defined a few theoretical terms and describing the notion of sound spheres, I will describe the performance's external conditions and focus on the urban sound milieus in which it took place. This will be followed by a presentation of the practical and technical aspects of the multichannel sound installation, followed by an analysis of pedestrian and citizen comments on the footbridge's removal. A final section will be devoted to the combination of sound, dance, and light—the intentions behind it and the issues involved—in a performance both improvised and composed.

Sound Spheres

I will first define a few expressions and terms related to the description of sound and its potential for interaction and mediation. These definitions are to ensure proper understanding of the following analysis, and they are only intended to apply to the artistic performance being described here.

Looking at outdoor performance from an anthropological point of view, we are naturally inclined to focus on the perception of sound's spatial and temporal properties rather than its intrinsic qualities (pitch and timbre, for example). This does not mean that these qualities were neglected in the preparation of sound materials; they were relevant but simply play a secondary role in the following analysis.

The aural experience of a particular place or route is shaped by culture, habitus, and knowledge. The book *Sonic Experience* (Augoyard and Torgue 2005) provides a concise and potentially exhaustive description of so-called "sound effects" analyzed through five disciplines: psychology and physiology of perception, physical and applied acoustics, architecture and urbanism, sociology and everyday culture, and musical aesthetics. Consequently, describing such an aural experience would involve a variety of aspects including aural culture, personal memories, degree of attentiveness, auditory spatial awareness (Blesser and Salter 2007), and the ability to identify and discriminate between sound sources and their movements (including being able to estimate distances). All these parameters are interdependent and variable.

The term "sphere" is applicable to acoustic waves emanating from a sound source in an open space, but here I suggest that it is also quite suitable for diagramming the aural experience of a listener surrounded by various types of sound sources. I suggest that the notion of sphere, which is broadly applicable to the study of people in their environment (Sloterdijk 2006), is thus logically also applicable to the study of people in their sound milieus, through the concept of "sonosphere"[3] or "aural sphere" that encompasses all the aforementioned parameters. In that sense, the center of a sonosphere, as a bare conceptual projection, would be halfway between the ears. For example, when a pedestrian leaves public transportation to enter the city, he might be focused on memories or thoughts that constitute his aural privacy (Blesser and Salter 2007)—his aural sphere is internal. Walking, seeing, perceiving things around him, his aural sphere opens and re-shapes itself, encompassing whatever sources attract his attention. In the context of a dance performance, Laban's exploration and description of the so-called "kinésphère" of dancers, quoted by Louppe (2004: 213), is also relevant. Note that the sonosphere is closely associated with the oral sphere or "phonosphere" (Féraud 2010), much like reading is linked to writing. But it should not be considered passive, since listening is an activity and might even be considered as a way of walking through sound (Voegelin 2010: 4). Sonospheres include both active listening and passive hearing.

> Sound source: An object or body producing sound. Sound sources have orientation, position/distance, strength/loudness, aperture/extent/spread. In the present case, "sound source" typically refers to speakers, cars, birds, planes, etc.

Focused source: A source with a peak in its directivity diagram, similar to a light cone.

Sound line: A road full of vehicles could be considered as a sound line.

Sound plane: It is common practice in theater or cinema to refer to "planes" for the construction of sets (its basic elements are background and foreground) (Deshays 2006).

Sound field: To be taken in its acoustic sense, which is the sum of all incidents of acoustic pressure from a set of sound sources (including reflected sounds) at each point in the universe. It is what a listener with closed eyes would hear, without trying to identify sound sources. From the listener's point of view this is an unattainable ideal situation, asymptotically approaching Schaeffer's *écoute réduite* ("reduced listening", 1966).

Sound space: A "built" sound field composed of a set of made or recorded sounds played at performance time.

Sound environment, Surrounding, or Milieu: A complex "uncontrolled" sound field composed of all sound sources and reflected sounds surrounding the performers and audience, which are in a sense out of their reach. In the context of the performance described here, it might be the resulting mixed sound of traffic noise, people walking and talking, a few birds singing, the hum of fans, or the noise of construction equipment. The acoustic properties of the footbridge, the road or the buildings should also be taken into account because they contribute considerably to the perceived sound field.

Figure 11.1 Three diagrams of a woman walking. Sketches of three sonospheres. From the left, the first two drawings show perfect spheres centered on the head. One is small, indicating little attention to surroundings, while the second one, larger, models general attention being paid to a larger surrounding area. The last sketch illustrates the deformed sonosphere, with peaks pointing toward focused sound sources.

Image: Vincent Rioux.

Urban Sound and Social Topography

Choisy-le-Roi's recent history (the latter half of the twentieth century) is a prime example of a rather unfortunate conjunction of strictly functional large-scale urban planning and economic instability. In the wake of the prosperous post-war period known as the "Glorious Thirty [years]" several large architectural projects were launched, mainly of utopian, technicist and functionalist inspiration. The construction of multilevel and multimodal (that is, with multiple forms of transportation) areas of flow was mainly planned to resolve the growing problem of road traffic congestion.

Following the impulse and ideas summed up in the 1933 Athens Charter and traceable to earlier writings (Le Corbusier 1924), the Choisy-le-Roi renewal project began in 1957. It was mainly articulated around the sharp separation of social spaces and transportation networks. A two-level city was to be built. A large concrete slab would create an upper story for pedestrians at the citywide scale, while motorized traffic would be confined to a ground or underground level. This vast and financially underestimated renewal project was finally abandoned in 1977. This slow failure (Capron and Garcia Sanchez 2002) finally led to a confused situation where less than a third of the planned projects actually saw the day. Of greatest importance to this article, a major road (the D86) cutting the city in half was ultimately not put underground as planned, so a footbridge had to be hastily built to connect the two halves of the city center.

The boundary of the city is geographically delimited by the river Seine (south-north) and two wide and busy roads (south-north, and east-west). The following diagram (Figure 11.2) displays average sound levels during daytime activity. As we expected, the two major roads (the D5 and D86) produce loud sound lines (70–75 dB).

The footbridge is located in the center of the city, spanning the D86 and linking two different parts of the city. To the northwest, a ground level "social area" is formed around a cathedral and an old market square surrounded by a high-rise public housing project, while to the southeast there is a "commercial area" built on the slab, with a shopping center and fast food and clothing shops scattered around it.

The footbridge is approximately 30 meters long and 7 meters wide (see Figure 11.3). Coming from the southeast entrance of the shopping mall, the footbridge starts to the left of the last shop (a rather old fashioned bar-restaurant). The first impression is rather ambiguous, between strange and ordinary (see Figure 11.4a). The bridge has two axes of symmetry (longitudinal and transversal). Four rows of concrete benches line each side. Two massive flower planters hem in each bench, and a metallic grillwork with vines runs along both sides. There is a public lighting system on one side of each bench (see Figure 11.4b).

Its overall ambiance at the time could be characterized by words such as cold, windy, rough, noisy, open, secure, old. The principal source of

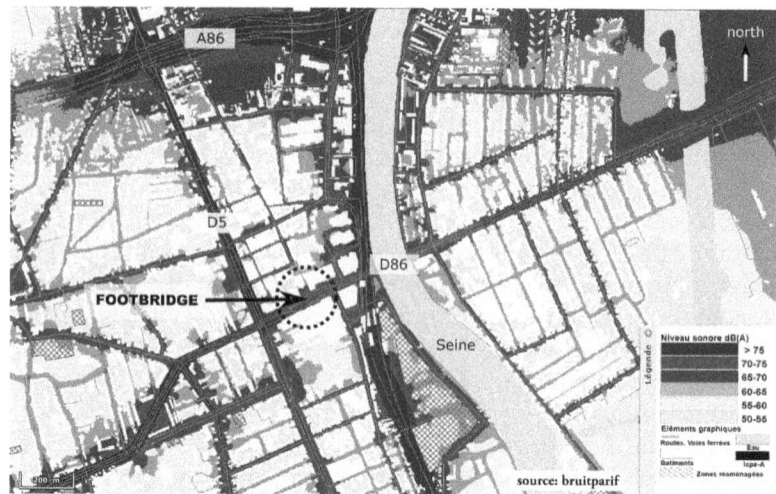

Figure 11.2 Noise map of Choisy-le-Roi (daytime levels, 2009), which complies with the Environmental Noise Directive (END; European directive 2002/49/CE). There is no industrial activity in this area. This map mainly represents road noise (mainly the D5 and D86, about 70–75 dB) and railway noise (track tangent to the Seine river with noise levels exceeding 75 dB). The footbridge is located close to the intersection between the D5 and D86 and parallel to the D5, oriented northwest-southeast. Note that this map was originally drawn using color codes. Choisy-le-Roi is also located about 4 kilometers northeast of Orly Airport.

Source: Bruitparif.

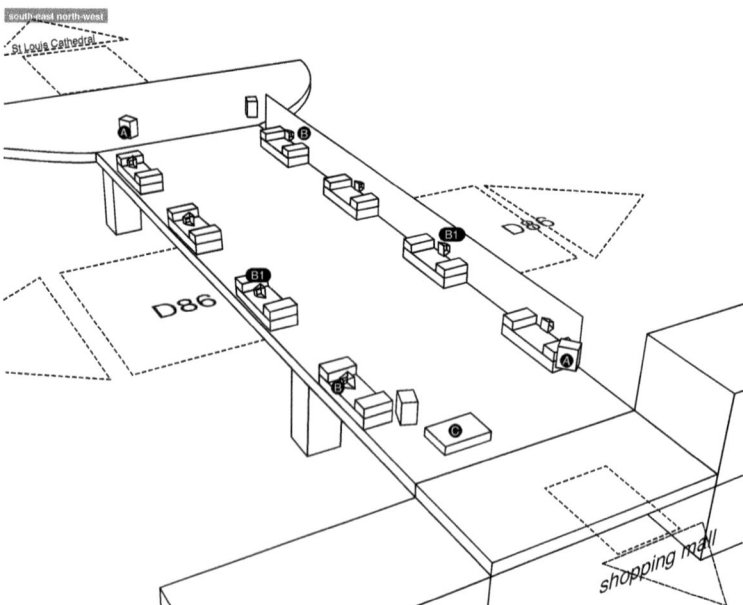

Figure 11.3 Perspective view of the footbridge.

Image: Vincent Rioux.

a. Four wide-band speakers.

b. Eight speakers in the medium range, arranged in facing pairs (e.g., same sound on each pair of speakers (B1), located above benches.

c. Placement of the mixing table, amplifiers, and computer.

b. bench and loudspeaker

a. footbridge with dancers

Figure 11.4 Pictures of the footbridge, November 2009.

a. Three pictures of dance situations.
b. A bench and its associated loudspeaker (corresponding to points B on Figure 11.3).

Courtesy of Jean-Christophe Cacouault.

sound heard on the footbridge is traffic, which is not constant and varies considerably according to the time of day. Peaks of traffic supposedly synchronize with pedestrian flow on the footbridge, mainly in the morning (6:00–10:00 a.m.) and afternoon (4:00–8:00 p.m.) rush hours.

Outdoor Multichannel Sound Improvisations

Set-Up

Figures 11.3 and 11.4b illustrate the spatial distribution and reduced visual impact of the arrangement of electro-acoustic sources. Two very different kinds of loudspeakers were used, and they had to be installed in an hour (very quickly for such an installation). The length of the audio cables linking speakers to the amplifiers at the main mixing point (see Figure 11.3, text dot C) was carefully prepared to facilitate a quick installation. One set was mainly dedicated to voices and sounds in the medium-frequency range, and consisted of an array of eight small speakers (green frustums in Figure 11.3b) covered in dark green plastic (hereafter referred to as "system B"). This cover was thin enough to let sound pass without noticeable frequency filtering, muffling, or distortion while providing cheap waterproofing and a fast and easy way to attach them to the metallic grilling. These sound sources were barely visible. Placed over the benches, they were ready to play the role of invisible people, sitting on a bench and talking about their footbridge.

These speakers were set up in facing pairs (across the bridge's width) to make four independent "sound lines." Put another way, pedestrians would discover a progression of four distinct voices, emanating from each pair of facing speakers, as they crossed the footbridge. It is important to point out that this system was not designed as a public address system, as voices were to be heard in a relatively narrow and intimate area.

A second set of four independent speakers (the red boxes in Figure 11.3), henceforth called "system A," placed at each corner of the footbridge, were used to be able to deliver powerful and low-frequency sounds. They were clearly visible (easily identifiable large black parallelepipeds) and were able to ensure a sense of envelopment (thanks to their power) and ubiquity (by generating low frequencies) (Augoyard and Torgue 2005).

Hence a system of eight independent channels (composed of a mixing table, sound card, and computer) was enough to run a system of twelve speakers in a way that would provide a satisfactory and creative rendering of an artificial acoustical space. This system provided a way to locally adapt a sound composition to a spatial progression (in the time-span of a walk, for example) as well as making it possible to reshape the general ambiance by creating an additional sound space superimposed on the sound milieu.

Invisible Voices

Sound material was collected through informal interviews of inhabitants.[4] They were asked to speak about the footbridge's usefulness, the reasons for its disappearance, and their spontaneous memories related to the place. They were not asked to focus on sound, so we did not use methods such as *parcours commenté* ("commented walks"; Thibaud 2004), but all interviews were conducted on site (i.e., the footbridge). We ended up with recordings of 23 people. Recorded audio files were carefully annotated[5] and edited to extract a few meaningful sentences for each person. Ultimately we created 114 sound files, running from 3 seconds to 1 minute.

  Excerpts of their statements are presented below (followed by our comments):

- **Document 1:** Person 1

  No, it's nice but it should be rebuilt. It makes noise when you walk, it's frightening. So there's that . . .
  This young woman was referring to the poor condition of the footbridge. The whole concrete slab was covered with large square pebbled tiles that had loosened up over time and moved when stepped on, thus producing a distinct muffled percussive sound that was an unmistakably idiosyncratic acoustic marker of the whole area.

- **Document 2:** Person 2

  It's the way to get to the station, to go everywhere. To go to the insurance office. But it's a rotten place . . . At first it was good, but they gave up in the end. It comes from the city hall, because here the city hall controls everything. The mayor and all this mess . . . I take it in the daytime, in the evening and at night . . . Thousands of people, thousands.
  This person emphasizes the fact that this footbridge was a "hotspot" for Choisy's population. He notes that the bridge was used for work-related movements (going to the train and bus stations, the insurance office, etc.) throughout the day.

- **Document 3:** Person 3

  To buy bread, to go to the market. I take this footbridge very often.
  Of course the footbridge was also used for domestic purposes (buying food, clothes, etc.). It became clear that all the citizens of Choisy used this path, and most likely people from outside Choisy as well.

- **Document 4:** Person 4

  I know that this footbridge has some problems. But from what I saw, the opening and the square below, with slowly rising staircases, this is going to be a space for pedestrians. From what I read on the panels below, with the trees, I can only be positive.

- **Document 5:** Person 5

  It's a good thing, it's good. The intermodal center, the station, it's all well thought out. They are going to take down this whole section in order to reconstruct the avenue Jean Jaurès for pedestrian circulation. I think it's good.

- **Document 6:** Person 6

  There is very little light starting at 6 at night, 8 at night. It is so isolated. It's a bit tricky in terms of security.

  These last three people are rather positive about the reconstruction process. It seems that they fully recognize the importance of new urban development for both aesthetic and practical reasons.

- **Document 7:** Person 7

  It would be more difficult, more of a nuisance to cross the road. No, there's no point.

- **Document 8:** Person 8

  We heard they are going to take the footbridge away. But the inhabitants are against it, we love this footbridge. Everyone takes it.

- **Document 9:** Person 9

  Even if there isn't a pretty view, we watch the cars, the people, everyone knows everyone else.

- **Document 10:** Person 10

  The footbridge bears no risk, even for young or old people.

- **Document 11:** Person 11

  Yes, I used to come here with my sweetheart before we got married. We would make dates here—we would meet near the station over there. See how beautiful it is, you can look at the church, it's too beautiful. And here, I don't know, when it's gone, when it's much noisier, we will be drawn to what's underneath . . .

  These people express their apprehensions about the destruction and reconstruction process. It is always difficult and unsettling to break habits (despite its ugliness, people loved the place). It is interesting to note that the footbridge created a rather homogeneous space, a sort of urban bubble where pedestrians were free to move and meet. In addition, the danger of crossing the road itself is clearly indicated.

As one might expect, opinions about the necessity of getting rid of the footbridge are rather mixed. But people generally tended to manifest a great interest in this place, especially because they recognized the value of the original urban planning project's premise of separating automobile and pedestrian flows. They dwell on the quick and secure path it provided between the two parts of the city. Moreover, several of them pointed out that the footbridge offered a good view of the surroundings and the road. Although the place is "rotten" (interestingly, quite associated with the sound of the broken pebble tiles), it still provides a sense of openness (vistas) and security (at least in the daytime). Despite the fact that sound and noise are hardly mentioned, it is obvious that the footbridge can also be considered as a "sound bridge," literally offering a path over a powerful sound line that essentially basically signals "danger." As a result walking on the footbridge and audibly feeling the source of danger (so close but assuredly out of reach) truly emphasizes feelings of comfort and security.

From a musician's point of view, it is rather important to clarify that it is more interesting to play with such excerpts of interviews in terms of timbre and prosody than it is in terms of the actual meanings of the words spoken. As Jaeglé demonstrated to remarkable effect in his "oral portrait of Gilles Deleuze" (Jaeglé 2005), the process of converting thought to actual words conveys very insightful information about the engagement of will, the possibility of action, and the quality of the speaker's moral position, not to mention the fact that voice also has the potential to perpetuate an individual's self-construction (Dolar 2006). Moreover the use of pre-recorded materials discreetly scattered along the bridge accentuated the fact that they actually were invisible voices (Castant 2010: 176), resembling ghost voices (Voegelin 2010: 11), casting a different dramatic character on the performance.

Live Coding on a Footbridge

As stated earlier, the twelve loudspeakers (systems A and B) were connected to a single diffusion console. In that sense, the selected configuration was much like a very small acousmonium, in electroacoustic jargon (the original GRM acousmonium was composed of 80 independent loudspeakers). But instead of running the sound system with pre-recorded tapes, we used an open-source software environment (running Linux) to compose the sound space over time.

The whole playing environment was implemented using SuperCollider (Wilson *et al.* 2011), a computer programming language entirely dedicated to sound synthesis and music composition. SuperCollider was chosen especially because it offers the remarkable possibility of the real-time (that is, during the performance) evaluation of lines of code describing not only synthesized sounds but also pseudo-random composition patterns. SuperCollider also makes it easy to use a large number of independent sound channels. These techniques are gaining popularity in the so-called "live coding"[6] scene, and were extremely useful, to the point of being a necessity, in this case. In addition to their apparent rigidity and finitude, computers offer very interesting paths for arriving at "improvised compositions," something that would resonate directly with how dancers were planning their performance on the footbridge (see last section).

Table 11.1 Pseudo-code to create a random selection of samples.

1—allocate audio buffer
2—launch in a parallel thread (a parallel task) the following steps:
3—read a file, randomly chosen among all 114 samples
4—play it on one (randomly chosen) pair of speakers of system A
5—wait for the end of this sound
6—wait from three to ten seconds
7—loop to point 3

For the sake of comparison with a classical musical instrument's physical configuration, this musical apparatus consisted of a table, a chair, a set of faders (mixing table), and a laptop computer screen, mouse, and keyboard. Of course the main instrument lies in the computer, so here we should think of algorithms and code as providing "new" or even meta-media (Manovich 2013), or in other terms, a "new" extension of the body (McLuhan and Lapham 1994).

Two main approaches were used. One was programming the computer to randomly choose which voice excerpt would be played at which position in space on system B, within a predetermined span of time and space. This was done using the following algorithm (here shown in pseudo-code format, not following the small-talk computer language syntax used in SuperCollider, for the sake of comprehension). The loop could be stopped or paused at any time. It was also possible to launch two or more loops simultaneously.

The second approach, for a larger sound space created by systems A and B, was built using sound objects (in Schaeffer's sense) that could be prescribed, built, and synthesized at will. Such sounds generally fall into typological categories such as pitched or noisy drones, harmonic layers, percussive sounds, unstable, chaotic, or slowly varying sounds, Theremin-like tones (a moving sine wave), and pre-recorded samples. Each sound object could then be sent to one or more speakers and move or circulate between all or a subset of speakers. The following example shows some basic commands used to produce sounds in real-time, implemented in SuperCollider[7] with the help of the JITLib library (Rohrhuber and De Campo 2009), especially conceived for live coding purposes. The user interface is reduced to a simple but powerful text editor called Emacs (Stallman 1981) that allows interesting interplay between written symbols, comments, structures, and the sounds produced. Each line of code can be "interpreted" at any time by pressing a combination of keys. Code can be modified or written from scratch at performance time. The demonstrative and extremely simple code shown in Table 11.2 can be heard in Document 12.

- **Document 12:** Supercollider/livecoding very simple demonstration

Table 11.2 Simple demonstration of a live coding session using the SuperCollider language.

---

p = ProxySpace.push(s.boot); // launch the server

~sig.ar(1); // allocate one channel of audio (used for actual sound generation)

~sig.fadeTime = 3; // make a three-second cross-fade between each sound change

~bruit.ar(4); // allocate a four-channel bus (used for routing sound)

~bruit = {PanAz.ar(4, ~sig.ar, LFSaw.kr(0.25))}; // routing the signal in a circular ring completed within a four-second cycle

~bruit.play; // play (this produces no sound, but creates the routes and spatial synths)

~sig = {Dust.ar(MouseX.kr(1,100))}; // defines "dusty" sounds made of very short pulses with density controlled by the x-axis of the mouse

~sig = {BrownNoise.ar(1)}; // a low-pass filtered white noise (sea-like sound)

Evaluating the last line allows to cross-fade from one sound (dusty) to another sound (sea-like) while maintaining the same spatial effect (circulating among four speakers).

Sound Space

The great combination of possible effects and the ability to call on them at will, made possible by the system described above, allowed the creation of an evolving sound space offering dialogue with the dancers, the pedestrians, and the sound milieu itself.

First, of course, comes silence (Cage 1973)—or rather "relative" silence, which Cage loved to point out was made of the incessant murmur of traffic—usually perceptible and hearable but barely listened to. Unsurprisingly, the footbridge's sound milieu was mainly composed of traffic noise (cars, buses, distant trains, and a few planes).

The sound performance was developed as a way to interact with the sound milieu and the actions of the dancers (see next section) by playing with congruencies, responses, and contrasts. The use of modulated noise sources (in space, time, and frequency) provided a flexible set of textures to play with to create an ever-changing ambiance. For example, scintillating percussive tonic sounds (high-pitched tones in Schaeffer's typology) emanating from all speakers at low volume were refreshing and discretely drew attention to the fact that something different was happening. Large bursts of white noise flowing up and down the footbridge were used to imaginatively accompany pedestrians' walks. Focused sources were used to provide light poetic touches when playing sound samples, such as an old southern Italian song played on a diatonic accordion.[8] And layers of sound were also added, such as the sounds of rattling train coupler chains or the Paris subway doors closing.

The recorded voices drew considerable attention and surprise because they contrasted sharply with the sound milieus in certain ways and were produced without identifiable bodies. This absence of visible bodies is rather commonplace for people versed in electro-acoustics, and I would be remiss if I did not cite composer-director Heiner Goebbels' masterpiece of the genre "Stifters Dinge", a theatrical play without actors, as a prime example.

The spatial progressions made possible by the aforementioned electro-acoustic system were of decisive importance. More than simulating a new sound milieu by producing a synthetic sound space, the idea, following musical thinking, was to produce a mixed emotional setting whose temporal and spatial characteristics would be perceptible to passing pedestrians. The way in which the sound space was prepared and eventually instantiated has much in common with how the dancing was planned, and could be described as improvised composition.

Bodies and Sounds[9]

The group of young dancers[10] knew each other well and had shared the experience of several performances in outdoor urban spaces. They were particularly attentive to and interested in the possibility of getting art forms to emerge from non-prepared scenes like train station platforms and town squares where there was a flow of crowds and everyday circulation.[11] They conceived of their work as loosely post-contact dance[12] consisting of composed interactions interspersed with opportunities for improvisation.

We woke up at sunrise and had only two hours to install the light and sound set-up the length of the footbridge (see Figure 11.3). The performance started around seven o'clock in the morning, when city traffic gives its first noticeable signs of thickening and a few people emerge from the darkness, forcing themselves to go to work with heads tucked low. It was very cold—indeed the temperature was an important factor in the improvisational process, being a parameter that is obviously relevant to the emergence of a particular mood (Toop 2001: 48). The overall ambiance was dark and silent, even desolate. The footbridge gave a square, rough, and stiff impression with its gray pebble paving tiles and its metallic grillwork. Dancers warmed up very slowly and began to draw longitudinal lines along the footbridge alternating walking and running with each passage, making approximately three passages per minute for the first half hour.

I was composing sound spaces with a light touch. Things were to move slowly. Invisible voices started making their ghostly presence known, waking up the still-drowsy pedestrians. Train sounds and "ritournelles" (piano, accordion, jingles) began their endless loops as if they had always been there.

Layers of sine waves were lightly drawing mysterious tapestries that floated on various parts of the bridge. Dancers were acting like pedestrians, or discreetly followed them as if to tell them a secret. Suddenly they would rush, running back and forth or side to side. Then improvised meetings in groups of two or three, falling at walkers' feet, gently obstructing their paths (Figure 11.4a), lying down for a couple of minutes in various positions. At one point there were five bodies on the ground. They climbed on the footbridge walls, upside down, on one side or the other—an improvised composition of a series of images.

They were accompanied by subtle sound lines. The footbridge was slowly waking up. Gradually, the pre-recorded voices started to be heard and dancers took pauses. Whether seated on a bench close to a little sphere of a nostalgic tune or half prone on the cold ground, they were composing an unusual agency of bodies. Loud sounds might suddenly erupt, like the electrical buzzing thunder-like drone that got Fabio in a sort of bare-chested trance, head stuck out obliquely, hands raised, shaking his whole body from top to bottom, in rhythm with the short clouds of needles produced by a supercollider.

After the morning session, we tried to warm down, get some rest, and prepare for the afternoon. Throughout the day, the nearby presence of (de)construction equipment delivered the full power of their engines' rattling noises to the space. The afternoon session was more fluid and energetic. More interestingly, on their way home, some pedestrians even stopped, staring at the dancers or wondering about the unusual sound ambiance. They hardly qualified as an audience or public, but we still felt fulfilled and emotional, and even today we have strong memories born of the shift of perspective that the performance context and indeed the footbridge itself led us to reveal.

Conclusion

By combining an electro-acoustically generated evolving sound space and a collective improvised dance composition, we tried to communicate a simple message of good-bye to the footbridge to passersby. The basic idea was to compose through improvisation an ambiance just slightly out of kilter with everyday life that would relate to a mode of modified presence (Thibaud 2004: 4). The tension between the dancers' bodies and the disembodied sounds was counterbalanced by the fact that dancers were not using touch, except between themselves. But sound is actually often said to be very similar to touch (Augoyard and Torgue 2005: 107), having the potential to establish fully sensual relations (Howes 2003).

With the growing attention to noise as a factor in health issues, we might be inclined to forget that sound is unimpeachable testimony to human activities in the present time and space. In a climate of complex and delicate political decision-making about regulating and coordinating our cities' sound milieus, we believe that artistic experiments, guided by a scientific understanding of contemporary sound, can play a key role in the search for bending conventional beliefs about a largely misunderstood medium and unlocking personal perceptions of one's own sound milieus.

It is our hope that this chapter will provide an interesting example of the interplay between art and science as well as a modest source of inspiration for people seeking relief from the downright spectacular in cracks and interstices outside the sphere of entertainment.

Notes

1 I want to acknowledge Guenola Capron and Pedro José Garcia Sanchez's article (Capron and Garcia Sanchez 2002), which was a revelation and really inspired and motivated me to share this experience with the scientific community.
2 I wish to thank Maxime Oudry, musician, who introduced me to the group of dancers.
3 I wish to express my gratitude here to the sound artist Gilles Malatray for spending time with me discussing the term *sonosphere*, which he has used in several past occasions (private communication).
4 Many thanks to Xavier Sauvage and his students for their sound recordings.
5 Using a computer program called e-sonoclaste, developed by the author (http://esonoclaste.net)
6 Live coding, coined by Collins, McLean, Rohrhuber, and Ward (Collins *et al.* 2003), refers to a set of powerful yet simple improvisational practices and computer languages that allow sensitive lines of code to be written, transformed, and evaluated at performance time. The authors stress that live coding requires very specific tools and has a significant element of risk. These risks are varied but can generally be summed up in categories such as improvisational mist (lack of orientation and/or direction), mistakes due to computer language syntax rigidity (prohibiting error-prone laziness), and real bugs (potentially leading to system freeze).
7 I wish to heartily thank the wonderful SuperCollider community, especially Alberto de Campo and Julian Rohrhuber.
8 For which we wish to thank the Calabrese musician Tonino Cavallo.
9 Thanks to the dancers Fabio Bello and Charlie Fouchier.
10 At the time, there were nine dancers in the Comipok' collective.
11 In that sense they are following the work of prestigious elders like Odile Duboc, Pierre Doussaint, Steve Paxton, and Trisha Brown.
12 "Contact improvisations are spontaneous physical dialogues that range from stillness to highly energetic exchanges. Alertness is developed in order to work in an energetic state of physical disorientation, trusting in one's basic survival instincts. It is a free play with balance, self-correcting the wrong moves and reinforcing the right ones, bringing forth a physical/emotional truth about a shared moment of movement that leaves the participants informed, centered, and enlivened."—early definition by Steve Paxton and his co-authors in *Contact Quarterly* 5 (1), 1979, cited at www.contactquarterly.com/ contact-improvisation/about/.

References

Augoyard, Jean-François and Henry Torgue. 2005. *Sonic Experience: A Guide to Everyday Sounds*. Translated by David Paquette and Andra McCartney. Montreal: McGill-Queen's University Press.

Blesser, Barry and Linda-Ruth Salter. 2007. *Spaces Speak, Are You Listening? Experiencing Aural Architecture*. Cambridge: MIT Press.

Cage, John. 1973. *Silence: Lectures and Writings*. Middletown: Wesleyan.

Capron, Guénola and José Pedro Garcia Sanchez. 2002. "L'urbanisme moderne de dalle, Histoire d'un lent échouage urbain: Le cas du centre-ville de Choisy-le-Roi." *Flux* 50 (4): 20–33.

Castant, Alexandre. 2010. *Planètes Sonores. Radiophonie, Arts, Cinéma*, revised and expanded edition. Blou: Monografik Editions.

Collins, Nick, Alex McLean, Julian Rohrhuber, and Adrian Ward. 2003. "Live Coding in Laptop Performance." *Organised Sound* 8 (3): 321–330.

Deshays, Daniel. 2006. *Pour Une Écriture Du Son*. Paris: Klincksieck.

Dolar, Mladen. 2006. *A Voice and Nothing More*. Cambridge: MIT Press.

Féraud, Olivier. 2010. *Voix publiques: Environnements sonores, représentations et usages d'habitation dans un quartier populaire de Naples*. PhD Thesis, Ecole des Hautes Etudes en Sciences Sociales, Paris.

Howes, David. 2003. *Sensual Relations Engaging the Senses in Culture and Social Theory*. Ann Arbor: University of Michigan Press.

Jaeglé, Claude. 2005. *Portrait oratoire de Gilles Deleuze aux yeux jaunes*. Paris: Presses universitaires de France.

Le Corbusier. 1924. *The City of Tomorrow and Its Planning*. Translated by Frederick Etchells. Mineola: Dover Publications.

Louppe, Laurence. 2004. *Poétique de la danse contemporaine*. Bruxelles: Contredanse.

Manovich, Lev. 2013. *Software Takes Command: Extending the Language of New Media*. New York: Continuum Publishing.

McLuhan, Marshall and Lewis H. Lapham. 1994. *Understanding Media: The Extensions of Man*, reprint edition. Cambridge: MIT Press.

Rohrhuber, Julian and Alberto De Campo. 2009. "Improvising Formalisation: Conversational Programming and Live Coding." In *New Computational Paradigms for Computer Music*, edited by Gérard Assayag and Andrew Gerzso, 113–124. Paris: Delatour France.

Schaeffer, Pierre. 1966. *Traité Des Objets Musicaux. Essai Interdisciplines. Nouvelle Édition*. Paris: Éditions du Seuil.

Sloterdijk, Peter. 2006. *Sphères: Tome 3, Écumes, Sphérologie plurielle*. Paris: Hachette.

Stallman, Richard M. 1981. "EMACS: The Extensible, Customizable, Self-Documenting Display Editor." *ACM SIGPLAN Notices* 16 (6): 147–156.

Thibaud, Jean-Paul. 2004. "Une approche pragmatique des ambiances urbaines." In *Ambiances en débats*, edited by Pascal Amphoux, Grégoire Chelkoff, and Jean-Paul Thibaud, 145–158. Grenoble: Éditions À la Croisée.

Toop, David. 2001. *Ocean of Sound: Aether Talk, Ambient Sound and Imaginary Worlds*. London: Serpent's Tail.

Voegelin, Salomé. 2010. *Listening to Noise and Silence: Towards a Philosophy of Sound Art*. New York: Continuum.

Wilson, Scott, David Cottle, Nick Collins, and James McCartney, eds. 2011. *The SuperCollider Book*. Cambridge: MIT Press.

Afterword

The Sonic Attunement of Social Life

Jean-Paul Thibaud

We are discovering that the world resounds. A wide variety of approaches have emerged taking an interest in the sonority of inhabited space, with talk of soundscapes, field recordings, sound studies, sound art, acoustemology, sound installation, auditory culture and even acoustic ecology. A whole field of research and practice is springing up—with its own publications, experiments, creative endeavours and journals—a field that sets out to lend an ear to everyday situations and learn to listen to our ways of being together. We could no doubt demonstrate that such attention is not new and that, on the contrary, it is underpinned by a long, underground history. But a genuine sensibility in tune with the audible world is nevertheless emerging, changing the sensory relationship we entertain with our everyday surroundings.

So, what can anthropology contribute to these efforts to listen to the world? In raising this question, our purpose is not to constrain a disciplinary posture, all the more so as the approaches involved already tend to complement and feed on one another, producing countless hybrid offshoots. Furthermore the world of human and social sciences increasingly enters into resonance with the art world to contribute to a socio-aesthetic of the sonic world, which is still in its very early days. On the contrary, our aim is to highlight a new line of research suggested by this collection of contributions: ambient sound. We should explain straight away that few of the articles make this concept their main theme, nor does it necessarily play a leading role in them. Rather it is present as a sort of watermark, disseminated in the descriptions and analyses, as if it were only nascent and barely sketched out. But it is no coincidence that this term features in the title of the publication. It invites the reader to listen to the ambient world, which cannot be reduced simply to the environment and landscape. What more is there to be said? How are we to specify, take stock of and accept the consequences of ambient sound?

As an introduction we may attempt to distinguish ambient sound from soundscape and auditory environment. All three terms are close, referring to a sonic experience, and are sometimes associated, indeed confused; they nevertheless correspond to different ways of listening to the world. In "soundscape", a term coined by R. Murray Schafer (1977), the idea of the composition of the sonic environment is uppermost, with the possibility of an aesthetic way of listening to the everyday world, which in turn entails the figure-ground relationship inherited from the visual landscape and rooted in a distinction between low and hi-fidelity soundscape. This brings us to a contemplative form of listening close to the experience of a viewer look-ing at a painting. In other words, the soundscape is based on a process of assessing and selecting which involves extracting from the sonic environment what is perceived as an aesthetic unity. With "auditory environment", it is more a case of immersion than a frontal relationship or a listening-to-music posture. This is emphasized by the word "environment", sound being a part of our surroundings, or our *in situ* experience. A wide range of work could stake a claim to an ambition of this sort, focusing attention on even the most ordinary situations and attempting to describe the sonic environments of daily life. Though the concept of "ambient sound" shares this aim, it seems to attach just as much importance to sonic actions as their perceptual coun-terparts, to the social modalities of producing the sonic environment as to those of its reception. In other words, and we may take this as our starting point, ambient sound above all concerns the pervasive noises of living in society and forms of social and emotional life insofar as they may be heard and make themselves audible to others.

Sound in Common

The sonic world is basically of an event-related order; it is indissociable from what is going on. Many authors have highlighted this characteristic, empha-sizing the capacity of sounds to tell us about what things and living beings are doing (Arnheim 1936), about the event-related nature of sound (Casati and Dokic 1994), and the primacy of the verbal field over the substantive with regard to sonic material (Flusser 2005). In short sound is the effect of an activity. As Walter Ong sums it up (1967: 112): "sound must be in active production in order to exist at all". These sonic productions are varied and diverse, relating to the manifestation of natural phenomena, the use of tech-nical tools, the operation of technological artefacts and the expression of the body in action (voices and all sorts of gestures).

We are thus immersed in a world of sound in which we take part and which everyone contributes to producing through their daily activities and actions. In this respect some sonic productions constitute genuine acts of presence in the urban space. Whether this means the festive use of firecrack-ers in Naples (see Féraud) or heckling voices in India (see Guillebaud), the aim is very certainly to make oneself heard and to mark space with one's presence. But although these phenomena are the result of deliberate, inten-tional sonic actions, targeting others, they enable us more generally to dem-onstrate the presential power of sound, its ability to embody the immediacy of existences. With sound, "it is easier for me to slip from the domain of representation to that of presence" (Sansot 1976: 21). Oral poetry admirably illustrates this point (see Depaule), putting the accent in particular on the expressiveness of the voice, the potential of a cry or a breath and the all-out exploration of sonic bodies.

But we also need to acknowledge the collective force of sound, its capacity for making the work of multiple beings audible (Serres 1995), grouping together (Quignard 1996), addressing a limitless number of individuals (Simmel 1981). This anthropology of ambient sound is therefore, through and through, a social and cultural anthropology constantly questioning the nature of life in sonic terms. There are many and various inputs to such a field of questioning, focusing on the makeup of an acoustic community or the audible forms of public sociability, the cultural filters affecting perception or the social representations of the sonic world. In short the question is to know how the sonic makes society and territory. Sound is consequently to be considered not so much as an object of social anthropology among others but rather as an operator and a condition for the possibility of social life itself. A consequence of prime epistemological importance deserves mention here. If the sonic world is a constitutive part of being together, if the sonic and social worlds are coextensive, then sound must be studied as one of the immanent modalities of the social bond (Augoyard 2003).

But the attention given to the audible forms of social life also necessitates the careful articulation of sonic perceptions and productions to the contexts and frameworks into which they fit. The public—even political—nature of the sonic worlds studied here depends upon it. Every sound is embedded in a set of codes, norms, practices, gestures, knowhow, customs, rituals, and interpretative schemes which must be brought to light with precision. It was certainly not by chance that Ludwig Wittgenstein used a sound-based metaphor to explain the following point. "How could human behaviour be described? Surely only by sketching the actions of a variety of humans, as they are all mixed up together. What determines our judgment, our concepts and reactions, is not what one man is doing now, an individual action, but the whole hurly-burly of human actions, the background against which we see any action" (Wittgenstein 1981: 567). So when we set about listening to sonic environments, we must not only take account of the sounds themselves but also the background and the conditions which make them possible.

The Audible Field

Any work on an anthropology of ambient sound also entails exploring the audible field. Each time we move between highly contrasted sonic cultures— from southern Italy to Ethiopia, from India to Scotland, Japan to Spain, Egypt to Portugal or France—we discover new ambient sonorities, new ways of listening to the world. There is certainly no cause to take this reasoning too far: our purpose is simply to note the huge diversity of situations at stake. This exploration of sonic worlds is based on the study of fields on a wide range of scales, each time raising specific questions and bringing into play investigative methods that are also very diverse. Thick ethnographic description, interpretation of old written texts, in situ sound recordings, sound preference tests, personal narratives, audio-ethnography and artistic performances can be found in this volume. The anthropology of ambient sound relies on numerous scientific disciplines and takes advantage of the heuristic power of pluridisciplinarity. Though the aim is definitely to come as close as possible to the experience of residents and local people, in every case to immerse oneself in a new ambient environment, the aim is also to acknowledge the plural modes in which sound exists. We should point out that much of the work presented here displays a genuine concern for methodological invention, seeking out original tools for investigation and analysis. For example, listening or sound recording is experimented while walking; new technological tools are developed to record or to listen in a new way; various types of audio, written and visual data are closely intertwined to document the complexity of a territory; auto-ethnography is incorporated in the data and the narratives. Methods are not given once and for all but on the contrary are always a challenge to meet.

Without claiming in any way that this work is exhaustive, several strands run through this research, opening up the audible field. The first strand concerns sonic productions at the two extremities of what is acoustically audible. Interest focuses on sonic sources that are particularly powerful—the noise of fireworks (see Féraud) or other saturated sounds (see Guillebaud, Battesti)— or on the contrary, barely perceptible—footsteps on the grounds and other murmurs (see Rioux, Guiu). In particular it seems necessary to rehabilitate the category of noise, all too often disparaged in work on sound. The theme of sonic comfort sometimes favors the existence of measured sounds, balanced sonic environments, but this anthropology of ambient sound reveals all there is to be gained from listening to noise and silence, ranging from the deafening to the almost imperceptible, from the hullaballoo associated with times of collective exuberance to the infinitesimal whispers by which we may hear the "wings of silence" (*coulisses du silence*) (Jankélévitch 1978).

Another strand invites us to rediscover sounds that are ordinary, habitual, non-descript, often going unnoticed because they are so integrated in daily life and blanked out by conscious perception (see Rioux, Uimonen, Depaule). Verging on the obvious, often taken for granted, these everyday sounds are fully entitled to a place in the sonic ambiance—indeed its existence may depend on them—and play a part in the relation of familiarity we entertain with our immediate environment. So it is a matter of describing as closely as possible what an ordinary sonic ambiance may be and of what it consists. Here we are very probably near to the ethnomethodology, which thematizes the ordinary character of social life and makes it a field of investigation in its own right (Sacks 1992). We are dealing with the sounds which feed an ambiance, which give it consistency and depth, and which may be heard without necessarily being noticed.

A third category of sounds emerges from this anthropology of ambient sound: those loaded with exceptional symbolic value and a particularly intense emotional charge. These sonic productions are close to the margins of what it is socially acceptable to hear. This means paying attention to sounds thought to be intolerable, associated with what one might hear in heaven or hell (see Damon-Guillot), or even obscene, such as bodily or intimate noises (see Chandola). Behind all these cases lurks a sonic environment which is supposed to be concealed or neutralized, as if it took us beyond the limits of what is bearable or seemly. Clearly, the sonic world is far from being neutral or free from affects and taboos. Rejoining some of the concerns of Georges Bataille's Collège de Sociologie, such work seeks to focus debate on the meeting point between the sacred and the poetic, between politics and intimacy. It opens the door to anything related to taboos and transgression and in so doing raises questions about what belongs in the public domain.

In their respective ways, these strands run along the borders of the sonic domain, defining its perimeter and frontiers, while at the same time opening up the full dimensions and potential of the audible field. In a way, the idea is to work on the thresholds of the sonic world, be they acoustic (ranging from the very noisy to the barely perceptible), attentional (from focus to lack of attention) or social (from the public to the personal). But also these sonic productions and listening modes only really make sense and become relevant when related to specific forms of life, concrete situations and clearly defined space-time frameworks. In other words cultures are conceptualized here as the dynamics of sonic sensitivity, as sensory-socialization processes.

The Power of Sound

The anthropology of ambient sound also enables us to recognize and study the varying powers exerted by sound. The sonic world really has the power to control, take hold and possess us, inevitably bringing into play forces and dynamics which affect us (Zuckerkandl 1956). This is very apparent in the German language, which establishes a direct link between *hören* (to hear) and *gehorchen* (to obey). Moreover, numerous examples remind us of the close affinity between sound and power, from the Sirens' song no one can resist (Homer) to the radio as an instrument for manipulating the people (Chakhotin). It is well known that *l'oreille n'a pas de paupière* ["there is no closing one's ears"], leaving us totally at the mercy of sounds. This is certainly the point made by Erwin Straus (1966), who emphasizes the presential character of sound and for whom "all hearing is presentic". "Tone has an activity all its own; it presses in on us, surrounds, seizes and embraces us. Only in a latter phase we are able to defend ourselves against sound, only after sound has already take possession of us, while in the visual sphere we begin to take flight before we have been prehended. The acoustical pursues us, we are at its mercy, unable to get away" (p. 16).

The power of sound reaches out in many directions, affecting our behavior and our surroundings, emotions and moods. This is true of the performative power of sound, the way it inflects gesture and action, imposing order on practices. Sound becomes a management tool, a means of capturing and disciplining attention, an instrument for rationalizing conduct and shaping routines. The example of electric bells in Japanese railway stations is a case in point (see Manea), much as drivers hooting their horns in Cairo to put pressure on police on point duty (see Battesti), vocal techniques of bus ticket collectors in India to get the clients' attention in order to be most efficient (see Guillebaud), the creation of a new sonic milieu to enforce a process of urban revitalization (see Sánchez) or the use of powerful sounds by missionaries to convert people (see Damon-Guillot). Sound is not an epiphenomenon of practical action; it is an integral part of it playing an active role. We should perhaps insist on the very special bond between time and sound: the time it takes for a sound to unfold and the time its listening lasts are co-extensive. In other words, the sound "dictates the temporality of its perception" (Sève 2002) and thus has the power to impose rhythm and duration on the course of actions. It also brings into play an ability to adjust and modulate the sequence of events. At issue here is the practical efficacy of sounds, making the sonic world a place of affordances, events, shifters and improvisations which all play their part in our carrying out our business.

But it is equally essential to register the formidable emotional power of sound. The various studies presented here make this clear, showing that the sonic world cannot be reduced to simply a functional, exclusively rational place. For example, the aim of some railway bells and whistles may be to control flows and make getting on or off easier, but they also set the tone for arrivals and departures, contributing to a sense of collective hysteria or enchantment, as the case may be (see Manea). But we could also cite—with very different degrees of intensity—certain utterances by Indian women in the slums they inhabit (see Chandola), the festive charge which is an essential component of the noisy celebrations in Naples (see Féraud) or indeed the various affective tonalities to be heard in Barcelona neighbourhoods (see Guiu). Sound is definitely a powerful medium on the basis of which affects and sensory atmospheres may be deployed, a modality particularly propitious to expressing the pathic component of sensory experience. It is here that emerges a particularly fecund meeting point between the sonic and ambient worlds. It really makes sense to talk about an ambient sound, the sound being a basic characteristic of how an ambiance is expressed (Thibaud 2011).

Sound's potential is also deployed in spatial terms. Sound is not only inscribed in a space—as the propagation of a physical signal in an environment—but also as a force for territorialisation (see Guiu) or cultural identity (see Uimonen). Gilles Deleuze and Félix Guattari (1980) demonstrated this feature with their *ritournelle* concept: it is the mark which makes the territory. Sound may tend to be impossible to delimit, slipping through all sorts of envelopes, but it nevertheless plays a part in territorial configuration: when certain sounds are identified with particular spaces, when certain sonic actions are only possible in specific places, when the forms of reverberation and other acoustic qualities constitute the signature of such and such an environment . . . These are all ways of affirming the capacity of sound to turn a space into a territory. Two points need to be made in this respect. First, sound can become an instrument of domination: taking possession of a territory by sound is also a way of asserting one's power over its inhabitants or controlling the experience of public spaces (see Sánchez). Second, sound is also related to a process of de-territorialization: it tends to leak out of a territory, emancipating itself and opening up to other connections, such as religion (see Damon-Guillot) or poetry (see Depaule). So the powers of sound are open, cannot be circumscribed and lend themselves to other lines of flight.

Listening to Ambiances

By listening to social life, we may in fact unveil a whole sensory atmosphere just waiting to be heard, with its rhythms and intensities, vibrations and pulsations, resonance and discordance. The aim is not so much to categorize attitudes or represent phenomena as to describe atmospheres and allow sensations to emerge. A modal anthropology attentive to the ways of being of the sonic world needs to be further developed (Laplantine 2005). Sound sets the tone for situations and territories, without contenting itself with focused listening. One of the lessons that could be drawn from these essays on sonic anthropology is that they are moving towards a posture which accords great importance to borderline sonorities, floating styles of listening and peripheral perceptions. If the aim is to develop our faculty for listening to ambient sonorities, the price to pay is a great deal work on de-focusing. What are therefore at stake are the fringes and margins of the sonic world, and what lends it consistency. Could the anthropology of ambient sound simply be another means of listening to ambiances?

References

Arnheim, Rudolf. 1936. *Radio*. London: Faber & Faber.

Augoyard, Jean-François. 2003. "Une sociabilité à entendre." *Espaces et Sociétés* 115: 25–42.

Casati, Roberto and Jérôme Dokic. 1994. *La philosophie du son*. Nîmes: Éditions Jacqueline Chambon.

Deleuze, Gilles and Félix Guattari. 1980. *Mille plateaux*. Paris: Minuit.

Flusser, Vilém. 2005. *Essais sur la nature et la culture*. Belval: Circé.

Jankélévitch, Vladimir. 1978. *Quelque part dans l'inachevé*. Paris: Gallimard.

Laplantine, François. 2005. *Le social et le sensible. Introduction à une anthropologie modale*. Paris: Téraèdre.

Ong, Walter. 1967. *The Presence of the Word*. Minneapolis: University of Minnesota Press.

Quignard, Pascal. 1996. *La haine de la musique*. Paris: Éditions Calmann-Lévy.

Sacks, Harvey. 1992. "On Doing Being Ordinary." In *Lectures on Conversation*. Vol. 2, edited by Gail Jefferson, 215–221. Oxford: Blackwell Publishers.

Sansot, Pierre. 1976. "Existence des bruits et bruits des existences." *Musique en Jeu* 24: 19–28.

Schafer, Murray R. 1977. *The Tuning of the World*. New York: Knopf.

Serres, Michel. 1995. *Genesis*. Translated by Geneviève James and James Nielson. Ann Arbor: University of Michigan Press.

Sève, Bernard. 2002. *L'altération musicale*. Paris: Éditions du Seuil.

Simmel, Georg. 1981 [1908]. "Essai sur la sociologie des sens." In *Sociologie et Epistémologie*, Introduction written by Julien Freund and translated by L. Gasparini, 223–238. Paris: PUF.

Straus, Erwin. 1966. "The Forms of Spatiality." In *Phenomenological Psychology: The Selected Papers of Erwin W. Straus*, 3–37. New York: Basic Books.

Thibaud, Jean-Paul. 2011. "A Sonic Paradigm of Urban Ambiances." *Journal of Sonic Studies* 1 (1). http://journal.sonicstudies.org/vol01/nr01/a02.

Wittgenstein, Ludwig. 1981. *Zettel*, second edition, edited by G.E.M. Anscombe and G.H.V. Wright. Oxford: Blackwell.

Zuckerkandl, Victor. 1956. *Sound and Symbol: Music and the External World*. New York: Pantheon.

Index

www.ingramcontent.com/pod-product-compliance
Ingram Content Group UK Ltd.
Pitfield, Milton Keynes, MK11 3LW, UK
UKHW022216290125
454372UK00017B/508